Frommer's

London day BY day®

5th Edition

by Donald Strachan

FrommerMedia LLC

Contents

THAMES PATH
EMBANKMENT

Published by:

Frommer Media LLC

ISBN: 978-1-628-87410-5 (paper); 978-1-628-87411-2 (ebk)

Editorial Director: Pauline Frommer
Development Editor: Alexis Lipsitz Flippin
Production Editor: Kelly Dobbs Henthorne
Photo Editor: Meghan Lamb
Cartographer: Roberta Stockwell
Indexer: Cheryl Lenser

Front cover photos, left to right: Big Ben and the Houses of Parliament. The band of the Coldstream Guards marches in front of Buckingham Palace during the Changing of the Guard ceremony. S.Borisov, David Steele / Shutterstock.com. Museum of Natural History. Melissa Baucom. Back cover photo: Tower Bridge. Samot.

For information on our other products and services, please go to Frommers.com.

Frommer's also publishes its books in a variety of electronic formats. Some content that appears in print may not be available in electronic formats.

Manufactured in China

5 4 3 2 1

About This Guide

Organizing your time. That's what this guide is all about.

Other guides give you long lists of things to see and do and then expect you to fit the pieces together. The Day by Day guides are different. These guides tell you the best of everything, and then they show you how to see it in the smartest, most time-efficient way. Our authors have designed detailed itineraries organized by time, neighborhood, or special interest. And each tour comes with a bulleted map that takes you from stop to stop.

Hoping to see where the Queen lives, or the global treasures of the British Museum? Planning a walk through swanky Chelsea, the "New London" of the East End, or the shopping streets of the West End? Whatever your interest or schedule, the Day by Days give you the smartest routes to follow. Not only do we take you to the top attractions, hotels, and restaurants, but we also help you access those special moments that locals get to experience— those "finds" that turn tourists into travelers.

The Day by Days are also your top choice if you're looking for one complete guide for all your travel needs. The best hotels and restaurants for every budget, the greatest shopping values, the wildest nightlife—it's all here.

Why should you trust our judgment? Because our authors personally visit each place they write about. They're an independent lot who say what they think and would never include places they wouldn't recommend to their best friends. They're also open to suggestions from readers. If you'd like to contact them, please send your comments our way at feedback@frommers.com, and we'll pass them on.

Enjoy your Day by Day guide—the most helpful travel companion you can buy. And have the trip of a lifetime.

About the Author

Donald Strachan is a writer and journalist whose work has been published worldwide, including in the UK *Telegraph* and *Guardian, National Geographic Traveller* magazine, and CNN.com. Over the years, he has written about everything London-related, from craft beer and coffee to shopping and spooky walks. He has authored or coauthored several guidebooks for Frommer's, including *Frommer's England & Scotland* and multiple editions of *Frommer's Italy*.

An Additional Note

Please be advised that travel information is subject to change at any time—and this is especially true of prices. We therefore suggest that you write or call ahead for confirmation when making your travel plans. The authors, editors, and publisher cannot be held responsible for the experiences of readers while traveling. Your safety is important to us, however, so we encourage you to stay alert and be aware of your surroundings.

Star Ratings, Icons & Abbreviations

Every hotel, restaurant, and attraction listing in this guide has been ranked for quality, value, service, amenities, and special features using a **star-rating system.** Hotels, restaurants, attractions, shopping, and nightlife are rated on a scale of zero stars (recommended) to three stars (exceptional). In addition to the star-rating system, we also use a kids **icon** to point out the best bets for families. Within each tour, we recommend cafes, bars, or restaurants where you can take a break. Each of these stops appears in a shaded box marked with a coffee-cup-shaped bullet.

The following **abbreviations** are used for credit cards:

AE	American Express	MC	MasterCard
DC	Diners Club	V	Visa

Frommers.com

Now that you have this guidebook to help you plan a great trip, visit our website at **www.frommers.com** for additional travel information on more than 4,000 destinations. We update features regularly to give you instant access to the most current trip-planning information available. At Frommers.com, you'll find scoops on the best airfares, lodging rates, and car rental bargains. You can even book your travel online through our reliable travel booking partners. Other popular features include:

- Online updates of our most popular guidebooks
- Vacation sweepstakes and contest giveaways
- Newsletters highlighting the hottest travel trends
- Online travel message boards with featured travel discussions

An Invitation to the Reader

In researching this book, we discovered many wonderful places—hotels, restaurants, shops, and more. We're sure you'll find others. Please tell us about them, so we can share the information with your fellow travelers in upcoming editions. If you were disappointed with a recommendation, we'd love to know that, too. Please write to: Support@FrommerMedia.com.

16 Favorite **Moments**

16 Favorite **Moments**

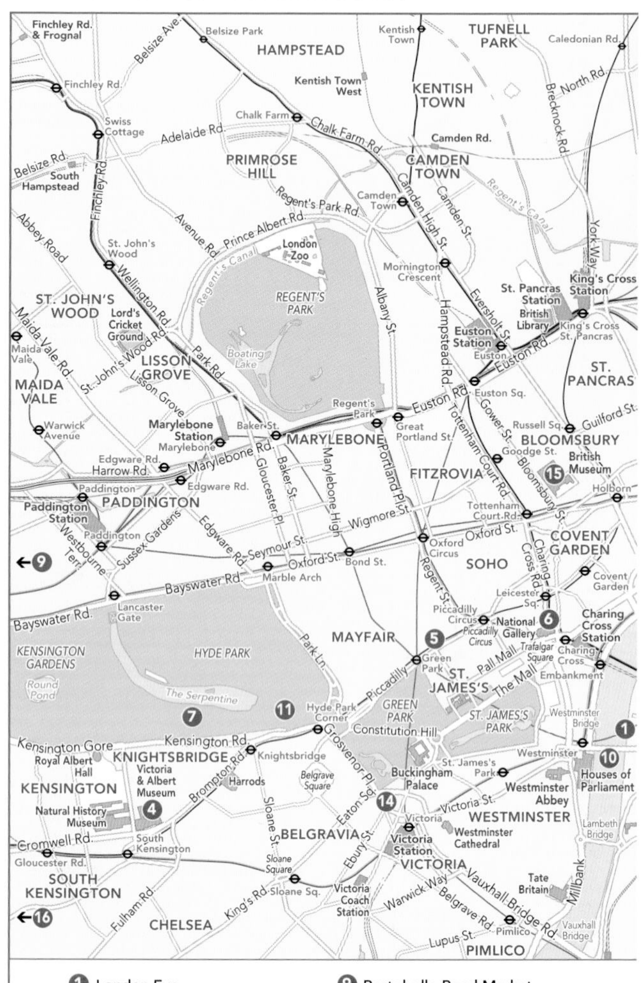

1. London Eye
2. Tate Boat
3. Pub crawl through the City
4. Friday Late at the V&A
5. The Wolseley
6. National Gallery
7. The Serpentine boat hire
8. Cocktails at the Sky Garden
9. Portobello Road Market
10. Big Ben
11. Hyde Park's Rotten Row
12. Millennium Bridge
13. Shakespeare's Globe Theatre
14. Tea at the Goring
15. The British Museum
16. Hampton Court Hedge Maze

Previous page: Riders enjoy views of the London cityscape from the London Eye Ferris wheel.

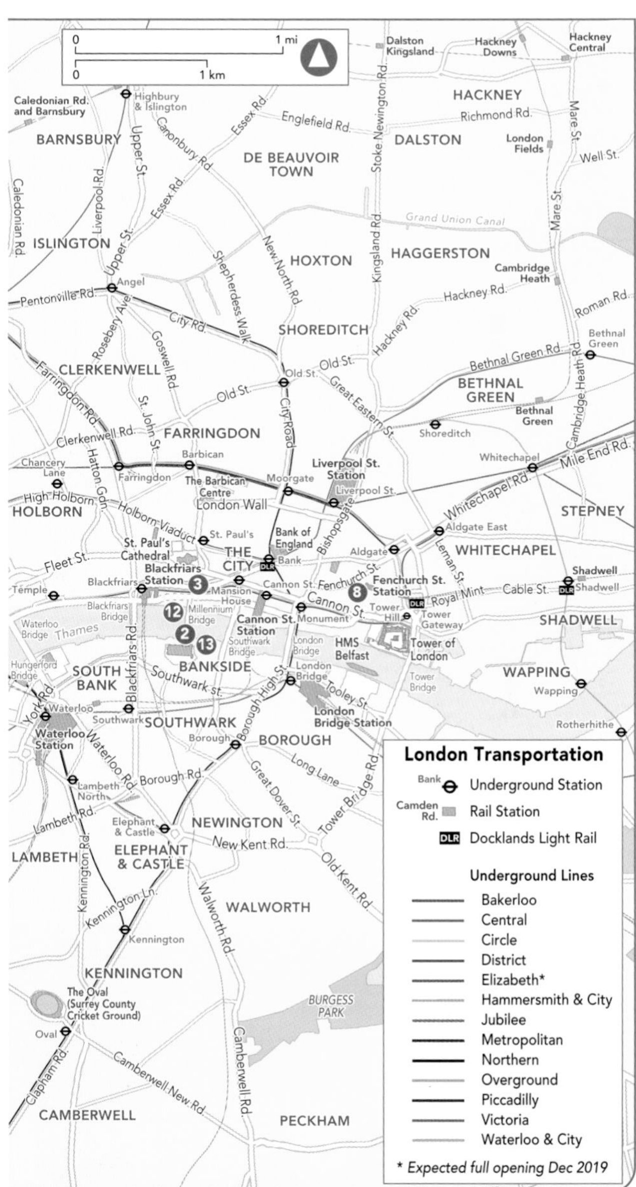
0
1 mi
0
1 km
London Transportation
Underground Station
Rail Station
Docklands Light Rail
Underground Lines
Bakerloo
Central
Circle
District
Elizabeth*
Hammersmith & City
Jubilee
Metropolitan
Northern
Overground
Piccadilly
Victoria
Waterloo & City
* Expected full opening Dec 2019
HACKNEY
DALSTON
DE BEAUVOIR TOWN
BARNSBURY
ISLINGTON
HOXTON
HAGGERSTON
SHOREDITCH
CLERKENWELL
BETHNAL GREEN
FARRINGDON
HOLBORN
THE CITY
STEPNEY
WHITECHAPEL
SHADWELL
WAPPING
SOUTH BANK
BANKSIDE
SOUTHWARK
BOROUGH
NEWINGTON
LAMBETH
ELEPHANT & CASTLE
WALWORTH
KENNINGTON
CAMBERWELL
PECKHAM
BURGESS PARK
Thames
Grand Union Canal
Dalston Kingsland
Hackney Downs
Hackney Central
Highbury & Islington
Caledonian Rd. and Barnsbury
London Fields
Cambridge Heath
Bethnal Green
Angel
Old St.
Shoreditch
Whitechapel
Chancery Lane
Farringdon
Barbican
Moorgate
Liverpool St. Station
Liverpool St.
The Barbican Centre
London Wall
St. Paul's
St. Paul's Cathedral
Bank of England
Bank
Aldgate
Aldgate East
Temple
Blackfriars
Blackfriars Station
Blackfriars Bridge
Mansion House
Cannon St.
Cannon St. Station
Monument
Fenchurch St. Station
Tower Hill
Tower Gateway
Tower of London
Tower Bridge
HMS Belfast
Shadwell
Wapping
Rotherhithe
Waterloo Bridge
Millennium Bridge
Southwark Bridge
London Bridge
London Bridge Station
Hungerford Bridge
Waterloo
Waterloo Station
Southwark
Borough
Lambeth North
Elephant & Castle
Kennington
The Oval (Surrey County Cricket Ground)
Oval
Englefield Rd.
Richmond Rd.
Mare St.
Well St.
Stoke Newington Rd.
Essex Rd.
Canonbury Rd.
Upper St.
Liverpool Rd.
Caledonian Rd.
Kingsland Rd.
New North Rd.
Shepherdess Walk
Pentonville Rd.
City Rd.
Rosebery Ave.
Goswell Rd.
Hackney Rd.
Roman Rd.
Bethnal Green Rd.
Cambridge Heath Rd.
Great Eastern St.
City Road
Farringdon Rd.
St. John St.
Clerkenwell Rd.
Hatton Gdn.
High Holborn
Holborn Viaduct
Mile End Rd.
Whitechapel Rd.
Bishopsgate
Leman St.
Fleet St.
Fenchurch St.
Royal Mint
Cable St.
Blackfriars Rd.
Southwark St.
Borough High St.
Tooley St.
York Rd.
Waterloo Rd.
Borough Rd.
Long Lane
Great Dover St.
Tower Bridge Rd.
Lambeth Rd.
New Kent Rd.
Old Kent Rd.
Kennington Rd.
Kennington Ln.
Walworth Rd.
Camberwell New Rd.
Camberwell Rd.
Clapham Rd.
3
8
12
2
13

You can explore the wonders of science, history, and nature at world-class museums, eat yourself to a bigger dress size at top-notch restaurants, marvel at just how much gold and jewelry fill the royal palaces and castles, and say you've "done" London. But to get to *know* London, you need to experience the special moments that reveal the city's true character. Below are some of the best.

❶ **Take photos from the top of the London Eye.** The top of this Ferris wheel is the best place to get a picture-perfect shot of London's far-reaching landscape. Any time is a good time for a ride, but for a truly breathtaking photo opportunity book a "night flight" for when the sun starts to sink and the lights come on across the city. *See p 11,* ❺.

❷ **Take an inter-art cruise aboard the Tate Boat.** Running between the sister art museums of Tate Britain and Tate Modern, the boat allows you to instantly swap an eyeful of paintings and installations for views of some of the Thames' iconic sights, including the London Eye and Big Ben. The boat itself is a work of art with a colorful spotted livery by Damien Hirst. *See p 18.*

❸ **Get to know Londoners in their natural habitat, with a pub crawl through the City.** A trip to a traditional boozer can combine many interests, such as history (many pubs have been going a *very* long time), dining, pub games, and of course, a wide range of beers and wines to sample. Be sure to pace yourself. *See p 130.*

❹ **Dig the music (classical, contemporary, or jazz) at Friday Late at the V&A,** played under the museum's extraordinary Chihuly chandelier on Friday evenings. Several of the renowned museum's galleries are open for exploring, and the relaxed atmosphere—helped by an open bar—makes for a leisurely and seductive visit. Pick up a ticket for one of the lectures, which start from 6:30pm, and round off the night with a browse at the gift shop. *See p 33.*

❺ **Dine next to a celebrity at the Wolseley,** but act unimpressed. Don't even think about autographs, Instagram, or gaping at this Piccadilly hot spot, where the modern British cuisine is good and the clientele often stellar. Make lunch and dinner reservations in advance of

A pub-crawl stop at the Coach & Horses in Covent Garden.

Spectacular blown-glass chandelier by artist Dale Chihuly greets visitors to the V&A Museum.

your visit. Weekdays and nights are better than weekends to catch sight of a celeb, and remember: Only Americans dine before 8pm. *See p 111.*

6 Print a poster of your favorite masterpiece at the National Gallery. The computers in the Sainsbury Wing offer virtual reconnaissance tours of this huge, world-renowned, treasure-packed museum and allow you to print high-quality posters of any painting in the gallery's collection in a variety of sizes. The database holds more than 2,000 works—it's a real kick to scroll through them. *See p 22,* **6**.

7 Crisscross the scenic Serpentine in a pedal boat on a sunny morning April through October, as ducks and geese wheel overhead. The little island on the north side is reputed to be local resident J. M. Barrie's inspiration for the Island of the Lost Boys in *Peter Pan.* Bring a camera. If you're not feeling too energetic, opt for a rowboat and let a companion do the work. *See p 90,* **5**.

8 Drink cocktails in the Sky Garden, a unique green space at the top of the "Walkie Talkie," one of the capital's newest skyscrapers. The bar provides the best opportunity to experience London from above, and to see even newer rival skyscrapers emerging across the skyline. *See p 123.*

9 Haggle for a bargain at Portobello Road Market, either at the open-air stalls or in its warrenlike indoor arcades. You may get 10% to 15% off the asking price, which everyone involved knows is set just for negotiation. Saturday's the big day for this famous antiques market, and part of the fun is sharing the street with seething crowds of bargain hunters and loiterers. *See p 86.*

10 Listen to Big Ben strike the hour. The bongs at midnight on December 31 will obviously get the biggest reaction, but this is a very London pleasure whatever the hour. It's the bell itself that's named Big Ben, even though most assign that name to the whole clock tower.

Dining at The Wolseley in Piccadilly.

Portobello Road Market in Notting Hill.

Although the bell has a crack in it and can't sound an E note, its chimed aria from Handel's *Messiah* is the undisputed aural symbol of London. *See p 10,* ❷.

⓫ **Ride down Hyde Park's Rotten Row on horseback** and you'll feel like a character in an 18th-century English novel—at least, if you ignore the passing joggers, in-line skaters, and cyclists. There's no better way to absorb the atmosphere of London's most popular park. Only skilled riders should let their horses try a canter; novices will still enjoy the experience at walking speed. *See p 90,* ❼.

⓬ **Stand in the middle of the Thames on the Millennium Bridge,** which spans not just the river but also the centuries, with St. Paul's Cathedral on one side and Tate Modern on the other. The views of the cityscape are impressive, especially at sunrise and sunset. *See p 13,* ❾.

⓭ **Become part of the play at Shakespeare's Globe Theatre** as one of the "groundlings" who stand in front of the stage, much as the rabble did during Shakespeare's time. You never know when the actors might mingle among you to bellow out their lines. It's a truly Elizabethan experience, minus the pickpockets and the spitting. *See p 141.*

⓮ **Stuff yourself with a full afternoon tea** at the Goring. This deluxe hotel rises to the task, impressing visitors with an array of sandwiches, scones with clotted cream, and cakes—all washed down with a cuppa from their vast tea menu. Don't make dinner plans: You won't be hungry. *See p 105.*

⓯ **Explore the breadth of the old Empire at the British Museum,** where priceless treasures acquired from all parts of the globe—including the Rosetta Stone and the Elgin Marbles—testify to the power that Britain once exerted over the farthest reaches of the world, and give an insight into just how greedy its adventurers were. *See p 24,* ⓫.

⓰ **Lose your way inside Hampton Court Palace's Hedge Maze,** with winding paths that cover nearly half a mile. When you extricate yourself from its clutches, stroll through centuries of architectural styles featured at this stunning palace, the country home of many an English monarch, including Henry VIII. Don't neglect the gift shops. *See p 50.* ●

Soldiers on horseback in Hyde Park.

1 The Best **Full-Day Tours**

The Best in One Day

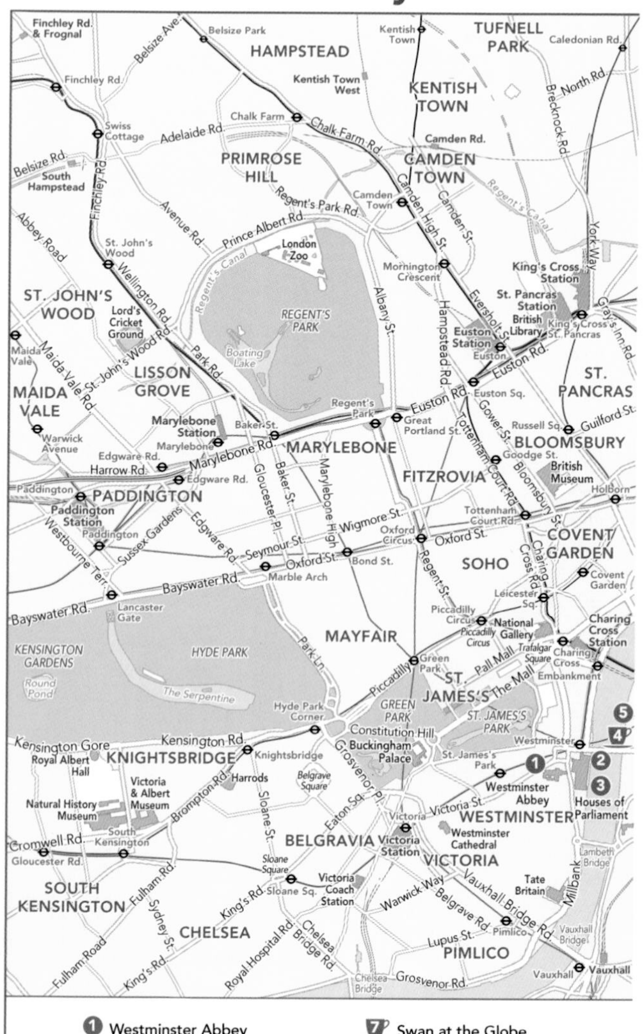

1. Westminster Abbey
2. Big Ben
3. Houses of Parliament
4. Izakaya Hannah
5. London Eye
6. Shakespeare's Globe Theatre
7. Swan at the Globe
8. The Shard
9. Millennium Bridge
10. St. Paul's Cathedral
11. Museum of London

Previous page: Westminster Abbey.

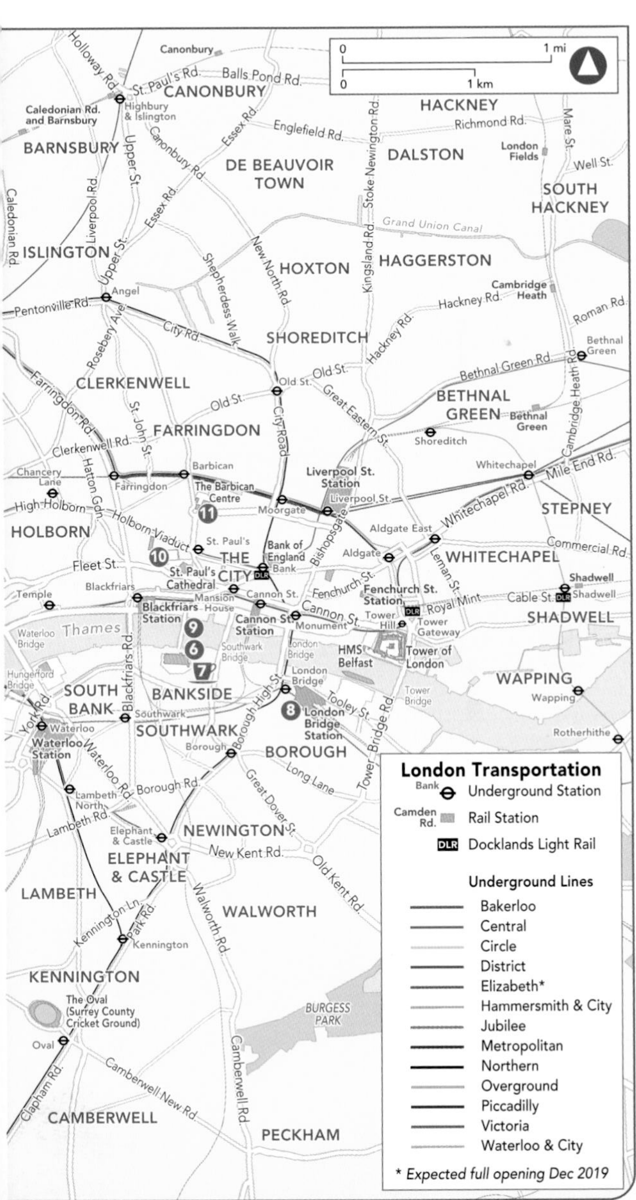
London Transportation
Underground Station
Rail Station
Docklands Light Rail
Underground Lines
Bakerloo
Central
Circle
District
Elizabeth*
Hammersmith & City
Jubilee
Metropolitan
Northern
Overground
Piccadilly
Victoria
Waterloo & City
* Expected full opening Dec 2019
CANONBURY
HACKNEY
BARNSBURY
DE BEAUVOIR TOWN
DALSTON
SOUTH HACKNEY
ISLINGTON
HOXTON
HAGGERSTON
SHOREDITCH
CLERKENWELL
BETHNAL GREEN
FARRINGDON
HOLBORN
STEPNEY
THE CITY
WHITECHAPEL
SHADWELL
WAPPING
SOUTH BANK
BANKSIDE
SOUTHWARK
BOROUGH
NEWINGTON
ELEPHANT & CASTLE
LAMBETH
WALWORTH
KENNINGTON
CAMBERWELL
PECKHAM
BURGESS PARK
Thames
The Oval (Surrey County Cricket Ground)
Tower of London
HMS Belfast
St. Paul's Cathedral
The Barbican Centre
Bank of England

This tour encapsulates "Iconic London." You'll be visiting attractions, including Westminster Abbey and St. Paul's, that have been familiar to Londoners for hundreds of years, as well as more recent arrivals, such as the London Eye, and modern re-creations of the past, like Shakespeare's Globe. Total time: 1 very busy day. Total history covered: More than 1,000 years. START: **Tube to Westminster.**

❶ ★★★ Westminster Abbey. The 1,000-year-old abbey is one of the finest examples of medieval architecture in Europe. Like a giant shrine to the nation, it contains some 3,300 memorials to monarchs, nobles, and other great British figures from down the ages. Edward III, Mary Queen of Scots, Elizabeth I (whose death mask was the model for her tomb's figure), and Henry V, the hero of Agincourt, all have elaborately decorated sarcophagi. Purcell and Elgar, Newton and Darwin, are also buried here. Don't miss the Gothic fan vault of the **Henry VIII Lady Chapel** (reflected in a large mirror for close-up viewing) and its elaborate carved choir stalls; England's oldest remaining door, from 1050, beside the **Chapter House**; and the treasure-filled **Queen's Diamond Jubilee Galleries**, opened in 2018. At **Poets' Corner** you'll find monuments and tombs of literary names such as Chaucer, Shakespeare, Austen, Henry James, and Dickens. 🕔 *1 ½ hr. Dean's Yard.* ☎ *020/7222-5152. www.westminster-abbey.org. £22 adults, £17 seniors & students, £9 children 6–16, £40–£45 family; half-price Wed after 4:30pm. Mon–Tues & Thurs–Fri 9:30am–4:30pm, Wed 9:30am–7pm, Sat 9:30am–2pm. Last admission 1 hr. before closing; arrive before 9:30am to avoid long lines. Tube: Westminster.*

❷ ★ Big Ben. The iconic clock tower of the Palace of Westminster is now officially named the Elizabeth Tower, to mark the queen's 60 years on the throne. Most, however, continue to call it by its nickname, Big Ben, even though that technically refers only to the tower's largest bell. This 14-tonne (15-ton) bell, installed in 1858, is believed to have been named after the rather portly commissioner of public works at the time, Sir Benjamin Hall. Once refurbishment is completed in 2021, visitors will once again be able to make an ascent up the tower's 334 spiral steps by special guided tour; for now, everyone

Houses of Parliament at dusk.

The London Eye.

must content themselves with a snapshot. ⏲ *5 min. Near St. Stephen's Entrance of Westminster Palace, Old Palace Yard. www.parliament.uk/visiting.*

❸ ★ Houses of Parliament. The immense 3-hectare (7.4-acre) Palace of Westminster, a splendid example of Gothic Revival architecture, dates back to 1840 (the original palace was all but destroyed by fire in 1834). It's home to the 600-plus M.P.s (Members of Parliament, the elected representatives of the people) of the House of Commons and the 700-plus appointed members of the House of Lords (who scrutinize the decisions made in the Commons). You may observe debates for free from the Strangers' Galleries in both houses, but the long lines usually make this attraction better for a quick photo opportunity than a lengthy visit. The only exceptions are on Saturdays throughout the year and Tuesday through Friday during Parliament's recess periods, when the palace is open for guided tours. ⏲ *5 min. Old Palace Yard.* ☎ *020/7219-4114. www.parliament.uk/visiting. Free admission to Commons debates: Mon–Tues 2:30–10:30pm, Wed 11:30am–7:30pm, Thurs 9:30am–5:30pm, Fri 9:30am–3pm. Guided tours (1½ hr.): £25.50 adults, £11 children 5–15; Sat 11am–4:15pm (check website for exact tour and opening times). Tube: Westminster.*

At the mammoth County Hall building you can snack Japanese style right by the London Eye in ❹ ★ **Izakaya Hannah**. The menu has sushi and sashimi, plus such hot favorites as katsu, chicken kara-age, and tempura. *Westminster Bridge Rd.* ☎ *020/3802-0402. www.izakayahannah.com. ££.*

❺ ★★★ kids London Eye. The huge Ferris wheel that solemnly rotates one revolution per half-hour is already an icon of the city, and is now begrudgingly loved by even the most hardened London traditionalist. You are encouraged to buy a timed ticket well in advance (thus securing a discount on the prices listed below), but your ride can end in disappointment if you get a gray and rainy day. Book yourself a "night flight" and you're guaranteed the twinkling lights of the city. Same-day tickets are sometimes available in the off-season. Show up 30 minutes before your scheduled departure time (15 if you have a Fast Track ticket). Don't forget your camera. ⏲ *1 hr. South Bank (at Westminster Bridge). www.londoneye.com. £27 adults, £22 children 3–15, £94 family. Prebook online for a 10% discount. Sept–Apr daily 11am–6pm, May–Aug 10am–8:30pm. Closed 3 weeks in Jan. Tube: Westminster or Waterloo.*

6 ★★ **Shakespeare's Globe Theatre.** Even if you don't have tickets to a play (p 141), the Globe is still a fascinating place to visit. It was rebuilt in painstaking detail on a parking lot near the site of the original theatre (and only those tools authentic to the period of the original were used in its construction). In the late 1500s/early 1600s Shakespeare's works were performed here to delight the nobility (who sat in the tiers) as well as the rabble (who stood before the stage). You can choose either option when purchasing tickets, weighing comfort versus proximity to the stage. Changing displays at the onsite exhibition focus on topics such as Elizabethan stagecraft, the frost fairs of medieval London (when the Thames would freeze solid and people would party on the river for days) or the juicy history of nearby Southwark, once a haven of prostitutes and thieves. *1 hr. 21 New Globe Walk. ☎ 020/7902-1400 (exhibition) or 020/7401-9919 (box office). www.shakespearesglobe.com. Admission to museum & exhibits: £17 adults, £15.50 seniors, £10 children 5–15, £46 family (2 adults & 3 children). Daily 9am–5pm (closed during afternoon theatre matinees when tours of the remains of the Rose Theatre may be offered instead—call for schedules). Tube: London Bridge or Southwark.*

Millennium Bridge.

The 7 ★ **Swan at the Globe** is a fine choice for a restorative break, and has a Thames-side view of London. The menu in the bar features reasonably priced English favorites, such as fish pie or sausages and mash, and cheese or meat sharing platters, while the restaurant is a fancier (and more expensive) affair. *21 Globe Walk (off Thames Path). ☎ 020/7928-9444. www.swanlondon.co.uk. £–££.*

View of the Shard from London Bridge.

8 ★★ **The Shard.** By far the most visible of London's recent building projects, this great, pointy, 72-story glass skyscraper is now Western Europe's tallest building. Standing 310m (1,017-ft.) high, it towers over the revamped London Bridge Station like a great shiny pyramid. Its upper observation decks (floors 69 and 72) have London's loftiest views, offering unprecedented (and giddying) panoramas over the city. From up here, the London Eye looks like a tiny toy spinning top. Prebook tickets for big savings (up to 30%) on the walk-up prices listed below. *1*

hr. London Bridge. ☎ *0344/499-7222. www.theviewfromtheshard.com. £31 adults, £25 children 5–15, £80 family. Thurs–Sat 10am–10pm, Sun–Wed 10am–7pm. Tube: London Bridge.*

9 ★ kids Millennium Bridge. This silver sliver of a footbridge connecting Bankside to the City is a wonderful spot from which to take photos of the surrounding landmarks (and note the incongruity of the Globe nestled among its 20th-century neighbors). When it first opened in 2000, it swayed and was temporarily shut down to be stabilized—but people still refer to it as the "wobbly bridge." 🕒 *10 min. Tube: Southwark or Blackfriars.*

10 ★★★ kids St. Paul's Cathedral. The dome of St. Paul's has been the defining icon of the London skyline since its construction after the Great Fire of 1666. It may not be the city's tallest structure anymore, but no modern skyscraper (even the much-admired "Gherkin") is held in such affection—or inspires the same awe— as Sir Christopher Wren's masterpiece. The cathedral was the culmination of Wren's unique and much-acclaimed fusion of classical (the exterior Greek-style columns) and baroque (the ornate interior decorations) architecture. The Whispering Gallery is a miracle of engineering, in which you can hear the murmurs of another person from across a large gallery. The 528 stairs to the Golden Gallery are demanding, but you'll be rewarded with a magnificent view not only of London but also of the interior of the cathedral 85m (279 ft.) below. Wren—who is buried in the cathedral's crypt alongside Admiral Lord Nelson, Wellington, and other military notables—considered it his ultimate achievement. Free audio guides are included in the admission price. 🕒 *1½ hr. Ludgate Hill (at Paternoster Sq.).* ☎ *020/7246-8357. www.stpauls.co.uk. £18 adults, £16 seniors & students, £8 children 6–17, £44 family. Mon–Sat 8:30am–4pm. Tube: St. Paul's.*

11 ★★ kids Museum of London. If it pertains to London's history, you'll find it here. Exhibits start at the prehistoric level and proceed to the 21st century, with interactive stops at all the great and terrible moments in London's long life, including "Roman London," the Great Fire, and the Swinging Sixties. Do not miss the ornate Lord Mayor's Coach, a 2.7-tonne (3-ton) gilt affair in which Cinderella would feel right at home. 🕒 *1½ hr. 150 London Wall (at Aldersgate St.).* ☎ *020/7001-9844. www.museumoflondon.org.uk. Free admission (except temporary exhibits). Daily 10am–6pm. Tube: Barbican or St. Paul's.*

St. Paul's Cathedral.

The Best in Two Days

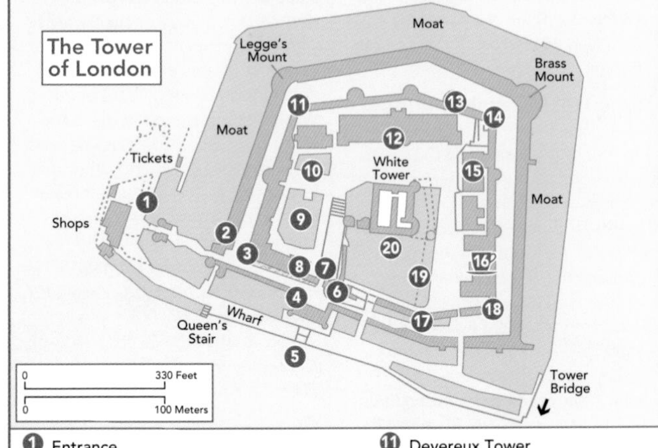

1. Entrance
2. Coins & Kings Exhibition
3. Bell Tower
4. Entrance to Medieval Palace & Wall Walks
5. Traitors' Gate
6. Wakefield Tower
7. Torture at the Tower Exhibition
8. Bloody Tower
9. Tower Green
10. Scaffold site
11. Devereux Tower
12. Crown Jewels Entrance
13. Royal Beasts Exhibition
14. Martin Tower
15. Fusiliers' Museum
16. New Armouries Cafe
17. Entrance to East Wall Walk
18. Salt Tower
19. Line of Roman City Wall
20. White Tower Entrance

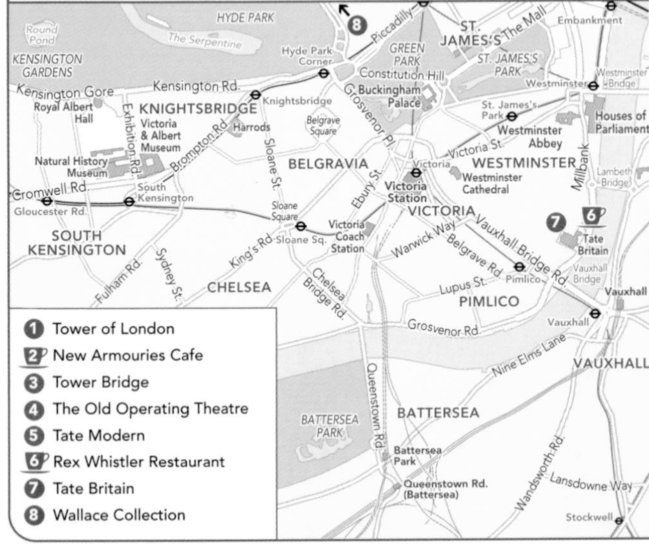

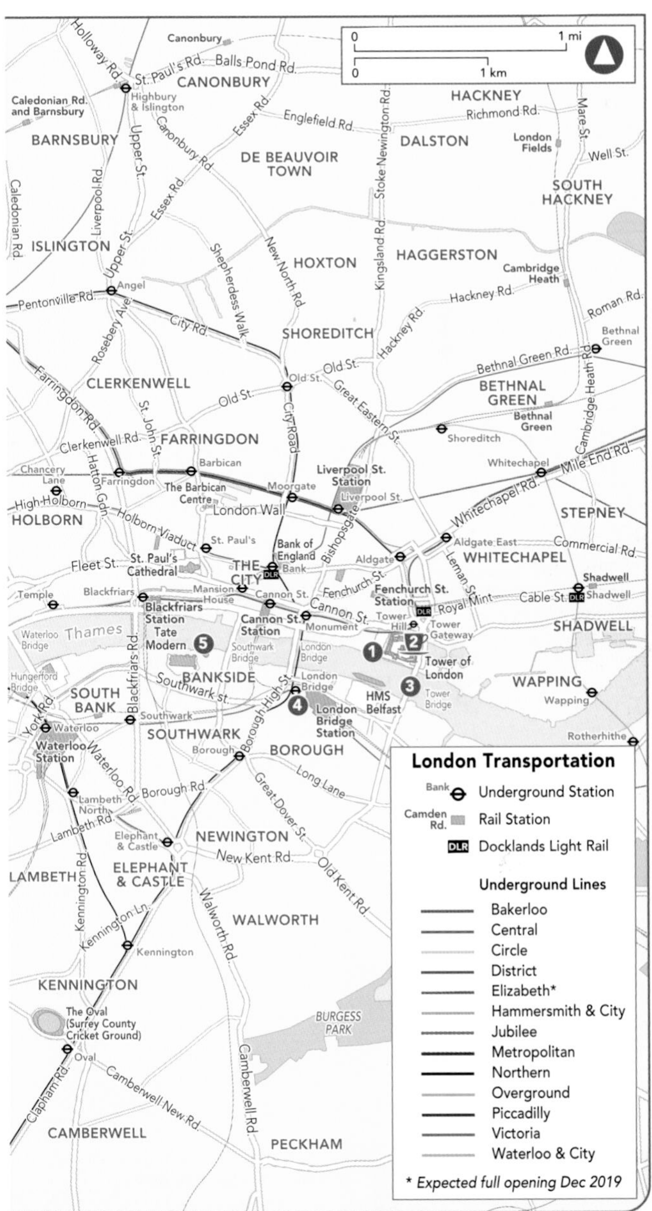
London Transportation
Bank Underground Station
Camden Rd. Rail Station
DLR Docklands Light Rail
Underground Lines
Bakerloo
Central
Circle
District
Elizabeth*
Hammersmith & City
Jubilee
Metropolitan
Northern
Overground
Piccadilly
Victoria
Waterloo & City
* Expected full opening Dec 2019
0 1 mi
0 1 km
CANONBURY
BARNSBURY
ISLINGTON
DE BEAUVOIR TOWN
HACKNEY
DALSTON
SOUTH HACKNEY
HOXTON
HAGGERSTON
SHOREDITCH
CLERKENWELL
FARRINGDON
BETHNAL GREEN
HOLBORN
THE CITY
STEPNEY
WHITECHAPEL
SHADWELL
WAPPING
SOUTH BANK
BANKSIDE
SOUTHWARK
BOROUGH
NEWINGTON
ELEPHANT & CASTLE
LAMBETH
WALWORTH
KENNINGTON
CAMBERWELL
PECKHAM
BURGESS PARK
The Oval (Surrey County Cricket Ground)
Thames
Tate Modern
Tower of London
HMS Belfast
Liverpool St. Station
Fenchurch St. Station
Cannon St. Station
Blackfriars Station
London Bridge Station
Waterloo Station
St. Paul's Cathedral
The Barbican Centre
Bank of England

On a second day you'll delve into the capital's history, exploring the buildings, jewels, and ghosts that make up the Tower of London; British art at Tate Britain; and the gruesome horrors of our medical past at the Old Operating Theatre. You'll also experience the new at the Tate Modern and traverse the Thames by boat, now (as always) the watery heart of the city. START: **Tube to Tower Hill.**

❶ ★★★ kids **Tower of London.** Begun by William the Conqueror in 1078, this fortress was added to by subsequent generations of kings and queens, and reflects the range of England's architectural styles over the last millennium. The Tower has a bloody past marked by power struggles, executions, and cruelty: The young nephews of Richard III were murdered here (probably) in 1483; two of Henry VIII's six wives (Anne Boleyn and Catherine Howard) were beheaded on Tower Green, as was England's 9-day queen, Lady Jane Grey. Yeoman Warders (or "Beefeaters") give gore-filled talks all day long, and actors offer living-history lessons as they wander about in period costume. The **Crown Jewels** are the most popular sight, just edging out the **Torture at the Tower** exhibit; the two together represent the awful accoutrements of power (and have the longest lines). The haunted—and haunting—Tower will thrill students of history and entertain kids too. *⏲ 2 hr. Tower Hill. ☎ 020/3166-6000. www.hrp.org.uk/TowerOfLondon. £21.50 adults, £16.40 seniors, £9.70 children 5–15, £38–£53 family. Tues–Sat 9am–5:30pm, Sun–Mon 10am–5:30pm, 'til 4:30pm Nov–Feb. Tube: Tower Hill.*

Tower Bridge.

Buy sandwiches at the ❷ **New Armouries Café** for an on-the-move picnic, or settle in for an early hot lunch of shepherd's pie, soup, or fish and chips. It's clean and pleasant though not hugely atmospheric, and by London standards isn't a rip-off. Snack kiosks are scattered around the Tower grounds, and the **Perkin Reveller** pub just outside has Thames views. *Inside Tower of London. ☎ 020/3166-6000. £.*

❸ ★ kids **Tower Bridge.** This picture-perfect bascule bridge—a term derived from the French for "seesaw"—has spanned the Thames since 1894. There's no denying the physical beauty of the neo-Gothic structure: Its skeleton of steel girders is clothed in ornate masonry using Cornish granite and Portland stone designed to harmonize elegantly with the nearby Tower of London. Its lower span opens and closes regularly thanks to some heavy-duty hydraulics (a board next to the bridge tells you when, or check www.towerbridge.org.uk/lift-times). Fnd out more at the **Tower Bridge Exhibition**, where you can also ascend to the bridge's

Tower Ghosts

The Tower of London, said to be the most haunted spot in England, fairly overflows with supernatural manifestations of tormented souls.

The ghost of Queen Anne Boleyn (executed in 1536 on a trumped-up charge of treason after she failed to produce a male heir for Henry VIII) is the most frequently spotted. The tragic shades of the Little Princes—allegedly murdered by Richard III in 1483—have been spied in the Bloody Tower. Ghostly reenactments of the Tower Green beheading of the Countess of Salisbury—who was slowly hacked to death by her inept executioner on May 27, 1541—have been seen on its anniversary. The screams of Guy Fawkes, who gave up his co-conspirators in the Gunpowder Plot under torture, reputedly still echo around the grounds.

Other spirits you may encounter (the no-nonsense Tower guards have had run-ins with them all) include Sir Walter Raleigh, Lady Jane Grey, and Henry VI.

top-level walkways for a bird's-eye view of the Tower of London and the Thames, 43m (141 ft.) below through a glass floor. (Acrophobics need not apply.) ⏲ *1 hr. Tower Bridge Rd.* ☎ *020/7403-3761. www.towerbridge.org.uk. £9.80 adults, £6.80 seniors, £4.20 children 5–15, £15–£27 family. Daily Apr–Sept 10am–5:30pm, Oct–Mar 9:30am–5pm. Tube: Tower Hill.*

❹ ★★ kids **The Old Operating Theatre.** A wooden table where operations—usually amputations—were performed without anesthetic or antiseptic (leather restraints held the patient in place, while pain relief was provided by alcohol and the speed of the surgeon); an early pair of forceps; and other instruments of outdated medical practices will fast cure any complaints you may have about modern medicine. ⏲ *30 min. 9a St. Thomas's St.* ☎ *020//7188-2679. www.oldoperatingtheatre.com. £6.50 adults, £5 seniors, £3.50 children 17 & under, £15 family. Daily 10:30am–5pm. Tube: London Bridge.*

❺ ★★★ kids **Tate Modern.** The world's most popular modern art museum, this offshoot of Tate Britain is housed in the gargantuan shell of a converted 1950s brick power station and its modern extension, the **Blavatnik Building**, which opened in 2016 (and resembles a twisted, truncated, brick pyramid). Through the main entrance, you enter a vast space, the **Turbine Hall**, where a succession of temporary exhibitions is held—the bigger

Vintage pill bottles in the Old Operating Theatre.

Sailing the Tate Boat

The Tate boat ferry service between the two Tate galleries on opposite banks of the Thames is one of London's most useful tourist creations. The same people who built the London Eye designed the ferry's dramatic Millbank Pier, and the colorful catamaran was decorated by a former *enfant terrible* of the British contemporary art scene, Damian Hirst. The 18-minute service—formally denoted as line RB2—stops off at the London Eye en route (p 11, ❺), and makes a convenient and scenic way to get from one to the other.

Alas, it's not free. One-way tickets cost £8.10 adults, £4.05 kids 5 to 15, free for kids 4 and under. If you have a London Travelcard (p 165), you get a good discount. Tickets can be bought online or at the Tate Britain or Tate Modern, or you can simply use the yellow Oyster reader (p 165). The Tate Boat runs daily every 40 minutes (more often in high season) between 9:45am and 6pm. For precise service times, call ☎ 020/7887-8888 or check www.tate.org.uk/visit/tate-boat.

and more ambitious, the better. Highlights have included 100 million ceramic sunflower seeds covering the floor (Ai Weiwei) and a maze made out of 14,000 polyethylene boxes (Rachel Whiteread). Spread over multiple levels, the permanent collection encompasses a great body of modern art dating from 1900 to right now. It covers all the heavy hitters, including Matisse, Pollock, Picasso, Dalí, Duchamp, and Warhol, and is arranged according to movement—Surrealism, Cubism, Expressionism—single artists (such as Bridget Riley), or innovatively curated themes (Rothko vs. Monet, for example). The large complex has multiple cafes and bars, plus one of London's best art bookshops. ⏱ *1½ hr. Bankside. ☎ 020/7887-8888. www.tate.org.uk/modern. Free admission, except for some temporary exhibitions. Sun–Thurs 10am–6pm, Fri–Sat 10am–10pm. Tube: Southwark, Blackfriars, St. Paul's, or London Bridge.*

Colorfully attired Beefeater at the Tower of London.

The Tate's own ❻ ★★ **Rex Whistler Restaurant** serves tasty modern British cuisine in a cheery dining room whose walls were decorated in 1927 with a vast mural executed by Whistler himself. *Inside Tate Britain. ☎ 020/7887-8825. ££.*

7 ★★ Tate Britain. Housed in a charming neoclassical building, which looks a bit like a miniature British Museum, Tate Britain opened in 1894 thanks to generous donations of money and art from sugar mogul Sir Henry Tate. It holds the country's finest collection of British art, covering the period from the 16th century to the present day, and has an unparalleled collection of works by revolutionary landscape painter J. M. W. Turner (1775–1851), who bequeathed most of his works to the museum. Other notable artists whose works adorn the walls include satirist William Hogarth, polymath William Blake, portraiture painters Thomas Gainsborough and Joshua Reynolds, and the members of the 19th-century Pre-Raphaelite Brotherhood. ⏲ *1½ hr. Millbank.* ☎ *020/7887-8888. www.tate.org.uk/britain. Free admission, except for temporary exhibitions. Daily 10am–6pm. Tube: Pimlico.*

8 ★ Wallace Collection. This collection offers an astonishing glimpse into the buying power of the English gentry following the French Revolution, when important art and furnishings were made homeless by the guillotine. In 1897, Lady Wallace left this entire mansion and its contents to the nation

Long Gallery at the Wallace Collection.

on the condition they be kept intact, without additions or subtractions. The paintings are outstanding, with works by Titian, Gainsborough, Rembrandt, and Hals (including his famous *Laughing Cavalier*). The collection also includes Sèvres porcelain, 18th-century French decorative art, and an array of European and Asian armaments that are works of art in their own right. There's also a pretty courtyard bar/restaurant. ⏲ *1 hr. Hertford House, Manchester Sq.* ☎ *020/7563-9500. www.wallacecollection.org. Free admission, except for some temporary exhibitions. Daily 10am–5pm. A free guided tour of the museum highlights is offered daily at 2:30pm. Tube: Bond St.*

Roy Lichtenstein's "Whaam!" at the Tate Modern.

The Best in Three Days

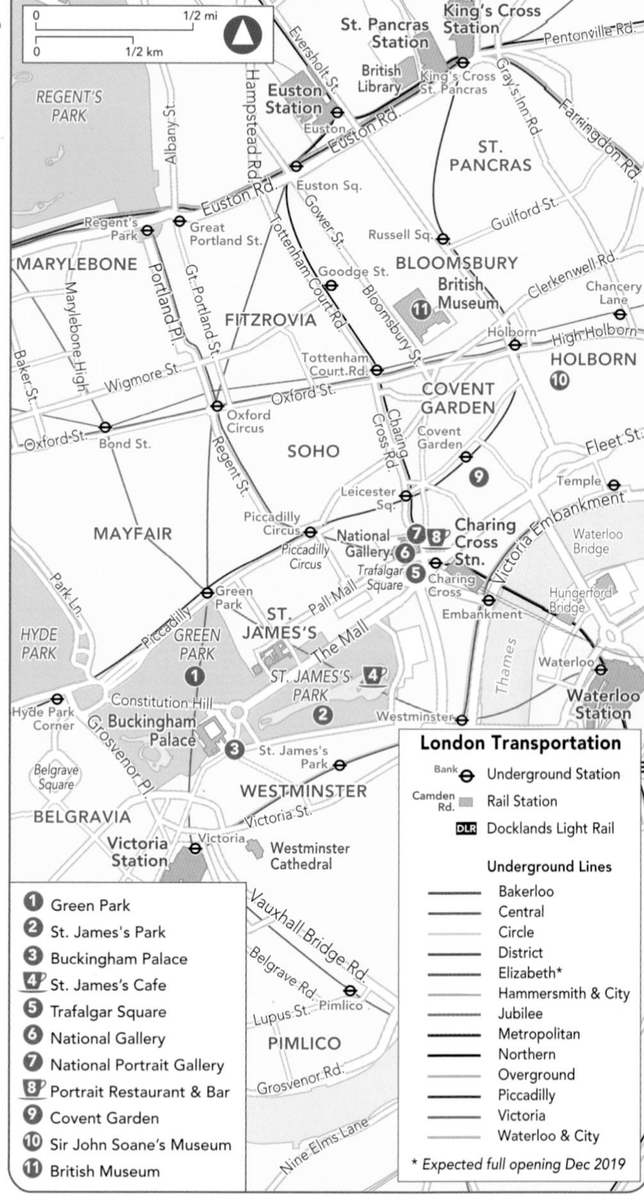

The tour begins with some of London's most utterly British attractions—sweeping royal parks and the pomp and ceremony of the Changing of the Guard—and finishes with gloriously elegant clutter at the Sir John Soane's Museum. In between are the National Gallery and perhaps the finest museum of human civilization, the British Museum. START: **Tube to Green Park.**

1 ★ kids Green Park. London's royal parks are often busy affairs, filled with flowerbeds, statues, ponds, playgrounds, and more, but all you'll find here are acres of rolling green lawns and tall, shady trees. In summer, scores of local workers sun their lunch hours away either on the grass or on the stripy deckchairs (£1.60/hr.) that represent the park's one formal facility. Founded in 1660 in order to allow Charles II to travel between St. James's Park and Hyde Park without leaving royal soil, the park's stripped-back nature supposedly dates from the time the queen caught Charles giving flowers from the park to another woman. In a rage, she had all the flowerbeds torn up. ⏲ *15 min. www.royalparks.org.uk. Tube: Green Park.*

2 ★★ kids St. James's Park. Southeast of Green Park, this is arguably London's prettiest park. It's certainly difficult to believe that this was, up until the 18th century, the center of a notorious scene, where prostitutes conducted their business and drunken rakes took unsteady aim at dueling opponents. It's now very respectable, with a wildfowl pond, weeping willows, very tame gray squirrels, and numerous flowerbeds. ⏲ *30 min. www.royalparks.org.uk.*

3 ★ Buckingham Palace. "Buck House," the queen's famous abode in London (if the yellow-and-red Royal standard is flying, it means she's home), is the setting for the pageantry of the **Changing of the Guard,** a London tradition that attracts more people than it warrants. A better place to see all the queen's horses and all the queen's men in action is at Horse Guards Parade (p 71, 3). But if you're determined to watch the guards change here, arrive a half-hour early to get a spot by the statue of Victoria; it offers a reasonably good view. The ceremony begins at 10:45am sharp every

Flowerbeds in bloom in St. James's Park.

A riot of tulips at Buckingham Palace.

Monday, Wednesday, Friday, and Sunday—in theory, anyway; it's often canceled in bad weather. *45 min.* *See p 35,* 1.

In the northeast sector of St. James's Park, 4 ★ kids **St. James's Café** is a light, modern spot with picturesque views of the London Eye and Whitehall from its pleasant roof terrace. *In St. James's Park.* ☎ *020/7839-1149. £.*

5 kids Trafalgar Square. Where a visit to this square once involved battling traffic and dodging pigeons, a part-pedestrianization and a ban on bird-feeding means it is now once again possible to appreciate the grand surroundings. Bordering the square are the **National Gallery** (see below) on the northern side, **St. Martin-in-the-Fields** to the east, and in the northwest corner, the "**Fourth Plinth,**" which supports (literally) temporary art installations. Towering above everything is **Nelson's Column,** a pillar topped with a statue of Britain's most revered naval commander, Horatio, Viscount Nelson. The square is named for his most famous and (for him) fatal victory, the 1805 Battle of Trafalgar. This is often the focal point of rallies, demonstrations, and celebrations. *15 min.*

6 ★★★ kids National Gallery. This outstanding art museum dominating the north side of Trafalgar Square sits roughly where the stables of King Henry VIII used to be. Founded in 1832 with a collection of 38 paintings bought by the British government, the National is now home to some 2,300 works representing the development of western European painting from 1250 to 1900.

The National Gallery in Trafalgar Square.

National Gallery Highlights

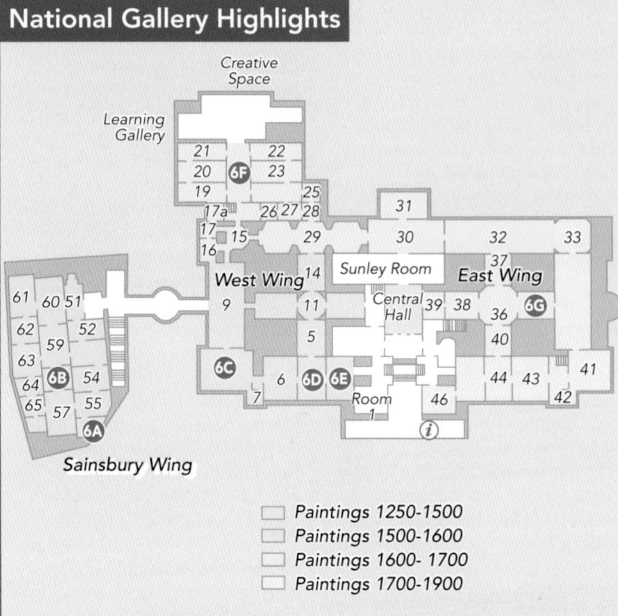

Start in the 6A ★★★ **Sainsbury Wing's Room 56,** where you'll find early European works, including Van Eyck's haunting *Arnolfini Portrait.* Note the words inscribed over the mirror: JAN VAN EYCK WAS HERE/1434. For a contrast in mood, go to 6B **Room 58** for Botticelli's voluptuous *Venus and Mars.* The 6C **West Wing's Room 8** has an ethereal Raphael painting known as *The Madonna of the Pinks* (1506) as well as a couple of Michelangelos. Holbein's *Ambassadors* is in 6D **Room 4;** the skull in the foreground looks distorted unless you look at it from the right-hand side. Pay your respects to Titian in 6E **Room 2,** and then leave the Renaissance for the 6F **North Wing** and Dutch, French, and Spanish masterpieces from 1600 to 1800, including Rembrandt's self-portrait at the age of 63 in Room 22 and Velazquez's controversial *Rokeby Venus* (Room 30). Finish at the 6G **East Wing** and the works of Impressionists van Gogh (including his *Chair* in Room 43), Monet, and Renoir, among others. *1½ hr. Trafalgar Sq. ☎ 020/7747-2885. www.nationalgallery.org.uk. Free admission, except for temporary exhibitions. Daily 10am–6pm, till 9pm Fri. Tube: Charing Cross or Leicester Sq.*

7 ★★ kids **National Portrait Gallery.** Beside the National Gallery, the NPG is the place to put faces to the names of those who have shaped Britain politically, socially, and culturally. The gallery's 10,000-plus portraits take in everyone from King Harold II (b. 1022),

Henry VIII, Shakespeare, and Charles Dickens to modern figures such as David Bowie and Princess Diana. Start at the top, where the earliest works are located. ⏲ *1 hr. St. Martin's Place.* ☎ *020/7306-0055. www.npg.org.uk. Free admission, except to temporary exhibitions. Sat–Wed 10am–6pm, Thurs–Fri 10am–9pm. Tube: Charing Cross or Leicester Sq.*

8 ★★ **Portrait Restaurant & Bar,** on the top floor of the NPG, commands spectacular views over Trafalgar Square. It's open through the day and for dinner (including a pre-theatre value deal) Thursday to Saturday, and serves afternoon tea. For cheaper snacks try the **Portrait Café**. *Inside National Portrait Gallery, St. Martin's Place.* ☎ *020/7312-2490. ££.*

9 ★ kids **Covent Garden.** The great fruit and vegetable market that used to form this area's centerpiece moved out in the early 1970s, but the glorious 19th-century market buildings remain. **Jubilee Market,** with inexpensive souvenirs, is set on the southern side of the arcade; at the western end you'll find antiques, crafts, and flea-market goods. A motley collection of jugglers and physical comedians perform on the Piazza, while in the main market building you can have a pint, grab a burger, or maybe experience an operatic performance by professionals from the **Royal Opera House** (p 139), which faces the arcade. ⏲ *30 min. Tube: Covent Garden.*

10 ★★ **Sir John Soane's Museum.** The distinguished British architect Sir John Soane (1753–1837) was also an avid hoarder. The bulk of his collection was amassed at the height of empire, when antiquities could be removed from their country of origin and displayed casually in one's home. Ancient tablets, sculptures, paintings (including William Hogarth's celebrated parable-painting, *A Rake's Progress*, and works by Turner and Canaletto), architectural models, and even an ancient Egyptian sarcophagus are strewn around in no particular order: This is essentially how he left it, and the haphazardness is part of the museum's charm. Small-group, curator-led museum tours (1 hr.; £10) are offered once or twice every day, but you'll need to book ahead—the popularity-to-size ratio here is insane, and justly so. ⏲ *1 hr. 12–13 Lincoln's Inn Fields.* ☎ *020/7405-2107. www.soane.org. Free admission. Wed–Sun 10am–5pm; monthly late-night opening till 9pm. Tube: Holborn or Chancery Lane.*

11 ★★★ kids **British Museum.** You could spend days exploring this world-renowned museum, but an hour or so is enough to get a flavor of what it has to offer. Visit on a Friday and you can stay 'til 8:30pm to enjoy a range of additional events, including films and lectures. ⏲ *1 hr.* *See tour p 26.* ●

2 The Best Special-Interest Tours

The British Museum

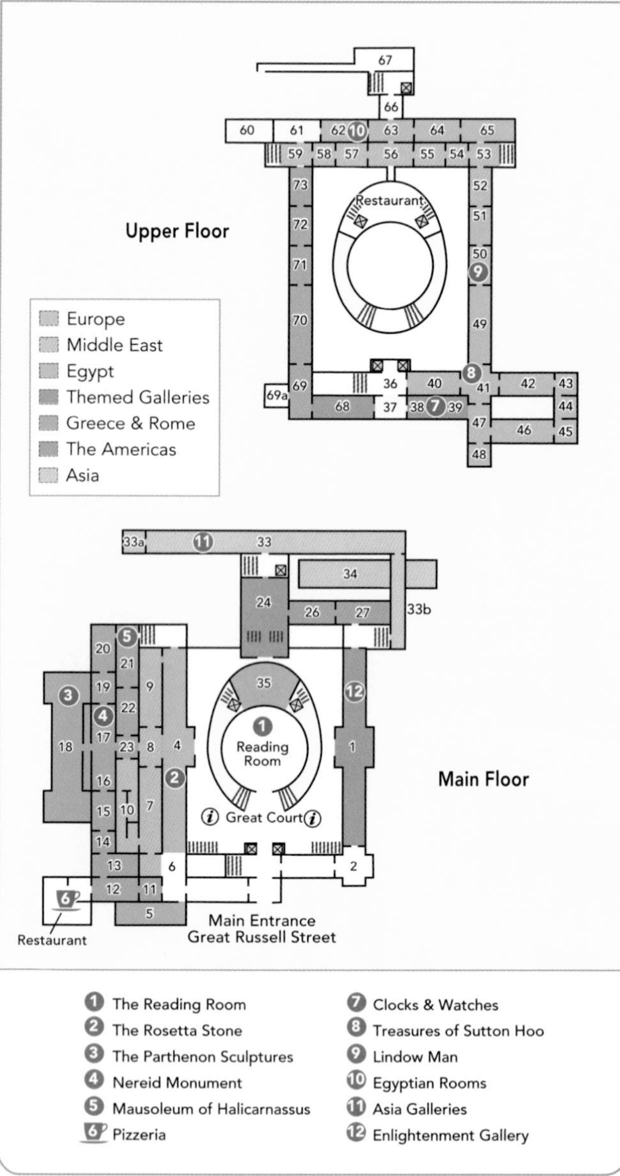

Previous page: The Great Hall of the British Museum.

The British Museum, started with a donation by the royal physician and collector Sir Hans Sloane in 1753, opened at a time when the expansion of the British Empire ensured its collection would be as eclectic as it was priceless. Note the frieze above the entrance—it signifies the museum's intention to encompass all the branches of science and the arts. START: **Tube to Holborn.**

1 ★★ The Reading Room. Located at the center of the **Great Court**, beneath the museum's crazy-paving-style glass roof, this was once the home of the British Library—now moved to more spacious, if rather less elegant, premises near St. Pancras Station (p 40). It was restored to its 1857 grandeur for the millennium, and today provides a sophisticated setting for temporary exhibitions (entrance fees usually apply). The authors listed on either side of the entrance doors, including Dickens, Marx, Tennyson, Kipling, and Darwin, all once sat within, composing some of history's finest works. ⏲ *15 min.*

2 ★★★ The Rosetta Stone. One of the museum's most prized artifacts is an ancient text engraved on a tablet in three parallel scripts (hieroglyphic, demotic, and Greek) that celebrates the virtues of 13-year-old pharaoh Ptolemy V, who lived in 196 B.C. The tablet was found in 1799 by Napoleon's troops and handed over to the British Army as part of the Alexandria Treaty of 1802. The text was deciphered in 1822, a breakthrough that allowed scholars to finally decode ancient Middle Eastern hieroglyphics. *Room 4.* ⏲ *5 min.*

3 ★★★ The Elgin Marbles. The Greek government has been fighting for 2 centuries to get these sculptures—taken from the **Parthenon** by Lord Elgin in 1805—returned to Athens. The B.M. argues that it has provided a safe home for these carvings (including 75m/246 ft. of the original temple frieze), which would otherwise have been chipped away by vandals or degraded by remaining in the open air. The marbles may yet be returned to the Parthenon (which would probably prove a disastrous precedent for the museum, filled as

The Rosetta Stone.

Practical Matters: The British Museum

The British Museum (☎ 020/7323-8000; http://britishmuseum.org) is located on Great Russell Street. Take the Tube to Tottenham Court Road, Russell Square, or Holborn.

Admission is free (donations appreciated), except to temporary exhibitions. The museum is open daily from 10am to 5:30pm; on Friday, select galleries remain open until 8:30pm, when special events are laid on. Specialty tours range from self-operated multimedia guides (£7) to regular lunchtime talks (usually 1:15pm) and free, 40-minute introductory "Eye-opener" tours that focus on a single theme or gallery; check the website for details or inquire at the Information Desk in the Great Court. The museum website provides details on thousands of objects in this astounding collection.

it is with the booty of the world), but don't expect this to happen anytime soon. *Room 18.* 🕓 *20 min.*

❹ ★ **Statues of the Nereid Monument.** This 4th-century-B.C. Lykian tomb from southwest Turkey arrived at the museum with the Elgin Marbles in 1816, and its life-like statuary is almost surreal. Even without their heads, the Nereids (daughters of the sea god Nereus) look as graceful as the ocean waves they personify. *Room 17.* 🕓 *5 min.*

❺ ★★ **Mausoleum of Halicarnassus.** These are the remains of one of the Seven Wonders of the Ancient World—the breathtaking Ionian Greek tomb built for King Maussollos, from whose name the word "mausoleum" is derived. The huge tomb, some 40m (130 ft.) high, remained undisturbed from 351 B.C. to medieval times, when it was damaged by an earthquake. In 1494, Crusaders used its stones to fortify a castle; in 1846, sections of the tomb's frieze were found at the castle and given to the B.M. Subsequent excavations turned up the remarkably lifelike horse sculpture and a series of lounging figures. *Room 21.* 🕓 *15 min.*

Modern Italian aromas of crispy crusts waft through the galleries of Ancient Mycenae as you approach the 6 ★ kids **Pizzeria,** a relaxed, cafeteria-style eatery. The made-to-order pizzas are reasonably priced, plus there are main-size salads and a kids' menu. *Off Room 12. £–££.*

❼ ★★ **Clocks & Watches.** The museum's outstanding collection of timepieces dating from the Middle Ages to the present day features the mind-blowing mechanical **Galleon (or "Nef") Clock**, which used to roll along a table announcing dinnertime to guests. Built (in 1585 in Germany) to resemble a medieval ship, the gilt-copper marvel played music, beat drums, and even fired tiny cannons. *Room 39.* 🕓 *10 min.*

❽ ★★★ **Treasures of Sutton Hoo.** Sutton Hoo was a burial ground of the early Anglo-Saxons (including one royal, who literally went down with his 30m [98-ft.] oak ship). When this tomb in Suffolk was excavated in 1939, previous beliefs about the inferior arts and crafts of England's Dark Ages (around A.D. 625) were confounded, as well-designed musical instruments, glassware, and armor (including the iconic Sutton Hoo helmet, here) were uncovered. *Room 41.* ⏲ *15 min.*

❾ ★★ kids **Lindow Man.** Don't miss the leathery cadaver of the "Bog Man" (aka "Pete Marsh"), found in 1984 preserved in a peat bog in Cheshire, where he had lain for nearly 2,000 years. The poor man had been struck on the head, garroted, knifed, and then put head-first into the bog. The excessive wounds suggest he died in a sacrificial ritual. *Start of Room 50, on your left.* ⏲ *5 min.*

❿ ★★★ kids **Egyptian Rooms.** Dedicated to death and the afterlife, rooms 62 and 63 are filled with coffins, sarcophagi, funerary objects, and, of course, mummies. There's even a **mummified cat**, and it's said the ghost of one of the 3,000-year-old bandaged corpses still haunts these rooms. ⏲ *20 min.*

⓫ ★★ **Asia Galleries.** Room 33 is an oasis of calm housing meditating Buddhas and the Dancing Shiva—a bronze depicting one of India's most famous icons. The intricate frieze of the **Great Amaravati Stupa** (Room 33a), carved in India in the 3rd century B.C., so closely resembles the Elgin Marbles, you'll wonder about an artistic zeitgeist that seemed to pass unaided across borders and cultures. There are statues of bodhisattvas, Buddhist archetypes, in every medium, from porcelain to metal. ⏲ *20 min.*

Bust of King Ramesses IV.

⓬ ★ **Enlightenment Gallery.** "Discovering the World in the 18th Century" is the subtitle of this permanent exhibit. Designed for George III by Sir Robert Smirke, the room is regarded as the finest and largest neoclassical interior hall in London. You'll be reaching for your pince-nez and quill pen as you marvel at the polished mahogany bookshelves stuffed with rare books. Display cases are filled with some 5,000 items that demonstrate the far-reaching, eclectic passions of the 18th-century Enlightenment scholar—the kind of person who helped make the British Museum possible. ⏲ *30 min.*

Victoria & Albert Museum

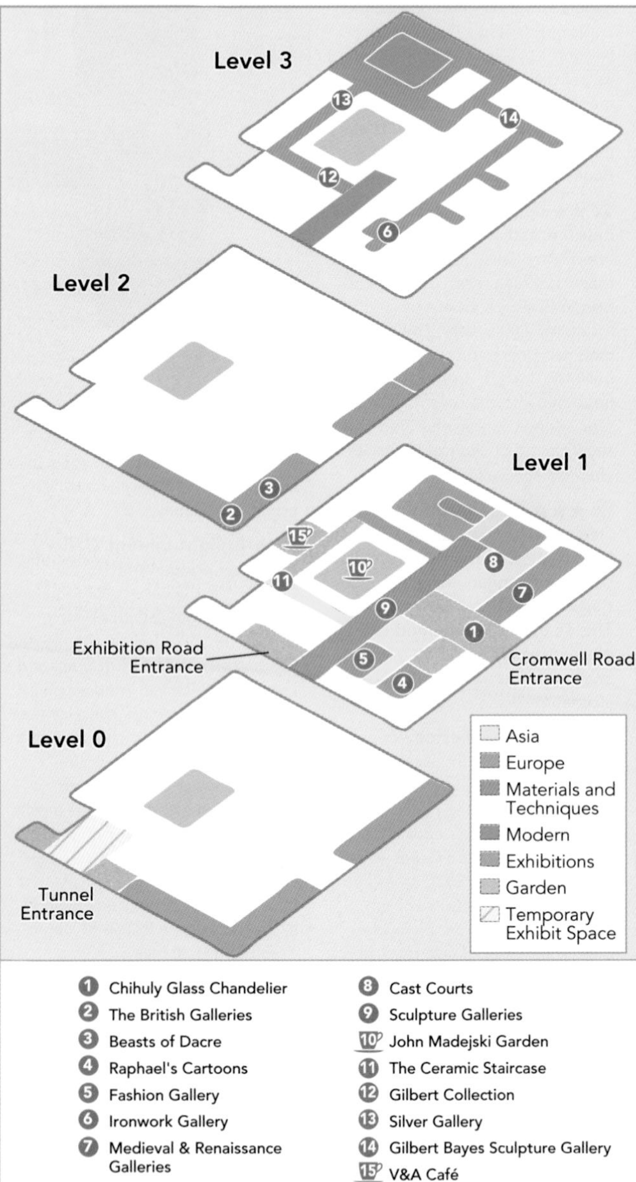

1 Chihuly Glass Chandelier
2 The British Galleries
3 Beasts of Dacre
4 Raphael's Cartoons
5 Fashion Gallery
6 Ironwork Gallery
7 Medieval & Renaissance Galleries
8 Cast Courts
9 Sculpture Galleries
10 John Madejski Garden
11 The Ceramic Staircase
12 Gilbert Collection
13 Silver Gallery
14 Gilbert Bayes Sculpture Gallery
15 V&A Café

This museum's 8 miles of galleries are resplendent with the world's greatest and most diverse collection of decorative arts. Opened in 1852 by Prince Albert, this glittering treasure trove, known colloquially as the V&A, is made up of millions of pieces of priceless arts and crafts. A massive refurbishment continues, and included the 2017 opening of the Exhibition Road Quarter and Sainsbury Gallery. START: **Tube to South Kensington.**

❶ ★★★ **Chihuly Glass Chandelier.** Renowned glass artist Dale Chihuly created this serpentine green-and-blue masterpiece (in the main entrance) specifically for the V&A in 2001, when an exhibition of his work was staged in the museum's outdoor courtyard. The chandelier is 8m (26 ft.) tall and made up of thousands of exquisite hand-blown glass baubles. Despite its airy effect, it weighs 1.7 metric tons (3,750 lbs.). *Foyer.* ⏲ *3 min.*

❷ ★★★ kids **The British Galleries.** This stellar example of 21st-century curatorship features some of England's greatest cultural treasures. The big draw is the **Great Bed of Ware** (Room 57), a masterpiece of woodcarving mentioned in Shakespeare's *Twelfth Night*. Built around 1590 as a sales gimmick for an inn, the bed is now covered in I WAS HERE graffiti and wax seals left by centuries of visitors. Another highlight is the *Portrait of Margaret Layton* (Room 56). The painting of the early-17th-century noblewoman is rather ordinary, but the fine jacket embroidered with silver thread and colored silks displayed alongside it is the very one worn in the portrait. ⏲ *45 min.*

❸ ★★ **Beasts of Dacre.** These four heraldic animals (gryphon, bull, dolphin, and ram) were carved for the Dacres, one of northern England's most important families, in 1520. The wooden figures survived a fire in 1844, only to be restored in a rather gaudy, Victorian carousel style. *Stairway C.* ⏲ *5 min.*

❹ ★★★ **Raphael's Cartoons.** Dating back to 1521, these immense and expertly rendered drawings ("cartoon" is derived from the Italian word for a large piece of paper, *cartone*) were used by the artist Raphael to plot a set of tapestries intended to hang in Rome's Sistine Chapel. *Room 48a.* ⏲ *15 min.*

❺ ★★ kids **Fashion Gallery.** Reopened after a major refurbishment, this is part of the world's largest collection of clothing, featuring everything from the dandy regalia of 18th-century aristocrats to bizarre creations by such 21st-century designers as Vivienne Westwood. *Room 40.* ⏲ *25 min.*

❻ ★★ **Ironwork Gallery.** Past the curlicued gates and nostalgic displays of cookie tins lining the

Interior of the V&A Museum.

museum's longest gallery, you'll find the stupendous **Hereford Screen,** a masterpiece of Victorian ironwork designed by the same man who devised the Albert Memorial (p 36, ❻). Check out a bird's-eye view of the foyer's chandelier. *Room 114.* ⏱ *20 min.*

❼ ★★★ **Medieval & Renaissance Galleries.** These galleries spread over three floors (0, 1, and 2) and aim to provide a complete overview of the progress of European art and culture from A.D. 300 to 1600; no mean ambition. The galleries comprise a mélange of tapestries, stained glass, statuary, glass, and metalwork. Notable items include Sir Paul Pindar's house, a rare wooden facade from a pre-Great Fire of London building; exhibits illustrating Donatello's revolution in sculpting stone (Room 64); and, in Room 64a, a densely packed notebook bursting with ideas from the mind of Leonardo da Vinci. ⏱ *40 min.*

❽ ★★★ kids **Cast Courts.** These two popular rooms contain plaster-cast copies of some of the most famous European sculptures throughout history, including Trajan's Column from Ancient Rome (in two giant pieces), a version of Michelangelo's iconic Renaissance *David* (whose nudity so shocked Queen Victoria that she had a fig leaf made for it—it's now displayed behind the statue), and a copy of Ghiberti's famous bronze doors for Florence's Baptistery. *Rooms 46a & 46b.* ⏱ *25 min.*

Nineteenth-century plaster cast of Trajan's Column in the Cast Courts.

❾ ★★ **Sculpture Galleries.** British garden and funerary sculptures from the 18th century fill rooms 22 to 24, and have been joined by another couple of galleries (rooms 26 and 27) of religious sculptures and carvings. Produced in Western Europe between 1300 and 1600, the wooden figures were vividly painted, giving them an almost hyper-real appearance. ⏱ *20 min.*

For a quick outdoor snack, grab a table or recline in the 10 kids **John Madejski Garden.** The water jets are great fun for kids, and on a sunny day you may not want to go back inside. *Inner Courtyard. Open summer only. £.*

⓫ ★★ **The Ceramic Staircase.** The V&A's first director, Henry Cole, designed these stairs, intending to doll up all the museum's staircases in this ceramics-gone-mad style. For better or worse, when costs spiraled out of control in 1870 the project was quietly dropped. *Staircase I.* ⏱ *10 min.*

⓬ ★★ **Gilbert Collection.** This shimmering array of gold jewelry, silvery statuary, mosaics, enamel portraits, and other historic *objets d'art* was put together by the British-born businessman Sir Arthur Gilbert and donated to the nation in 1996. A 19th-century ceramic tabletop illustrating where to spend "24 Hours in Rome" is like an early

The V&A: Practical Matters

The Victoria & Albert Museum (☎ 020/7942-2000; www.vam.ac.uk) is located on Cromwell Road, at the corner of Exhibition Road. Ride the Tube to South Kensington and follow signs to the museum.

Admission is free, except to special exhibitions (many of which are well worth seeing, with creative curation that justifies sometimes steep admission prices). The museum is open daily from 10am to 5:45pm. On Friday, the V&A stays open until 10pm. The last Friday of the month (except May and Dec) is **Friday Late**, with live music, guided tours of the collection, and talks (it's best without kids). On weekends and during school breaks, there are activities to engage kids of all ages.

travel guide. Stars of the show are the almost ridiculously opulent jewel-encrusted 18th-century snuffboxes; magnifying glasses are supplied if you want a closer look. *Rooms 70–73.* ⏲ *25 min.*

⑬ ★★ **Silver Gallery.** This hall displays a dazzling (literally) array of some 10,000 silver objects from the past 600 years, ranging from baby rattles and candelabras to bath-size punch bowls. Highlights include a 15th-century German reliquary depicting an arrow-pierced St. Sebastian, Elizabethan gambling counters, and ornate 17th-century Swedish drinking tankards. Interactive educational displays reveal some secrets of silver smithery. Keeping these rooms polished must be a full-time job. *Rooms 65–70a.* ⏲ *25 min.*

⑭ ★ **Gilbert Bayes Sculpture Gallery.** This narrow gallery takes a look at the craft of sculpture, showing each stage of the creative process with pieces selected from different eras to showcase the various techniques and materials (including stone, bronze, and ivory) used by sculptors. It also gives you a treetop view down into the Cast Courts. *Room 111.* ⏲ *20 min.*

The splendid 15 ★★★ **V&A Café** incorporates the original 19th-century Arts and Crafts refreshment rooms (the world's first museum restaurant) and is overlooked by stained glass and ornate ceramics and tiles. The food is traditional hot English fare, plus sandwiches and salads. *Ground Level. £–££.*

Royal London

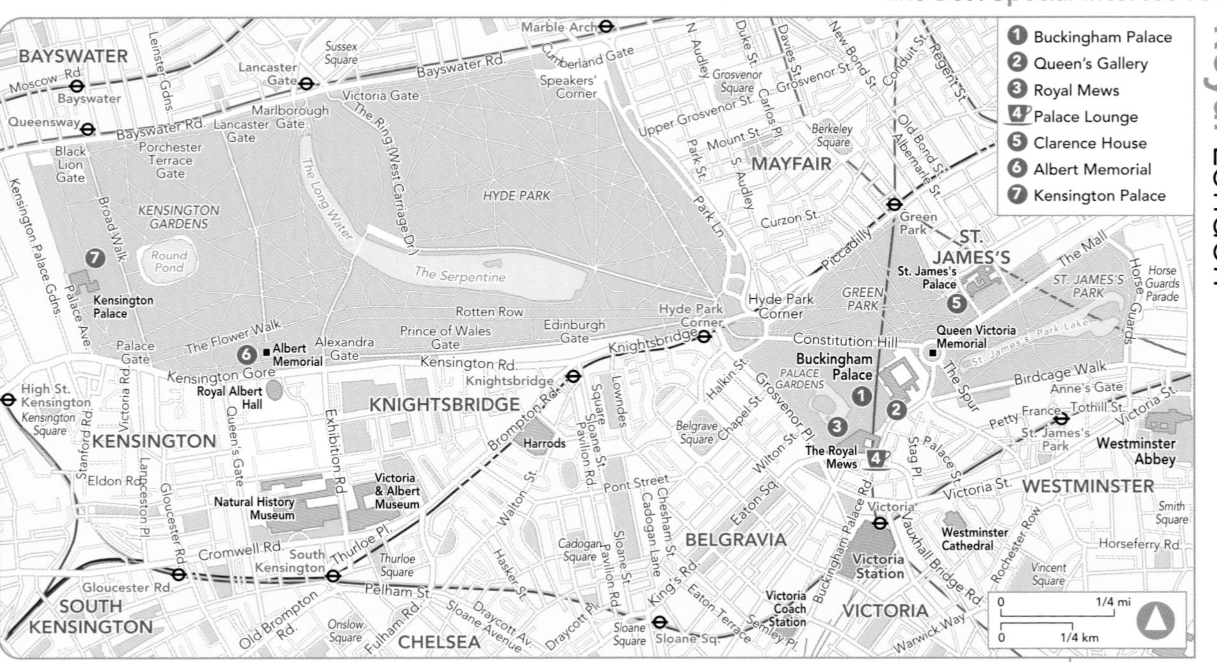

The various justifications for keeping the institution of the British monarchy often come down to the entertainment of tourists, who can't get enough of the wealth, history, and gossip that have always defined royalty. This full-day tour serves up some of the city's royal highlights and offers a glimpse into the London lives of royals past and present. START: **Tube to Green Park.**

1 ★ Buckingham Palace. Our tour starts at the top, at Buckingham Palace, the main residence of Queen Elizabeth II. The palace was originally built for the Duke of Buckingham and sold in 1761 to King George III (who needed the space for his 15 children). George IV had it remodeled by famed architect John Nash in the 1820s. For most of the year, you'll have to content yourself with views through the railings of its rather boxy exterior and the **Changing of the Guard** (p 21, 3). However, for 10 weeks from late July to September, when the monarch is elsewhere, a few of the palace's lavish 500-plus rooms are opened up for guided tours, including the State Rooms, Grand Staircase, and Throne Room. You can also take a walk across the famous palace garden. The palace has an aloofness that makes it difficult to love, but it still provides a fascinating glimpse inside one of the gilded cages of British royalty. Book the earliest timed tour possible via the website to avoid the worst of the lines. *2 hr. Buckingham Palace Rd. www.royalcollection.org.uk. Admission (includes self-guided audio tour) £24 adults, £22 seniors, £13.50 children 5–16, £61.50 family. Late July–Sept daily 9:45am–7pm (last admission 4:15pm). Tube: Victoria or St. James's Park.*

2 ★★ Queen's Gallery. This well-curated museum answers the question of how one furnishes and decorates a palace or two. Priceless treasures from the monarch's private collection of paintings, jewelry, furniture, and bibelots are displayed in sumptuous Georgian-style surroundings. The exhibits rotate (the Queen's holdings include, among other items, 10,000 Old Masters and enough *objets d'art* to fill several palaces—which they do, when they aren't here), but whatever is on display will be top-notch. You'll also find the city's best gift shop for royalty-related items, both affordable and budget-busting. *1 hr. Buckingham Palace Rd. www.royalcollection.org.uk. Timed tickets necessary in summer. £11 adults, £10 seniors, £5.50 children 5–16. Daily 10am–5:30pm (last admission 4:15pm). Closed for 2 weeks when temporary exhibitions rotate in/out. Tube: Victoria or St. James's Park.*

3 ★ kids Royal Mews. This oddly affecting royal experience is a great diversion if you're waiting for your timed entry slot to Buckingham Palace. Even if you're not

Visitors admiring Vermeer's "A Lady at the Virginal with a Gentleman, 'A Music Lesson,'" in the Queen's Gallery.

into horses, you'll be fascinated by this peek into the lives of the Queen's privileged equines. The stalls at this working stable are roomy, the tack is pristine, and the ceremonial carriages (including the ornate **Gold State Coach** and the coach that both princesses Diana and Catherine rode in after their weddings to their respective princes) are eye-popping. A small exhibit tells you about the role the Queen's horses have played in the past and present; old sepia-toned pictures show various royals and their four-footed friends. ⏱ *45 min. Buckingham Gate. www.royal collection.org.uk. £11 adults, £10 seniors, £6.40 children 5–16, £28.40 family. Apr–Oct daily 10am–5pm, Nov & Feb–Mar Mon–Sat 10am–4pm. Closed Dec–Jan. Tube: Victoria or St. James's Park.*

Overlooking the entrance to the Royal Mews is the 4 **Palace Lounge,** an atmospheric spot to take a refined afternoon tea (£39 per adult, kids' tea £15) or a light meal. You may get a glimpse of deliveries being made to Buckingham Palace in old-fashioned wagons. *Inside Rubens at the Palace Hotel, 39 Buckingham Palace Rd.* ☎ *020/7834-6600. www.rubens hotel.com. ££.*

5 ★ **Clarence House.** The list of former inhabitants of this rather staid mansion reads like a who's who of recent royals. It was designed in the 1820s by John Nash, the Royal Family's then favorite architect, for the Duke of Clarence, who continued residing there during his brief 7-year reign as William IV. In 1947 it was home to Princess Elizabeth following her marriage to Prince Philip. Before she succeeded to the throne she had given way to her mother, the "Queen Mother," who lived here until her death in 2002. Today, it's the official residence of Prince Charles and the Duchess of Cornwall, who are responsible for its current tastefully jumbled interior. In August visitors can take a guided tour of five state rooms, where a good deal of the royal collection of art and furniture is displayed. ⏱ *45 min. St. James's Palace. www.royal collection.org.uk. £10.30 adults, £6.20 children 5–16. Aug Mon–Fri 10am–4:30pm, Sat–Sun 10am–5:30pm. Tube: Green Park or St. James's Park.*

6 ★ kids **Albert Memorial.** An inconsolable Queen Victoria spent an obscene amount of public money on this 55m-tall (180 ft.) gaudy neo-Gothic shrine to her husband, Albert, who died of typhoid fever in 1861. The project (completed in 1876) didn't go down too well with her ministers, but Victoria was not a woman to whom one said no. The excessively ornate mass of gilt, marble, statuary, and mosaics set in Kensington Gardens stands in all its dubious glory across the street from the equally fabulous (and much more useful) **Royal Albert Hall**. The book Albert is holding is a catalogue from the Great Exhibition, of which he was patron. The Great Exhibition formed the seed from which grew the great museums of South Kensington. ⏱ *20 min. Kensington Gardens (west of Exhibition Rd.). Free admission. Daily dawn–dusk. Tube: High St. Kensington.*

7 ★★★ kids **Kensington Palace.** A royal palace since the late 17th century, when the original Jacobean mansion was given a thorough makeover by Sir Christopher Wren for the new king, William III, this provides a much more satisfying visit than Buckingham Palace (and it's open year-round). The

The gardens at Kensington Palace.

palace is smaller, and curators go out of their way to entertain and inform visitors. Following its most significant revamp in more than a century, palace gardens are now connected to Kensington Gardens for the first time since the 19th century. The King's (George II, patron of the composer Handel) and Queen's State Apartments have been "reimagined" elegantly, including with multimedia installations, theatrical exhibits, and items from the Royal Ceremonial Dress Collection. The lives of the late 17th- and early 18th-century queens Mary II and Anne are explored, and the "Victoria Revealed" exhibition inhabits the very rooms where she presided over her first Privy Council meeting. The life of Princess Diana is examined through the lens of fashion. ⌚ *2 hr. Kensington Gardens.* ☎ *020/3166-6000. www.hrp.org.uk/kensington-palace. £17 adults, free for children 15 & under. Daily Mar–Oct 10am–6pm, Nov–Feb 10am–4pm. Tube: High St. Kensington or Queensway.*

Literary London

1. Temple Church
2. Dr. Johnson's House
3. Charles Dickens Museum
4. Platform 9 ¾
5. British Library
6. 50 Gordon Square
7. Senate House
8. Fitzroy Tavern
9. Charing Cross Bookstores
10. Westminster Abbey
11. Shakespeare's Globe
12. House

From Shakespeare premiering plays at the Globe to Dickens illuminating the plight of the backstreet poor, London and literature have long gone together like a good book and a comfy armchair. This tour takes you to sites associated with the city's most illustrious writers, as well as places where you can take a closer look at the works themselves. START: **Tube to Temple.**

❶ ★ **Temple Church.** Its pivotal role in *The Da Vinci Code*, the biggest-selling English language book of the 21st century, saw this 12th-century church enjoy a huge spike in visitor numbers. It was built by the Knights Templar, a group of warrior priests who fought in the Crusades. The distinctive circular nave is based on the Church of the Holy Sepulcher in Jerusalem. Within are effigy tombs of various crusaders. ⏱ *30 min. King's Bench Walk.* ☎ *020/7353-3470. www.templechurch.com. £5 adults; £3 seniors & students; free children 16 & under. Mon–Fri 10am–4pm; check website as changes (including weekend opening dates) are common. Tube: Temple or Blackfriars.*

❷ ★★ **Dr. Johnson's House.** Travel writers have long been grateful to Dr. Samuel Johnson. His proud maxim, "When a man is tired of London, he is tired of life...," has kicked off many an introduction to the city. But Johnson was more than a mere quotation machine. One of the great scholars of the 18th century, he was also a poet, a biographer, a critic, and the compiler of one of the first and most influential English-language dictionaries. He worked on his mighty tome over a period of 9 years at this Queen Anne house, which has been restored to its mid-18th-century prime and is filled with Johnson-related paraphernalia. A bronze of Johnson's cat Hodge—"a very fine cat indeed"—faces his old home across Gough Square. ⏱ *30 min. 17 Gough Sq.* ☎ *020/7353-3745. www.drjohnsonshouse.org. £6 adults, £5 seniors, £2.50 children 5–17. Oct–Apr Mon–Sat 11am–5pm, May–Sept Mon–Sat 11am–5:30pm. Tube: Chancery Lane.*

Temple Church was originally the precinct of the Knights Templar.

❸ ★★ **Charles Dickens Museum.** Revamped and expanded in 2012 for the bicentennial of Dickens' birth, this museum occupies the one London house of the great Victorian novelist still standing. He lived here only from 1837 to 1840, but this being Dickens, it was more than enough time to churn out several sizeable classics, including *Nicholas Nickleby* and *Oliver Twist*. The rooms have been restored in period style and are adorned with various mementoes from his life, including a number of original manuscripts and his (presumably reinforced) quill pen. Costumed tours of the house and other family-focused events usually happen on Sundays. 1 hr. *48 Doughty St.* ☎ *020/7405-2127. www.dickensmuseum.com. £9 adults, £7 seniors, £4 children 6–16. Tues–Sun 10am–5pm (Dec also open Mon). Tube: Russell Sq.*

4 ★ kids **Platform 9¾.** All aboard for the Hogwarts Express! J.K. Rowling's famous fictional train departure point, Platform 9 ¾, has been brought to (sort of) life at King's Cross Station in the form of a sign and a luggage trolley seemingly stuck halfway through a wall, as if magically passing through. Cameras at the ready! There is (of course) a Harry Potter shop right beside it. *10 min. Western Departures Concourse, King's Cross Station, Euston Rd. www.harrypotterplatform934.com. Tube: King's Cross.*

5 ★★ kids **British Library.** The ultimate repository of British literature, the B.L. receives a copy of every single book published in the U.K., amounting to some 14 million volumes stored on 400 miles of bookshelves (largely belowground). The library's current home may be less elegant than its predecessor at the British Museum (p 26), but it's much more user-friendly. At the free "Treasures of the British Library" exhibition, you can see some of its most precious possessions, including Shakespeare's *First Folio*, Jane Austen's writing desk, and Lewis Carroll's diary. Paid temporary exhibitions are well worth checking out. *1 hr. 96 Euston Rd.* ☎ *01937/546-546. www.bl.uk. Free admission. Mon–Thurs 9:30am–8pm, Fri 9:30am–6pm, Sat 9:30am–5pm, Sun 11am–5pm. Tube: Euston or King's Cross.*

6 **50 Gordon Square.** A brown plaque marks the headquarters of the Bloomsbury Group, a collective of writers, artists, and economists, including Virginia Woolf, E.M. Forster, and John Maynard Keynes, who met here in the early 20th century when Bloomsbury was the unofficial capital of literary London. *10 min. Tube: Euston or Euston Sq.*

Shakespeare statue in Poets' Corner.

7 **Senate House.** Exit the southwest corner of Gordon Square and to the south you'll see a sinister-looking, roughly pyramidal building with long, narrow windows. This is Senate House, the inspiration for the "Ministry of Truth" in George Orwell's *1984*, and where Orwell's wife, Evelyn Waugh, and Dorothy L. Sayers worked during World War II. It's now part of the University of London. *5 min. Malet St. Tube: Goodge St.*

Between the 1920s and 1950s **8** ★★ **The Fitzroy Tavern** was a noted boozy hangout for writers including George Orwell and Dylan Thomas (there's a picture on the wall of Thomas drinking in the pub). This Victorian original, complete with wooden screens and etched glass, is now owned by the Sam Smith's Brewery chain and offers reasonably priced drinks and simple pub food. *16 Charlotte St.* ☎ *020/7580-3714. £.*

9 ★ Charing Cross Bookstores. The stretch of Charing Cross Road running south from Oxford Street toward Leicester Square has for decades been the spiritual center of the London book trade. The mighty, multistory Foyles (see "Shopping," p 79) is here, and several venerable secondhand and antiquarian bookstores are hanging on in the Internet age, including in atmospheric little passageways that connect with St. Martin's Lane just south of the Leicester Square Tube Station. ⏱ *20 min. Tube: Tottenham Court Rd. or Leicester Sq.*

10 ★★★ Westminster Abbey. Poets' Corner in the Abbey's south transept is a memorial smorgasbord of illustrious dead British writers. Chaucer, Dickens, Hardy, Tennyson, and Kipling (among others) are all buried here, while clustered around are memorials to many of the country's other great men (and a few women) of letters, including Milton, Robert Burns, the Brontë sisters, Keats, Jane Austen, D. H. Lawrence and, of course, the big fella himself, Shakespeare. ⏱ *1½ hr. See p 10, 1.*

11 ★★ Shakespeare's Globe. At the onsite exhibition you can find out all about Shakespeare, Shakespeare's London, and the theatres (both past and present) where his works have been performed. Guided tours are offered daily in the off-season. From May to September, they are usually only available in the morning. In the afternoon, when matinee performances are taking place, alternative tours to the rather limited remains of the Rose Theatre, the Globe's predecessor, are sometimes offered instead. ⏱ *1 hr. See p 12, 6.*

The National Theatre's 12 ★★ **House** restaurant is the ideal place to fortify yourself before a night at the theatre. The menu is modern European, the mezzanine setting atmospheric and minimal, and the food comes out quickly, to get you seated as soon as possible in front of one of this famous venue's three stages. *Two courses for £22. National Theatre, South Bank.* ☎ *020/7452-3600. ££.*

Shakespeare's Globe.

Kids' London

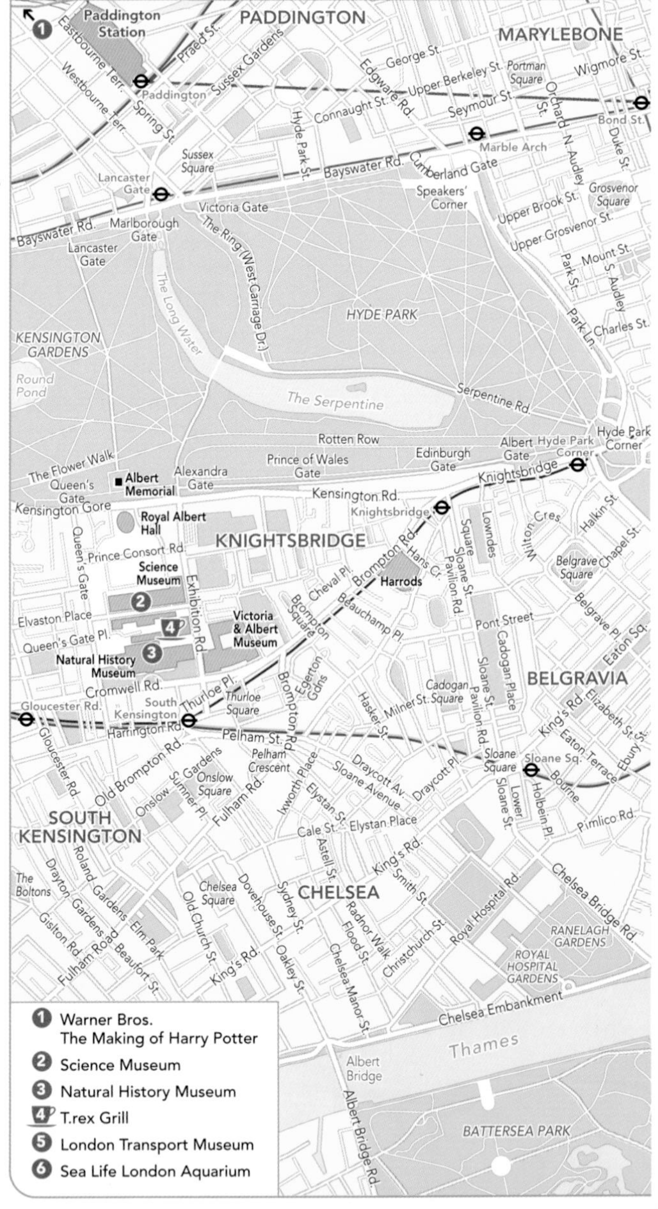
PADDINGTON
MARYLEBONE
Paddington Station
Paddington
Eastbourne Terr.
Westbourne Terr.
Praed St.
Sussex Gardens
Spring St.
Sussex Square
George St.
Edgware Rd.
Connaught St.
Upper Berkeley St.
Portman Square
Wigmore St.
Seymour St.
Orchard St.
Bond St.
Duke St.
N. Audley St.
Marble Arch
Hyde Park St.
Bayswater Rd.
Cumberland Gate
Speakers' Corner
Grosvenor Square
Upper Brook St.
Upper Grosvenor St.
Lancaster Gate
Victoria Gate
Marlborough Gate
The Ring (West Carriage Dr.)
The Long Water
Mount St.
S. Audley St.
Park St.
Park Ln.
Charles St.
HYDE PARK
KENSINGTON GARDENS
Round Pond
The Serpentine
Serpentine Rd.
Rotten Row
Hyde Park Corner
Albert Gate
Edinburgh Gate
Prince of Wales Gate
Alexandra Gate
The Flower Walk
Queen's Gate
Albert Memorial
Kensington Gore
Kensington Rd.
Knightsbridge
Royal Albert Hall
KNIGHTSBRIDGE
Prince Consort Rd.
Science Museum
Exhibition Rd.
Victoria & Albert Museum
Natural History Museum
Elvaston Place
Queen's Gate Pl.
Cromwell Rd.
Brompton Rd.
Brompton Square
Cheval Pl.
Hans Cr.
Harrods
Beauchamp Pl.
Sloane St.
Pavilion Rd.
Lowndes Square
Wilton Cres.
Halkin St.
Chapel St.
Belgrave Square
Belgrave Pl.
Eaton Sq.
Pont Street
Cadogan Place
Cadogan Square
BELGRAVIA
Egerton Gdns
Hasker St.
Milner St.
Thurloe Pl.
Thurloe Square
South Kensington
Gloucester Rd.
Harrington Rd.
Pelham St.
Pelham Crescent
Draycott Av.
Draycott Pl.
Sloane Avenue
Sloane Square
Sloane Sq.
King's Rd.
Elizabeth St.
Eaton Terrace
Ebury St.
Bourne St.
Holbein Pl.
Lower Sloane St.
Pimlico Rd.
Old Brompton Rd.
Onslow Gardens
Onslow Square
Sumner Pl.
Fulham Rd.
Ixworth Place
Elystan St.
Elystan Place
Cale St.
SOUTH KENSINGTON
Roland Gardens
The Boltons
Drayton Gardens
Gilston Rd.
Fulham Road
Elm Park
Beaufort St.
Old Church St.
Chelsea Square
Dovehouse St.
Sydney St.
CHELSEA
Astell St.
Smith St.
Radnor Walk
Flood St.
Christchurch St.
Royal Hospital Rd.
Chelsea Bridge Rd.
RANELAGH GARDENS
ROYAL HOSPITAL GARDENS
Oakley St.
Chelsea Manor St.
Chelsea Embankment
Thames
Albert Bridge
Albert Bridge Rd.
BATTERSEA PARK
1 Warner Bros. The Making of Harry Potter
2 Science Museum
3 Natural History Museum
4 T.rex Grill
5 London Transport Museum
6 Sea Life London Aquarium

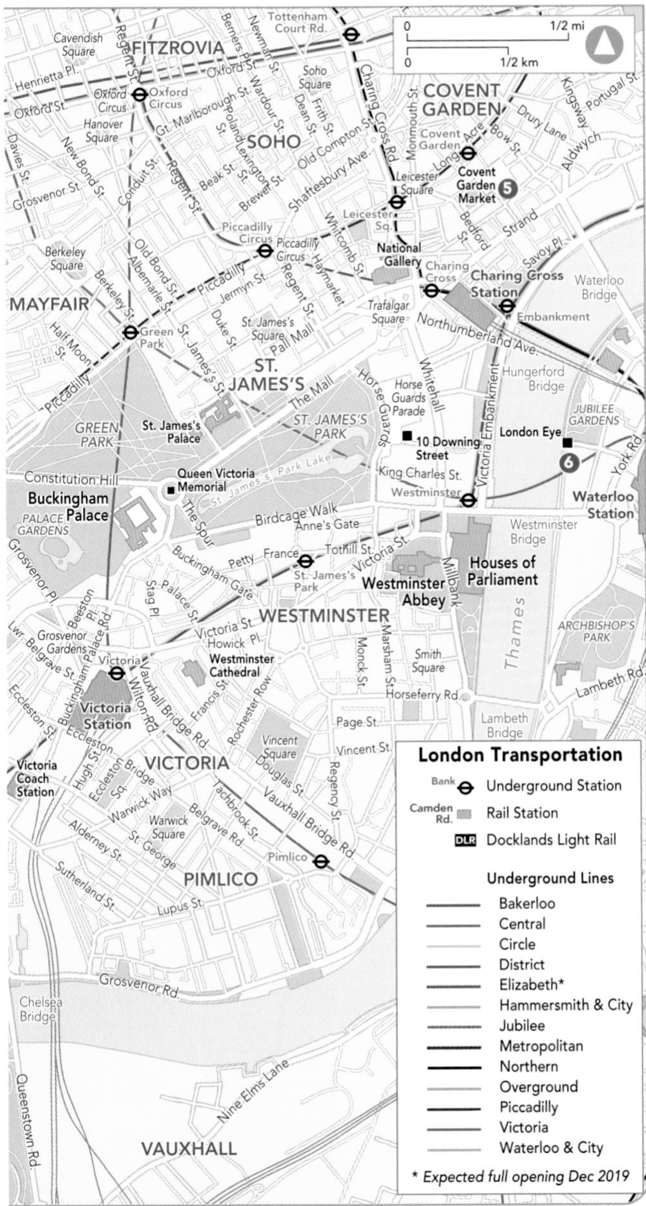
0 1/2 mi
0 1/2 km
FITZROVIA
SOHO
COVENT GARDEN
MAYFAIR
ST. JAMES'S
WESTMINSTER
VICTORIA
PIMLICO
VAUXHALL
Tottenham Court Rd.
Cavendish Square
Henrietta Pl.
Oxford St.
Oxford Circus
Hanover Square
Regent St.
Berners St.
Newman St.
Wardour St.
Soho Square
Dean St.
Frith St.
Gt. Marlborough St.
Poland St.
Lexington St.
Beak St.
Brewer St.
Old Compton St.
Shaftesbury Ave.
Charing Cross Rd.
Monmouth St.
Covent Garden
Long Acre
Bow St.
Drury Lane
Kingsway
Portugal St.
Aldwych
Leicester Square
Leicester Sq.
Covent Garden Market
5
Bedford St.
Strand
Savoy Pl.
Davies St.
New Bond St.
Grosvenor St.
Conduit St.
Piccadilly Circus
Whitcomb St.
National Gallery
Charing Cross
Charing Cross Station
Waterloo Bridge
Embankment
Berkeley Square
Old Bond St.
Albemarle St.
Piccadilly
Jermyn St.
Haymarket
Trafalgar Square
Northumberland Ave.
Berkeley St.
Green Park
Half Moon St.
St. James's Square
Pall Mall
Duke St.
St. James's St.
Hungerford Bridge
The Mall
Horse Guards
Horse Guards Parade
Whitehall
Victoria Embankment
JUBILEE GARDENS
GREEN PARK
St. James's Palace
ST. JAMES'S PARK
10 Downing Street
London Eye
6
York Rd.
Constitution Hill
Queen Victoria Memorial
St. James's Park Lake
King Charles St.
Westminster
Waterloo Station
Buckingham Palace
PALACE GARDENS
The Spur
Birdcage Walk
Anne's Gate
Westminster Bridge
Grosvenor Pl.
Buckingham Gate
Petty France
Tothill St.
Victoria St.
St. James's Park
Houses of Parliament
Westminster Abbey
Millbank
Stag Pl.
Palace St.
Beeston Pl.
Thames
ARCHBISHOP'S PARK
Grosvenor Gardens
Lwr. Belgrave St.
Buckingham Palace Rd.
Victoria
Howick Pl.
Westminster Cathedral
Monck St.
Marsham St.
Smith Square
Vauxhall Bridge Rd.
Wilton Rd.
Francis St.
Rochester Row
Horseferry Rd.
Lambeth Rd.
Eccleston St.
Victoria Station
Eccleston
Page St.
Lambeth Bridge
Vincent Square
Vincent St.
Victoria Coach Station
Hugh St.
Eccleston Sq.
Eccleston Bridge
Douglas St.
Regency St.
Warwick Way
Warwick Square
Belgrave Rd.
Tachbrook St.
Alderney St.
St. George
Pimlico
Sutherland St.
Lupus St.
Grosvenor Rd.
Chelsea Bridge
Nine Elms Lane
Queenstown Rd.
London Transportation
Bank Underground Station
Camden Rd. Rail Station
DLR Docklands Light Rail
Underground Lines
Bakerloo
Central
Circle
District
Elizabeth*
Hammersmith & City
Jubilee
Metropolitan
Northern
Overground
Piccadilly
Victoria
Waterloo & City
* Expected full opening Dec 2019

London is one of Europe's top playgrounds for kids. Nearly all major museums have well-thought-out trails and activities to entertain and inspire children, and to show off the collections to their best advantage. Some even have dedicated apps. Whether you make it to all the venues on this tour obviously depends on the ages and temperaments of your kids; you may prefer to split it over 2 slower-paced days instead. START: **Tube to South Kensington.**

1 ★★★ kids Warner Bros. The Making of Harry Potter. Visitors make a pilgrimage from the center to explore the universe of Harry Potter. Vast studios house the genuine sets where scenes from all 8 of the original movies were filmed. After a half-hour talk and tour of the **Great Hall**, you're set free to explore at your pace, which takes at least 2 hours. You'll walk along **Diagon Alley**, board the **Hogwarts Express,** and see thousands of the props, costumes, and animatronic creatures that every fan knows. There's also lots of insight into the craft of moviemaking. ***Note:*** Booking a timeslot in advance is essential. *3 hr. Leavesden. ☎ 0345/084-0900. www.wbstudiotour.co.uk. £41 adults, £33 children 5–15, £132 family ticket. Daily: first tour 9am/10am, last tour btwn. 2:30pm & 6:30pm (depending on season). Train: Watford Junction, then shuttle bus (£2.50).*

2 ★★★ kids Science Museum. Packed with hands-on fun, this great institution appeals to children (and adults) of all ages, with seven levels of exhibits tracing the progress of technology and providing plenty of buttons to press and levers to pull along the way. Dedicated sections for kids include the **Garden**, an interactive play area for 3- to 6-year-olds on the Lower Ground Floor, and **Wonderlab,** with more than 50 hands-on experiments. The museum stages numerous free events for children and offers daily tours of the galleries, a VR experience, and an IMAX cinema. Plus, the gift shop is almost as interesting as the exhibits. *2 hr. Visit on weekdays to avoid weekend crowds. Exhibition Rd. ☎ 0333/241-4000. www.sciencemuseum.org.uk. Free admission, except for special exhibitions/experiences, IMAX & Wonderlab (£9, £7 children). Daily 10am–6pm. Tube: S. Kensington.*

3 ★★★ kids Natural History Museum. This museum's 19th-century building alone is worth a look, with relief statues of beasts incorporated into its terracotta facade; it's been a favorite of moviemakers from *One of Our Dinosaurs is Missing* (1975) to the 21st-century *Paddington* films. Although not as edgy as the Science Museum next door, this collection is no fossil. Exhibits include a growling, prowling T. rex and other animatronic beasts, an

Exploring the Natural History Museum.

The underwater tunnel "Shark Walk" at Sea Life London Aquarium.

interactive rainforest, and topnotch mineral and meteorite displays. The old animal dioramas are still around, but the Darwin Centre's 8-story **Cocoon** has left them in the dust; its highlights include audiovisual shows and interactive events with naturalists and photographers (not to mention its 28 million insects and 6 million plant specimens). The museum's free app is a great way for kids to pick and pinpoint specific exhibits. ***Note:*** The line is almost always shorter if you use the side entrance on Exhibition Road. ⏱ *1½ hr. Cromwell Rd. (at Exhibition Rd.).* ☎ *020/7942-5000. www.nhm.ac.uk. Free admission, except for temporary exhibits. Daily 10am–5:50pm. Tube: S. Kensington.*

4 kids **T.rex Grill,** set next to the Natural History Museum's Creepy Crawlies exhibit, has a children's menu, high chairs, and extra space for buggies. The food is basic fare—pizza, burgers, sandwiches, and so on—but decently prepared. Prices are not too deadly. *Inside Natural History Museum. £.*

5 ★★★ kids London Transport Museum. If only the real London Transport system were as up to date and child-friendly as this superb museum. Tracing the technological and social history of the capital's public transport network, the museum gives everyone the chance to climb aboard a stagecoach, ride a double-decker Omnibus, and peer inside an old-fashioned Underground train. Family trails are available at the front desk, and there's a dedicated All Aboard play area for children 0–7. The admission ticket allows unlimited entry for a year. ⏱ *1½ hr. The Piazza, Covent Garden.* ☎ *020/7379-6344. www.ltmuseum.co.uk. £17.50 adults, £15 seniors & students, free for children 17 & under. Daily 10am–6pm. Tube: Covent Garden.*

6 ★ kids Sea Life London Aquarium. On the ground floor of the historic County Hall building, beside the Thames, this is filled with an array of marine wonders, including an underwater tunnel, a "Shark Walk" (on reinforced glass over a tank filled with fearsome-looking creatures), a Ray Lagoon, and a petting Rockpool. Talks, feedings, and behind-the-scenes tours are available, and for the very brave, an opportunity to go snorkeling with Brown and Black Tip Reef Sharks. ⏱ *1 hr. County Hall, Westminster Bridge Rd. www.visitsealife.com/london. £26 adults, £21 children 3–15, £22 per person family admission. 20% discount for purchasing tickets online. Snorkel with Sharks £130 (includes admission). Mon–Fri 10am–6pm, Sat–Sun 9:30am–7pm. Tube: Westminster or Waterloo.*

Hampton Court Palace

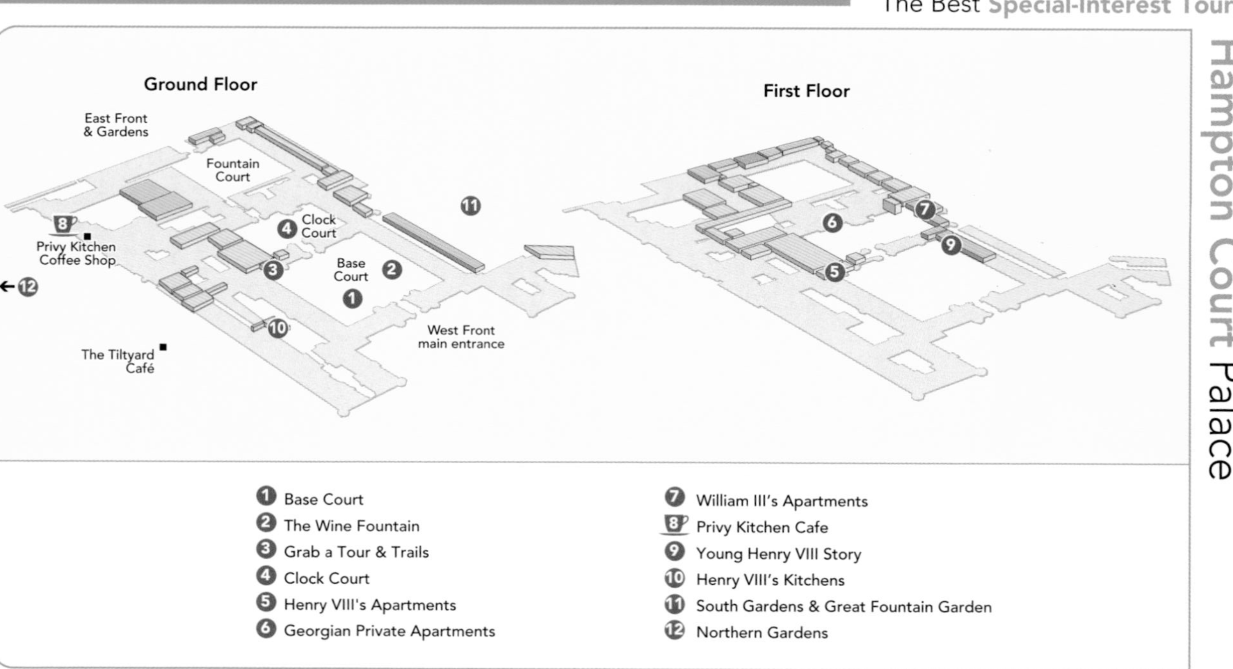

This Tudor masterpiece was built by Cardinal Thomas Wolsey in 1514, only to be snatched up by Henry VIII (r. 1509–47) when Wolsey fell out of favor. Encompassing some 1,500 rooms (about 70 are open to visitors) and 500 miles of corridors, it's one of the biggest palaces ever built and served as a royal residence from 1528 to 1737. Here you can tread the same paths as Elizabeth I, William III, and George II as you learn about life at court through the centuries. START: **Waterloo Station for Hampton Court.**

❶ ★ **Base Court.** Monarchs arrived at Hampton Court on the River Thames and entered via the South Gardens (⓫). Visitors today, however, pass through a gatehouse built by Henry VIII for the common folk, and into this Tudor-style courtyard, which is almost exactly as it was when Cardinal Wolsey first built it in 1515. The turrets surrounding the courtyard sport the insignia of Henry VIII and Elizabeth I (who both resided here), as well as numerous carved heads of Roman emperors. ⏲ *10 min.*

❷ ★ **The Wine Fountain.** In 2010 a replica wine fountain was built over the foundations of a Tudor original, discovered 2 years previously on the south side of the Base Court. The design is based on a representation of the *Field of the Cloth of Gold* painting, which hangs in the Young Henry VIII Story (❾) inside the palace. For most of the year the 4m (13-ft.) high fountain, adorned with 40 gilded lions' heads, pours water from its eight taps, but has been adapted to occasionally serve something a little stronger—just as in Henry's day. ⏲ *10 min.*

❸ ★★ kids **Grab a Tour & Trails.** Stop in at the Information Centre in the Undercroft on the north side of **Base Court** to grab an audioguide or book a spot on one of the day's costumed talks and tours (included with your admission fee). You must book in person; do so on arrival, as space on some tours is limited. Palace guides are knowledgeable and entertaining, and the themes chosen for these free tours are wonderfully eclectic—from Tudor dancing for kids to the suffragette "threat" to Hampton Court in the 1910s.

Hampton Court Palace.

How to Get to Hampton Court

Hampton Court Palace is located in East Molesey, Surrey, 13 miles west of London. Trains from London's Waterloo Station to Hampton Court Station take 35 minutes; when you exit the station, turn right and follow the signs to the palace, a 5-minute walk away. The adult roundtrip fare is around £14.50 (kids travel half-price). Alternatively, **Westminster Passenger Service Association** (☎ **020/7930-2062;** www.wpsa.co.uk; Tube: Westminster) operates a **riverboat** service from Westminster Pier to Hampton Court between April and October. Boats usually leave daily at 10:30am, 11:15am, and noon. Journey time varies between an hour and 3 hours, depending on the tide. Roundtrip tickets cost £25 for adults, £12.50 for children aged 4 to 14, and £62.50 for a family ticket; one child aged 3 or younger accompanied by an adult goes free.

Kids might also want to download the Time Explorers app (using the free hotspot) to play a digital mission game as they tour the rooms. 🕓 *10 min.*

❹ ★★ **Clock Court.** From Base Court, pass through the **Anne Boleyn Gatehouse** (built in the 1800s, centuries after the beheaded queen's execution) and into Clock Court, which encompasses several architectural styles, ranging from Tudor (the north side) to 18th-century Gothic (the east side). Its major attraction is the elaborate **Astronomical Clock**, built for Henry VIII. Note the sun revolving around the Earth—the clock was built before Galileo and Copernicus debunked that myth. 🕓 *15 min.*

❺ ★★★ **Henry VIII's Apartments.** Even though Sir Christopher Wren modified some of them, these rooms represent the best examples of Tudor style in England. Don't miss the elaborately gilded ceiling of the **Chapel Royal,** a still-functioning royal church where Henry was informed of the "misconduct" of his adulterous fifth wife, Catherine Howard, and later married wife number six, Catherine Parr. An exact replica of Henry's crown is displayed on the Royal Pew. Just off the chapel is the **Haunted Gallery,** where Howard's spectre reportedly still pleads for her life (though if you believe the many ghost stories, this "Haunted Gallery" may be one of the least haunted rooms in the whole palace). The **Watching Chamber,** where senior courtiers would dine, is the only one of Henry VIII's many English estate rooms in something close to its original form (the fireplace and stained glass are not originals). Also impressive is the **Great Hall,** with a set of tapestries (real gold and silver thread) that cost Henry as much as his naval fleet. 🕓 *45 min.*

❻ ★★ **Georgian Private Apartments.** The private apartments of George II and Queen Caroline still look as they did in 1737, when Caroline died and the royal court left this palace forever. (When George had been Prince of Wales, these same rooms witnessed a father/son struggle for popularity and influence that remains notorious in royal history.) The **Presence Chamber** of the 10-year-old Duke of Cumberland (George's second son) is the only room at the palace that's fully paneled, gilded, and painted. A portion of the ceiling of the **Wolsey Closet** survives from the Tudor era, with the rest decorated in the Renaissance style. The state bed in the **Queen's Bedchamber** is a reproduction. If the king and queen wanted to sleep together in privacy (no mean feat for the royal couple), it was to this room they retired, thanks to a rather sophisticated door lock. ⏲ *45 min.*

7 ★★★ William III's Apartments. These baroque rooms (among the finest of their kind) were designed by Sir Christopher Wren for William III (r. 1689–1702), who did more to shape the palace than any other monarch, although he died shortly after moving in. The apartments were badly damaged in a 1986 fire but have been fully restored. All the rooms in this wing are impressive, notably the **King's Guard Chamber,** with a spectacular collection of nearly 3,000 weapons mounted on its walls. The **Presence Chamber** has an exquisite rock-crystal chandelier; the **Great Bedchamber** (ceremonial only—the king slept elsewhere) is loaded with gilded furniture, priceless tapestries, and a magnificent red-velvet canopy bed; and the relatively snug, ground-floor **Private Dining Room** has a reproduction of the king's gold-plated dining service. ⏲ *1 hr.*

The 8 ★ kids **Privy Kitchen Cafe** has a real Tudor atmosphere—original kitchens with wooden tables, flagstones, and 16th-century-style chandeliers—along with decent pastries, light lunches, and afternoon tea. **£.**

9 ★ Young Henry VIII Story. Established in 2009 for the 500th anniversary of Henry's accession to the throne, this self-contained multimedia exhibition focuses on the king during his lesser-known "pinup" years, as a fit young sportsman who was married to his first wife for 20 years. Gluttony (for food *and* wives) later took hold, and he became the rotund despot of legend. ⏲ *20 min.*

10 ★★★ Henry VIII's Kitchens. At its peak, Hampton Court's kitchen staff catered two meals a day to a household of 600—more than almost any modern hotel. An enormous effort of labor prepared

One of Hampton Court's many kitchens.

Practical Matters: Hampton Court

Admission to the palace and gardens costs £18 adults, £9 children 5 to 16, £15.40 seniors and students, £47 family (2 adults, 3 children). You can easily fill most of a day with just this single outing. To avoid waiting in line, and to obtain around a 15% discount per person, book your tickets on the website (☎ **020/3166-6000;** www.hrp.org.uk). The admission fee also includes a self-guided audio tour; collect it at the information center off Base Court (3).

The palace is open daily April to October (the best time to visit) from 10am to 6pm, and daily November to March from 10am to 4:30pm. The gardens are open 7am until dusk. Closed December 24, 25, and 26. Arrive at opening time to beat peak-season crowds.

and served up some 8,200 sheep, 1,240 oxen, and 600,000 gallons of beer a year. Once the palace lost its popularity with the royal set, these 50-room kitchens were converted into apartments. They were restored authentically in 1991, and today live Tudor cookery demonstrations are put on throughout the year. Check the website for dates. *45 min.*

11 ★★★ The South Gardens & Great Fountain Garden. The palace's southern gardens are home to William III's **Privy Garden,** with its elaborate baroque ironwork screen; the box-hedged **Knot Garden,** which resembles a traditional Tudor garden; and the lovely sunken **Pond Gardens.** The **Great Vine** is one of the oldest (planted in 1768) and largest grape vines in the world. Its annual 270kg (600 lb.) crop is sold in the palace shops after the August Bank Holiday. The **Orangery** displays Mantegna's nine-painting masterpiece, *Triumphs of Caesar,* an important work of the Italian Renaissance. *30 min.*

A live interpreter in the role of Henry VIII, wearing a re-created version of the king's Crown of State.

12 ★★ kids The Northern Gardens. Renowned for their spring bulbs and **Rose Garden** (blooms peak in June), the Northern Gardens are where you'll find the world's most famous **Hedge Maze,** whose labyrinthine paths cover nearly a half-mile. Planted in 1702, the maze has trapped many a visitor in its clutches. When you do escape, stroll to the adjacent **Tiltyard** (jousting area), where you'll find several walled gardens, as well as the only surviving tiltyard tower (used to seat spectators at tournaments) built for Henry VIII. *45 min.* ●

3 The Best Neighborhood Walks

Chelsea

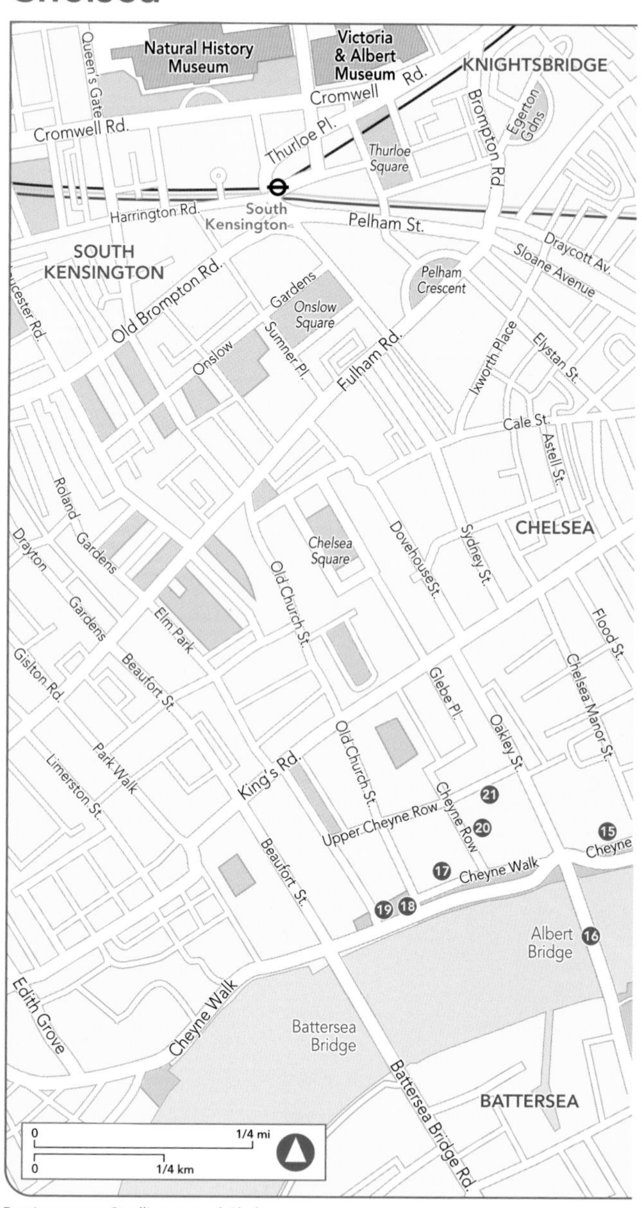

Previous page: Strolling around Chelsea.

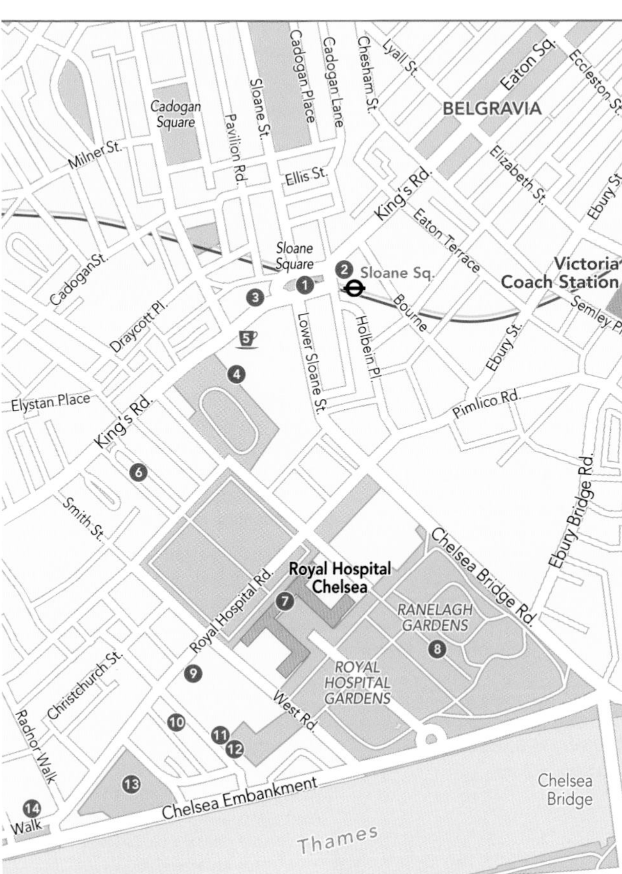

1 Sloane Square
2 Royal Court Theatre
3 King's Road
4 Saatchi Gallery
5 Polpo
6 Royal Avenue
7 Royal Hospital Chelsea
8 Ranelagh Gardens
9 National Army Museum
10 Oscar Wilde's Home
11 John Singer Sargent's Home
12 Augustus John's Studio
13 Chelsea Physic Garden
14 George Eliot's Home
15 Dante Gabriel Rossetti's Home
16 Albert Bridge
17 Carlyle Mansions
18 Statue of Sir Thomas More
19 Chelsea Old Church
20 Thomas Carlyle's House
21 Leigh Hunt's Home

Since the 16th century, when Henry VIII and Thomas More built country manors on its riverbanks, Chelsea has had a long tradition of eccentricity, aristocracy, and artisanship. This posh district is great for a stroll. Keep an eye peeled for blue plaques affixed to houses; they reveal the many historical figures who once called this neighborhood home. START: **Tube to Sloane Square.**

❶ **Sloane Square.** Royal physician Sir Hans Sloane (1660–1753), who helped found the British Museum, is the namesake of this busy square, marking the boundary between two well-to-do districts, Chelsea and Belgravia. In addition to his educational and medical achievements, Sloane discovered the milk-chocolate recipe that became the basis of the Cadbury chocolate empire. *Intersection of Sloane St. & King's Rd.*

❷ ★★ **Royal Court Theatre.** This restored theatre, originally built in 1888, is famous for showcasing playwrights such as George Bernard Shaw, John Osborne, and Harold Pinter. Nowadays, the work of today's most promising dramatists is performed on the two stages. *A few steps to the right of the Sloane Sq. Tube exit.* ☎ *020/7565-5000. www.royalcourttheatre.com.*

Sloane Square.

❸ ★★ **King's Road.** Chelsea's main road was once an exclusive royal passage used by Charles II to travel from Whitehall to Hampton Court. It was also a favorite route of highwaymen looking to "liberate" royal goods. An echo of these King's Road robbers can be found in the extortionate prices of its chi-chi stores that once helped the 1960s' swing and '70s' punks look the part, and today attracts free-spending members of London's upper social strata. *Runs from Sloane Sq. southwest to Putney Bridge.*

❹ ★★★ **Saatchi Gallery.** The capital's largest contemporary art gallery stands just off the King's Road. The brainchild of ad mogul and mega-collector Charles Saatchi, it lays on a succession of temporary exhibitions dedicated to all that is best, brightest, and most challenging in the modern art world. Whatever's on display when you visit, it's liable to be controversial—or else the gallery isn't really doing its job. *Duke of York's Headquarters, King's Rd. www.saatchigallery.com. Free admission. Daily 10am–6pm.*

Duke of York Square has a number of dining spots, but you can't go wrong at this branch of 5 ★ **Polpo.** The stylish London take on a Venetian bàcaro serves tapaslike small plates for brunch, lunch, or dinner appetites. *81 Duke of York Sq. (off King's Rd.). 020/7730-8900. ££.*

❻ ★ **Royal Avenue.** This small, picturesque road was not quite what William III intended in the 1690s. He wanted it to run all the way from the nearby Chelsea Royal Hospital to Kensington Palace, but construction was cut short after his death. Still, it proved just the ticket for its most famous fictional resident, Ian Fleming's James Bond. *Between St. Leonard's Terrace & King's Rd.*

❼ ★★ **Royal Hospital Chelsea.** This Christopher Wren masterpiece, commissioned by Charles II in 1686 as a retirement estate for injured and old soldiers, is still home to 400-plus "Chelsea Pensioners," who dress in traditional red uniforms and offer informative tours of the historic grounds and chapel. There's also a small onsite museum. The grounds host the prestigious Chelsea Flower Show, held every May since 1912. *Royal Hospital Rd.* ☎ *020/7881-5200. www.chelsea-pensioners.co.uk. Free admission. Guided tours by prior arrangement only. Museum: Mon–Fri 10am–4pm. Chapel services open to public, Sun 11am.*

❽ ★ **Ranelagh Gardens.** Once centered round a large rotunda (demolished in 1805), these gardens (some of the prettiest in London) were a favorite of 18th-century socialites who were occasionally entertained here by a young Mozart. *At Chelsea Royal Hospital. Free admission. Mon–Sat 10am–4pm, Sun 2–4pm.*

Kids Zone in the National Army Museum.

❾ ★★ kids **National Army Museum.** Home to the Duke of Wellington's shaving mirror and Florence Nightingale's lamp, plus plenty of assorted weapons, this museum follows the history of Britain's fighting forces from 1066 to the present. *Royal Hospital Rd. www.nam.ac.uk. Free admission. Daily 10am–5:30pm (until 8pm first Wed of month).*

Polpo restaurant in Duke of York Square.

⑩ ★ **Oscar Wilde's Home.** The eccentricities of Oscar and his wife, Constance (they lived here from 1885–95), were well known to neighbors, who would often see them on the street dressed in velvet (him) and a huge Gainsborough hat (her). Street boys would shout, "'Ere comes 'Amlet and Ophelia!" The house is not open to the public, but is marked with a blue plaque. *34 Tite St.*

⑪ ★ **John Singer Sargent's Home.** The renowned American portraitist of the high and mighty lived and worked at this address (the former abode of the equally famous James McNeill Whistler) from 1901 until his death in 1925. *31 Tite St.*

⑫ **Augustus John's Studio.** A renowned Welsh painter (1878–1961), John was one of Chelsea's most illustrious artists. His insightful portraits and landscapes made him famous, while his bohemian lifestyle and love affairs (including one with the mother of James Bond creator Ian Fleming) earned him notoriety. *33 Tite St.*

⑬ ★★ **Chelsea Physic Garden.** This garden was established in 1673 by the Apothecaries' Company to cultivate medicinal plants and herbs. Cotton seeds from the garden were sent to America in 1732, and slavery was their eventual harvest. *66 Royal Hospital Rd.* ☎ *020/7352-5646. www.chelseaphysicgarden.co.uk. £7.50 adults, £5 children 5–15. Apr–Oct Sun–Fri 11–6pm; winter Mon–Fri 11am–3pm.*

⑭ **George Eliot's Home.** The famous Victorian novelist, born Mary Ann Evans in 1819, moved into this house with her new and much younger husband, John Cross, only a few months before her death in December 1880. *4 Cheyne Walk.*

⑮ **Dante Gabriel Rossetti's Home.** The eccentric Pre-Raphaelite poet and painter (1828–82) lived here after the death of his wife in 1862. He kept a menagerie of exotic animals, including kangaroos, a white bull, peacocks, and a wombat that inspired his friend, Lewis Carroll, to create the Dormouse for *Alice in Wonderland.* *16 Cheyne Walk.*

⑯ ★★ **Albert Bridge.** Designed by R. M. Ordish, this picturesque suspension bridge linking Battersea and Chelsea was completed in

Albert Bridge.

1873. Conservationists saved the bridge from destruction in the 1950s. In 1973, the cast-iron structure had new supports installed so it could cope with the rigors of modern traffic, though it still tends to shake when things get busy (hence its nickname, the "Trembling Lady"). At night it's illuminated by 4,000 bulbs.

⑰ **Carlyle Mansions.** Over the past century or so, this redbrick apartment complex has been home to Henry James (1843–1916), who breathed his last here, T. S. Eliot (1888–1965), Ian Fleming (1908–1964), and Somerset Maugham (1874–1965). No wonder it's nicknamed "The Writers' Block." *Cheyne Walk.*

⑱ ★ **Statue of Sir Thomas More.** Despite his long friendship with Henry VIII, Lord Chancellor Thomas More (1478–1535) refused to accept Henry as head of the Church of England after the king's notorious break with the Roman Catholic Church. More paid for his religious convictions with his life—he was tried and subsequently beheaded for treason. In 1935, the Roman Catholic Church canonized him as the patron saint of lawyers and politicians. This statue of More, with its slightly odd gilded face, was erected outside Chelsea Old Church in 1969. *Old Church St.*

⑲ ★ **Chelsea Old Church.** A church has stood on this site since 1157. Though the structure suffered serious damage during the Blitz, it has since been rebuilt and restored. Sir Thomas More worshiped here (he built the South Chapel in 1528), and it was the setting for Henry

Statue of Sir Thomas More.

VIII's secret marriage to third wife Jane Seymour in 1536. *64 Cheyne Walk.* ☎ *020/7795-1019. www.chelseaoldchurch.org.uk. Free admission. Tues, Wed & Thurs 2–4pm.*

⑳ ★★ **Thomas Carlyle's House.** The famous Scottish historian (1795–1881) and his wife, Jane, entertained their friends Dickens and Chopin here. It was in this remarkably well-preserved Victorian home that the "Sage of Chelsea" finished his landmark *History of the French Revolution. 24 Cheyne Row.* ☎ *020/7352-7087. www.nationaltrust.org.uk/carlyles-house. £6.50 adults, £3.25 children 5–16. Mar–Oct Wed–Sun 11am–5pm.*

㉑ **Leigh Hunt's Home.** From 1833 to 1840, the noted poet and essayist (a friend of Byron and Keats) lived here, and was well known for pestering neighbors for loans. His wife infuriated Jane Carlyle, the celebrated Victorian letter writer and wife of historian Thomas, by incessantly borrowing household items. *22 Upper Cheyne Row.*

Mayfair

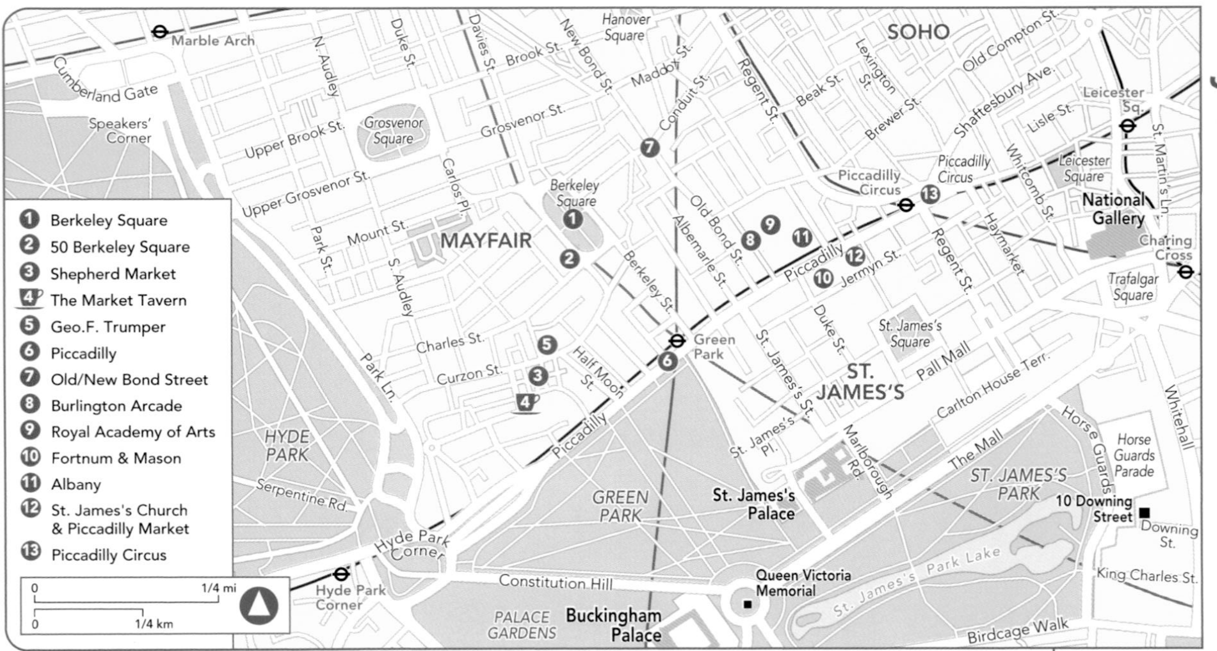

1 Berkeley Square
2 50 Berkeley Square
3 Shepherd Market
4 The Market Tavern
5 Geo.F. Trumper
6 Piccadilly
7 Old/New Bond Street
8 Burlington Arcade
9 Royal Academy of Arts
10 Fortnum & Mason
11 Albany
12 St. James's Church & Piccadilly Market
13 Piccadilly Circus
0 1/4 mi
0 1/4 km
Marble Arch
Cumberland Gate
Speakers' Corner
N. Audley
Duke St.
Grosvenor Square
Upper Brook St.
Upper Grosvenor St.
Davies St.
Brook St.
Grosvenor St.
Carlos Pl.
Park St.
Mount St.
S. Audley
MAYFAIR
Berkeley Square
New Bond St.
Hanover Square
Maddox St.
Conduit St.
Old Bond St.
Albemarle St.
Berkeley St.
Charles St.
Curzon St.
Half Moon St.
Park Ln.
HYDE PARK
Serpentine Rd.
Hyde Park Corner
Piccadilly
Green Park
GREEN PARK
Constitution Hill
PALACE GARDENS
Buckingham Palace
Queen Victoria Memorial
St. James's Palace
St. James's Pl.
St. James's St.
Marlborough Rd.
ST. JAMES'S
Duke St.
St. James's Square
Pall Mall
Carlton House Terr.
The Mall
ST. JAMES'S PARK
St. James's Park Lake
Birdcage Walk
Horse Guards
Horse Guards Parade
10 Downing Street
Downing St.
King Charles St.
Whitehall
Regent St.
Jermyn St.
Haymarket
Whitcomb St.
Trafalgar Square
Charing Cross
National Gallery
Leicester Square
Leicester Sq.
St. Martin's Ln.
Lisle St.
Shaftesbury Ave.
Old Compton St.
SOHO
Lexington St.
Beak St.
Brewer St.
Piccadilly Circus

For more than 3 centuries, Mayfair has been an exclusive neighborhood of the aristocracy, who lived in grand style inside elegant mansions run by armies of servants. Enough of these urban palaces survive to make a walk around Mayfair a fascinating glimpse into how London's rich lived—and in part, still live. This walk focuses on the southern part of Mayfair. START: **Green Park Tube Station.**

❶ ★ **Berkeley Square.** Laid out in the 18th century on part of Lord Berkeley's London estate, this grand square has long been one of the capital's most-sought-after addresses. Notables who have called the square home include prime ministers Winston Churchill (who lived at No. 48 as a boy) and George Canning (who resided briefly at No. 50; see ❷). The modern east side is now undistinguished office buildings. The plane trees surrounding the square were planted in 1789 and are among the oldest in the city.

❷ **50 Berkeley Square.** This Georgian-style building was famed as the "most haunted house in London" in the 19th century, when sightings of a bewigged man and sounds of an unearthly nature kept the house untenanted. Although strange happenings have been reported here in recent years, the worst of it seems to have taken place in Victorian days, when an evil presence so terrified a visitor that he threw himself out the window and was impaled on the railings below.

Berkeley Square.

❸ ★★ **Shepherd Market.** In the mid-18th century, the riotous May Fair (the neighborhood's namesake) was banned and the land was redeveloped by architect Edward Shepherd. The result was much what you see now: charming yet humble buildings from the days when this area was the hub of the servant classes in Mayfair. Today it's filled with traditional pubs, including the 1730s-built Shepherds Tavern, and restaurants serving various different cuisines: French, Italian, Lebanese, Mexican, Japanese, and more.

A favorite with the after-work crowd, ❹ ★ **The Market Tavern** is a homey pub with wooden floors, a diverse wine list, and such elevated English comfort food as steak and smoked Cheddar pie. *7 Shepherd St. ☎ 020/7491-0910. www.themarkettavernmayfair.co.uk. £–££.*

❺ ★ **Geo. F. Trumper.** This English institution opened in 1875, and still offers traditional wet shaves with straight razors and hot towels, mustache trimming, and—in a concession to metrosexual modernity—manicures. Even if you don't need a shave or toiletries, do have a look around the wonderful shop. *9 Curzon St.* ☎ *020/7499-1850. www.trumpers.com.*

6 ★★ **Piccadilly.** The name Piccadilly is said to have come from the word "picadil," a stiff collar manufactured by an early-17th-century tailor who bought a great parcel of land here on which he built a grand home. Lest the upstart forget his humble beginnings, it was sneeringly referred to as "Piccadilly Hall." In the 18th and 19th centuries, many great mansions were built along the street facing Green Park. Head east on Piccadilly so you can admire the elaborate gates surrounding Green Park and the carved classical-style heads on the Parisian-inspired facade of the Ritz Hotel.

7 ★★ **Old & New Bond Street.** Perhaps the smartest shopping street in London, lined end to end with boutiques from some of the biggest names in fashion and jewelry (Prada, Tiffany, Louis Vuitton, Bulgari) and not a price tag in sight (if you have to ask…). The point where Old Bond Street meets New is marked with a statue showing President Franklin Roosevelt and prime minister Churchill chatting on a bench.

8 ★★★ **Burlington Arcade.** Opened in the early 19th century, this is a very *haute* mall, with around 40 elegant shops (with curved glass windows and mahogany fronts) selling upmarket clothing, shoes, art, and antiques. Top-hatted, frock-coated guards are employed to make sure nobody does anything as uncouth as running, whistling, or singing in the arcade. *51 Piccadilly.* ☎ *020/7493-1764. www.burlingtonarcade.com.*

Burlington Arcade opened in 1819.

9 ★★★ **Royal Academy of Arts.** Burlington House, built in the 1660s, was a magnificent estate later purchased by the government (in 1854) to house England's oldest arts society. The Royal Academy has staged a "Summer Exhibition" for more than 200 years now, making this the home of the world's longest-running open-submission competition. These days, however, its major draws are blockbuster

Mayfair's circa-1730s Shepherds Tavern.

temporary exhibitions, often showcasing the biggest names from art's past or present. In 2018, the RA celebrated its 250th birthday with an expanded offering and more free access to its permanent collection: Check the website for rotating exhibits. *Burlington House, Piccadilly.* ☎ *020/7300-8000. www.royalacademy.org.uk. Daily 10am–6pm. Admission prices vary by exhibition (typically £12–£20).*

⑩ ★★ **Fortnum & Mason.** A famous partnership began in 1705 when shop owner Hugh Mason let a room to William Fortnum, a footman for Queen Anne at the Palace of St. James. The enterprising Fortnum "recycled" candle ends from the palace (the queen required fresh candles nightly) and sold them to Mason. From this humble beginning, Fortnum & Mason grew to rule Britannia (or at least Piccadilly) with one of the earliest globally recognized brand names. Its hampers are legendary. For a refined (if pricey) afternoon tea, try the **Diamond Jubilee Tea Salon** on the fourth floor. *181 Piccadilly. www.fortnumandmason.com.* *See also p 82.*

⑪ **Albany.** Built in the 1770s by architect William Chambers for Lord Melbourne, this grand Georgian building was turned into a residence for gentlemen in 1802. Since then, many poets (Lord Byron), authors (Graham Greene), playwrights, and politicians have called this prime Piccadilly bachelor patch home. Marking a revolutionary leap into the modern world, women are now allowed to live here (but no children under 14). Traditional values are maintained via the rigid use of terminology: Dwellings are not flats or apartments, but "sets," and the building is strictly "Albany" never "*The* Albany." *At Albany Yard, off Piccadilly.*

⑫ ★ **St. James's Church & Piccadilly Market.** This unprepossessing redbrick church is one of Christopher Wren's simplest, said by Charles Dickens to be "not one of the master's happiest efforts." The poet William Blake was baptized here, as was William Pitt, the first earl of Chatham, who became England's youngest prime minister at the age of 24. You are welcome to enter and sit in its quiet interior, or enjoy the free (donations requested) lunchtime recitals. A market in the forecourt sells crafts, clothes, and collectibles Monday through Saturday. *197 Piccadilly.* ☎ *020/7734-4511. www.sjp.org.uk. Recitals usually 1pm Mon, Wed & Fri.*

⑬ ★ **Piccadilly Circus.** London's slightly underwhelming answer to New York's Times Square was the first place in the city to have electrical signage, and its glaring neon billboards have graced a million postcards. The word "circus" refers to a circular juncture at an intersection of streets, and the plaza was built in 1819 to connect two of London's major shopping streets: Regent Street and Piccadilly. The statue popularly known as Eros (though, trivia fans, it's actually Anteros, the Greek god of requited love) on the central island is a favorite meeting place.

Shopping in Fortnum & Mason.

Hampstead

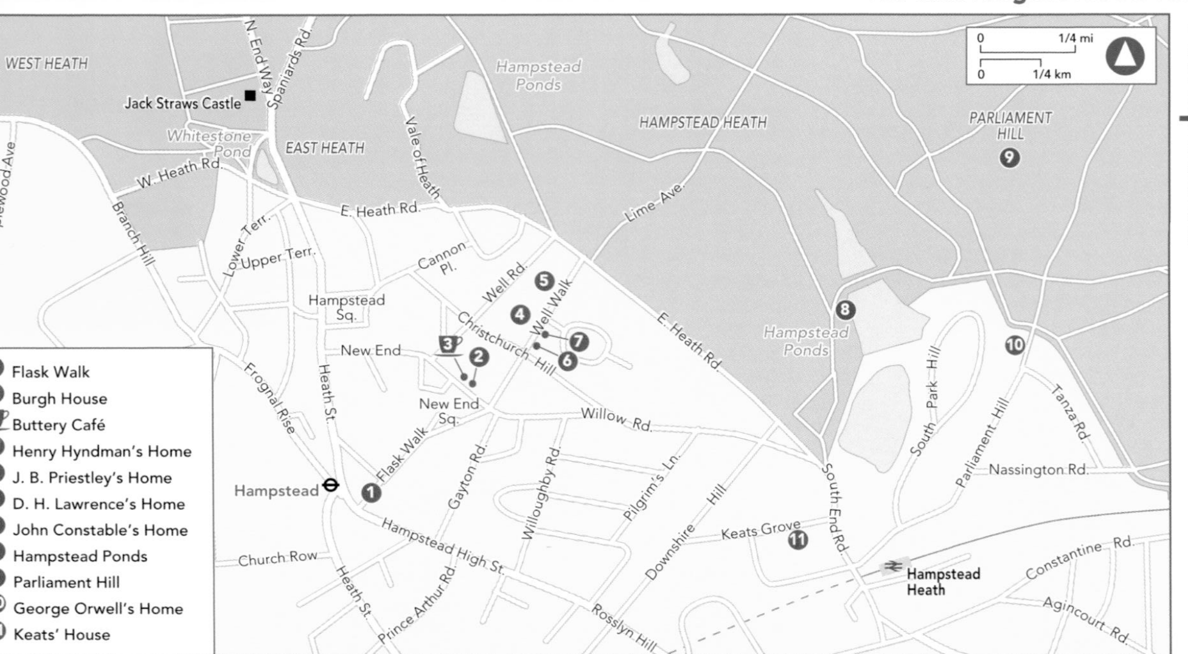
0 1/4 mi
0 1/4 km
WEST HEATH
Jack Straws Castle
N. End Way
Spaniards Rd.
Whitestone Pond
EAST HEATH
W. Heath Rd.
Templewood Ave
Branch Hill
Hampstead Ponds
Vale of Heath
HAMPSTEAD HEATH
PARLIAMENT HILL
Lime Ave.
E. Heath Rd.
Lower Terr.
Upper Terr.
Cannon Pl.
Well Rd.
Well Walk
Hampstead Sq.
Christchurch Hill
New End
New End Sq.
Willow Rd.
Frognal Rise
Heath St.
Flask Walk
Gayton Rd.
Willoughby Rd.
Pilgrim's Ln.
Downshire Hill
Keats Grove
South End Rd.
South Park Hill
Parliament Hill
Tanza Rd.
Nassington Rd.
Hampstead
Church Row
Hampstead High St.
Prince Arthur Rd.
Rosslyn Hill
Hampstead Heath
Constantine Rd.
Agincourt Rd.
1 Flask Walk
2 Burgh House
3 Buttery Café
4 Henry Hyndman's Home
5 J. B. Priestley's Home
6 D. H. Lawrence's Home
7 John Constable's Home
8 Hampstead Ponds
9 Parliament Hill
10 George Orwell's Home
11 Keats' House

Hampstead first became popular during the Great Plague of 1665, when well-to-do Londoners escaped here from the contagion of their neighborhoods. Today, it is still a charming refuge, known for its historic buildings, rich artistic and literary legacy, and proximity to the Heath, 324 hectares (800 acres) of loosely managed wilderness and far-reaching views. START: **Tube to Hampstead.**

❶ ★ **Flask Walk.** Now a narrow alley of chichi shops leading to a street of expensive homes, Flask Walk was the site of early-18th-century fairs and also home to year-round establishments for drinking and gambling—all built to entertain the crush of Londoners escaping the fetid city streets for Hampstead's fresh air. The street was named after a now-defunct tavern that bottled the village's pure water and sold it throughout London.

❷ ★★ **Burgh House.** Built in 1704, this restored Queen Anne structure, the former home of spa physician Dr. William Gibbon, now houses a museum specializing in Hampstead's history. It offers literary-themed walks through the town (and across the common) and talks, and stages classical music concerts. *30 min. New End Sq. ☎ 020/7431-0144. www.burghhouse.org.uk. Free admission. Wed–Fri & Sun noon–5pm. Tube: Hampstead.*

Found in the Burgh House basement, the 3 ★★ **Buttery Café** serves great home-made cakes and afternoon tea from 3pm, as well as some heartier traditional British and European dishes. The garden is a great place for a slow lunch on a sunny afternoon. *New End Sq. ☎ 020/7794-3943. MC, V. ££.*

❹ ★ **Henry Hyndman's Home.** A journalist, politician, and public speaker, Hyndman (1842–1921) founded the Social Democratic Federation, England's first socialist party, in 1881. He lived in this house until his death in 1921. *13 Well Walk.*

❺ **J. B. Priestley's Home.** One of England's most prolific men of letters, Priestley (1894–1984) was an essayist, playwright, biographer, historian, and social commentator who refused a knighthood and peerage. He lived in this Queen Anne–style house from 1928 to 1932. *27 Well Walk.*

❻ **D. H. Lawrence's Home.** During World War I, Lawrence (1885–1930) hoboed around Hampstead, including here, after being kicked out of Cornwall when his wife was unjustly accused of being a German spy. He left in 1919 for Italy, where he wrote his most famous novel, *Lady Chatterley's Lover,* in 1928. The book was banned in Britain on charges of indecency and wasn't published here uncensored until 1960. *32 Well Walk.*

Flask Walk.

The Loos of London

London once had plenty of public lavatories. Time was when nearly every high street boasted its own well-maintained public convenience, but now they're few and far between. The old-fashioned tiled underground facilities have almost completely disappeared (they're too expensive for councils to maintain) while the free-standing kiosks (known locally as "super loos") are increasingly thin on the ground. If you get caught short, however, many of the capital's major train and Tube stations have public lavatories, typically costing around 30p to 50p. Other options include museums, galleries, and art centers, most of which are free and offer good-standard facilities, or public parks. Department stores are another good bet, as are fast-food restaurants. Come the evening, however, your best option may be to nip into the nearest pub, though you should probably buy a little something to become a customer first.

7 John Constable's Home. The well-known British landscape and portrait painter resided here from 1827 until his death in 1837. It was in his many studies of nearby Hampstead Heath that Constable mastered the depiction of weather in landscapes, tirelessly painting the same scene under different climatic conditions. The house is marked with a blue plaque. ***40 Well Walk.***

Swimming in the mixed pond at Hampstead.

8 ★★ Hampstead Ponds. Hampstead boasts three lovely wooded swimming ponds (actually former reservoirs dug in the mid-19th century) where you can take a refreshing open-air dip (the water is often cold). There's a men's pond, a ladies' pond, and a mixed pond, which gets particularly busy in summer. *Hampstead Heath. ☎ 020/7485-3873. www.cityoflondon.gov.uk. £2 adults, £1 seniors & children 15 & under. Daily 7am–dusk (times can vary; call ahead); mixed pond closed in winter. Overground: Hampstead Heath.*

9 ★★★ Parliament Hill. According to legend, the men behind the 1605 Gunpowder Plot planned to watch Parliament blown sky-high from this elevated vantage point. Fittingly, it's now one of the best places to watch the fireworks staged every November 5 to commemorate the foiling of the plot.

Parliament Hill, overlooking London.

Daytime views are no less dramatic; a map on the site identifies the buildings in the distance. *Inside Hampstead Heath.*

⑩ ★ George Orwell's Home. The author of *Animal Farm, 1984,* and *Down and Out in Paris and London* wrote the satirical *Keep the Aspidistra Flying* in a back room on an upper floor of this house. He lived here for only 6 months in 1935 while working part-time at Booklover's Corner, a small bookstore on South End Green (now a chain bakery). *77 Parliament Hill.*

⑪ ★★ Keats' House. Keats lived just 2 years at this Regency house, but found enough time to write some of his most famous works, including *Ode to a Nightingale,* and fall in love with next-door neighbor Fanny Brawne, his eventual fiancée (and the muse behind much of his best poetry). In 1820, he traveled to Italy, where he died of tuberculosis only a few months later. The house is now a museum dedicated to the poet's life and displays original manuscripts and portraits. You can join a free, 30-minute guided tour of the house at 3pm. 🕓 *1 hr. 10 Keats Grove.* ☎ *020/7435-2062. www.cityoflondon.gov.uk. £6.50 adults, free children 17 & under. Wed–Sun 11am–5pm (also open Mon holidays). Overground: Hampstead Heath.*

Shops in Hampstead Heath.

The City & East End

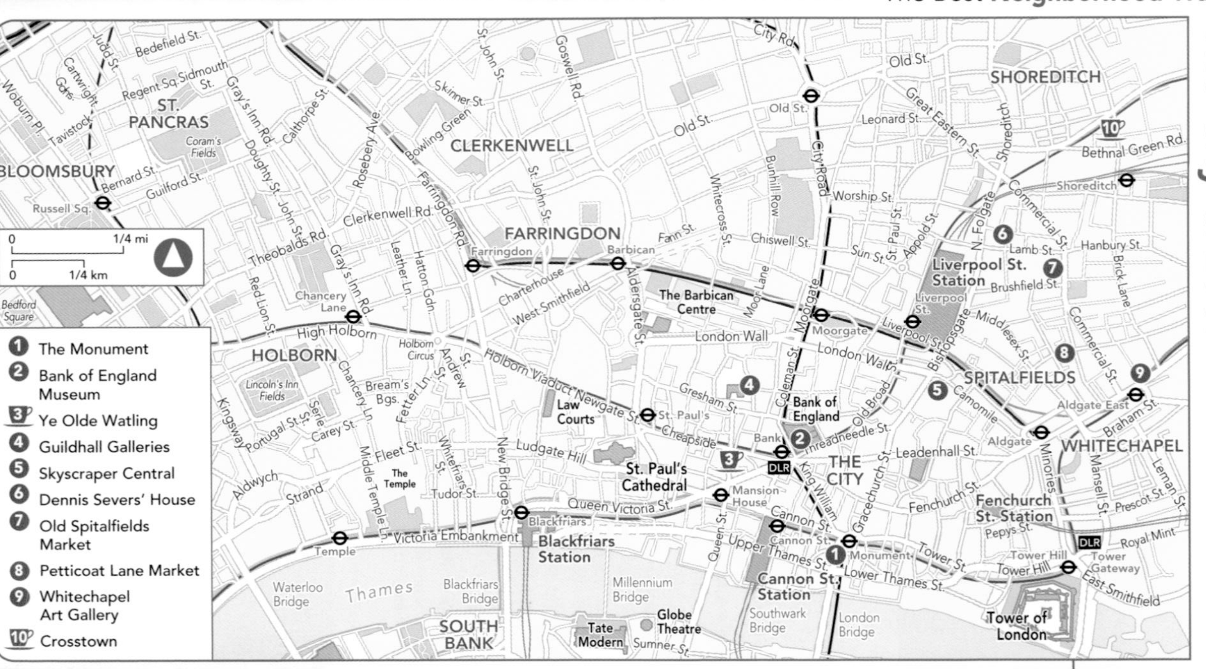

This walk starts where it all began: in the Square Mile, also known as "the City." The site of the first London settlement founded by the Romans 2,000 years ago continues to thrive as the center of the country's financial services. Onward from here is the East End, where many exciting developments in the arts, shopping, and entertainment take place. START: **Monument Tube Station.**

1 ★★★ kids The Monument. Sir Christopher Wren designed this 62m-high (203-ft.) Doric stone column—topped with a gilded fiery urn—to commemorate the Great Fire of 1666. That tragic disaster started on September 2 inside the house of a baker on Pudding Lane (the height of the tower corresponds to the distance from its base to the fire's starting point). A stiff wind ignited the old timber-and-thatch houses of the City; more than 13,000 homes and 87 churches were reduced to smoldering ashes. It's 311 steps to the top, from where the views are among the finest in the City. *40 min. Monument St. www.themonument.info. £4.50 adults, £3 seniors, £2.30 children 5–15. Daily 9:30am–5:30pm (Oct–Mar 'til 5pm). Tube: Monument.*

2 ★★ kids Bank of England Museum. Take a close-up look at the glue that holds the Square Mile together: money. Exhibits include old notes and coins and a re-creation of an 18th-century banking hall. The highlight is a genuine gold bar that can be touched but—no matter how you wiggle your hand inside the Perspex box—not removed. *45 min. Bartholomew Lane. ☎ 020/3461-5545. www.bankofengland.co.uk/museum. Free admission. Mon–Fri 10am–5pm. Tube: Bank.*

Just south of St. Mary-le-Bow, the "Cockney Church," is London's oldest road, Watling Street, which 1,900 years ago linked the capital with the coast. Here you'll find the aged—if not quite so venerable—**3 ★ Ye Olde Watling.** Built in the 17th century out of ships' timbers, it serves some decent pub grub and a range of ales. *29 Watling St. ☎ 020/7248-8935. www.nicholsonspubs.co.uk. £.*

The Monument.

4 ★★ kids Guildhall Galleries. A 1990s extension of the City's medieval and much-restored Guildhall holds an art gallery showcasing a rotating selection from its 4,000-plus London-related works, including Pre-Raphaelite paintings. The building also contains a small police history museum and, in the basement, the remains of London's Roman amphitheatre. *1 hr. Guildhall Yard, off Gresham St. ☎ 020/7332-3700. www.cityoflondon.gov.uk/guildhallgalleries. Free admission. Mon–Sat 10am–5pm, Sun noon–4pm. Tube: Bank.*

5 ★ kids Skyscraper Central. Just off Bishopsgate, the small square of Great St. Helen's neatly encapsulates how the City's skyline has changed over the centuries. At its center is the small, almost fragile-looking, 13th-century **St. Helen's church,** while on all sides stand giant glass-and-steel skyscrapers. From the church courtyard, you can see to the west **Tower 42**, formerly the City's tallest building (check out the views from the top at the Vertigo 42 champagne bar; see p 123), to the east the **Gherkin** (more formally, 30 St. Mary Axe), and to the north, the **Heron Tower,** which at 230m (755 ft.) is currently the tallest building in the Square Mile. To the south, the City's so-called "Eastern Cluster" adds new giants at a rapid rate, including buildings imaginatively nicknamed the **Cheesegrater** (122 Leadenhall St.) and the **Walkie-Talkie** (20 Fenchurch St.; home to the Sky Garden, p 123). *10 min. Gt. St. Helen's. Tube: Bank or Liverpool St.*

The Gherkin skyscraper.

6 ★★ Dennis Severs' House. From 1979 until his death in 1999, the American expat Dennis Severs not only restored his Spitalfields townhouse to its early-18th-century prime but also created a fictional back story for it, as a refuge for the Jervises, a family of Huguenots who fled persecution in France. The rooms have been arranged as if just vacated by these occupants, and the result is fascinatingly odd. Note the limited opening hours. *45 min. 18 Folgate St. ☎ 020/7247-4013. www.dennisseversshouse.co.uk. Adults £10 Sun & Mon daytime visit (no reservations); £15 "Silent Night" visit (reservations essential). Sun noon–4pm, Mon noon–2pm; "Silent Night" Mon, Wed & Fri 5–9pm. Tube: Liverpool St.*

7 ★ Old Spitalfields Market. Although now surrounded by a modern, upscale development of high-end shops, restaurants, and delis, the craft market is still holding strong, with stalls selling clothes, secondhand books and records, home-made jewelry, hats, and an assortment of esoteric arts and crafts. Saturdays focus primarily on one-off clothes and accessories. At the northern end of the covered building is a row of cheap street-food stalls offering cuisine from every corner of the globe. There's been a market on this site for more than 350 years. *45 min. Commercial St. ☎ 020/7377-1496. www.*

Market Sundays

Sundays are a browser's paradise in the East End. Although many markets stay open (sometimes in low-key fashion) through the week, on a Sunday morning **Spitalfields** will be in full swing, while **Petticoat Lane** will have spilled beyond its usual Wentworth Street parameters onto the surrounding roads with cheap clothes and jewelry. Just to the east is Brick Lane, the heart of London's Bangladeshi community, and on Sunday its central stretch is given over to the **UpMarket** (www.sundayupmarket.co.uk), held since 2004 in and around the Old Truman Brewery buildings. This succession of busy flea markets sells everything from crafts and furniture, vintage clothes, and designer accessories to vinyl records and street food. If you fancy stretching your legs, a 5-minute walk north up Brick Lane takes you toward **Columbia Road** and its famous Sunday-morning flower market, its stalls piled high with colorful blooms. (See also "Shopping," chapter 5.)

spitalfields.co.uk. Open daily. Tube: Liverpool St.

8 ★ Petticoat Lane Market. This ever-popular market selling cheap clothes, leather goods, and jewelry was founded more than 400 years ago by Huguenots from France who sold lace items, including the eponymous undergarments. The name was changed to Wentworth Street in the 19th century so as to avoid offending delicate Victorian sensibilities, but market traders have long memories, and London's premier cheap-clothes market continues to be known by its slightly racier moniker. ⏱ *45 min. Wentworth & Middlesex sts.* ☎ *020/7364-1717. Mon–Fri 8am–4pm, Sun 9am–2pm. Tube: Liverpool St. or Aldgate East.*

9 ★★★ Whitechapel Art Gallery. This museum has been the East End's artistic touchstone for more than a century. Always as close to the cutting edge as possible, it offers constantly changing exhibitions of the best and most challenging contemporary visual art, as well as a program of talks, film screenings, and concerts. There's always an art-themed event (and late bar opening) on the first Thursday of the month. ⏱ *1½ hr. 77–82 Whitechapel High St.* ☎ *020/7522-7888. www.whitechapelgallery.org. Free admission. Tues–Sun 11am–6pm ('til 9pm on "First Thursdays"). Tube: Aldgate East.*

At **10 ★ Crosstown** you'll find creatively flavored donuts to die for (regular and vegan), plus a damn fine cup of any espresso-based coffee you like — or chill-filtered if you prefer. *157 Brick Lane.* ☎ *020/7729-3417. www.crosstowndoughnuts.com. £.*

Whitehall

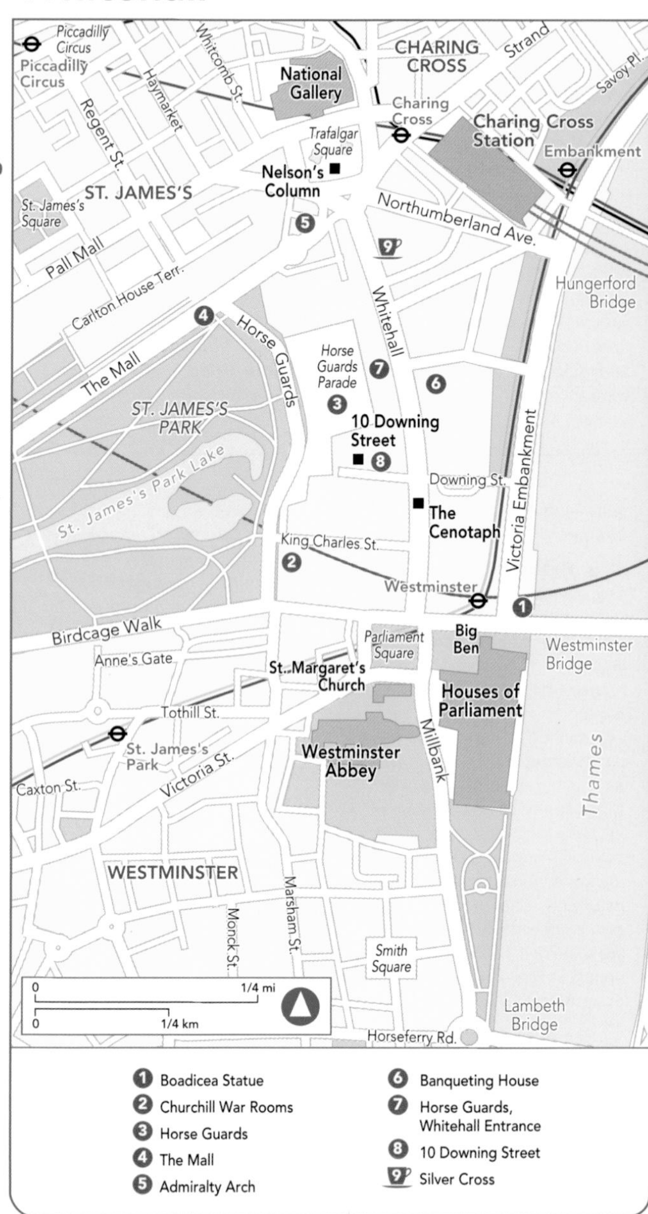
Piccadilly Circus
Piccadilly Circus
Haymarket
Whitcomb St.
Regent St.
National Gallery
CHARING CROSS
Strand
Savoy Pl.
Charing Cross
Charing Cross Station
Embankment
Trafalgar Square
Nelson's Column
ST. JAMES'S
St. James's Square
Pall Mall
Carlton House Terr.
Northumberland Ave.
Hungerford Bridge
Whitehall
Horse Guards
Horse Guards Parade
The Mall
ST. JAMES'S PARK
St. James's Park Lake
10 Downing Street
Downing St.
The Cenotaph
Victoria Embankment
King Charles St.
Westminster
Birdcage Walk
Anne's Gate
Parliament Square
Big Ben
Westminster Bridge
St. Margaret's Church
Houses of Parliament
Tothill St.
St. James's Park
Caxton St.
Victoria St.
Westminster Abbey
Millbank
Thames
WESTMINSTER
Marsham St.
Monck St.
Smith Square
Lambeth Bridge
Horseferry Rd.
0
1/4 mi
0
1/4 km
1 Boadicea Statue
2 Churchill War Rooms
3 Horse Guards
4 The Mall
5 Admiralty Arch
6 Banqueting House
7 Horse Guards, Whitehall Entrance
8 10 Downing Street
9 Silver Cross

Once the site of the vast Palace of Whitehall—London's chief royal residence from 1530 to 1698—this area is now a grand neighborhood of government buildings whose architecture confers a certain beauty to the dull business of bureaucracy. This walk is best in the morning; time things to arrive at Horse Guards Parade to see the Changing of the Guard. START: **Westminster Tube Station.**

❶ **Boadicea Statue.** A tall and ferocious queen of the Iceni tribe of East Anglia, Boadicea waged battle against Britain's 1st-century Roman invaders, nailing captured soldiers to trees and flaying them alive. In A.D. 61, her forces temporarily retook Londinium before they were thoroughly defeated by the Roman army. The queen (whose name means victorious) became a heroic figure of Victorian England. This statue by Thomas Thornycroft was erected in 1902. *Bridge St. & Victoria Embankment.*

❷ ★★ kids **Churchill War Rooms.** Winston Churchill directed World War II from this underground shelter as German bombs rained down on London. The basements of these Civil Service buildings were redesigned in the war to house a hospital, a cafeteria, sleeping quarters, and even a shooting range. After the war, the area was locked and left untouched until1984, when Churchill's quarters were turned into a museum; all the items you see are the genuine article. 🕓 *1 hr. Clive Steps, King Charles St.* ☎ *020/7930-6961. www.iwm.org.uk. £21 adults, £17 seniors, £10.50 children 5–15. Daily 9:30am–6pm.*

❸ ★★ kids **Horse Guards.** This grand 18th-century building is the headquarters of the Household Cavalry Mounted Regiment, the chief bodyguards of the reigning monarch. At a small on-site museum, you can see members tending to their horses in the adjacent stables, through a glass partition. The large parade ground out front is the site for the annual **Trooping the Colour** ceremony. Every day at 11am (10am on Sun) there's a **Changing of the Life Guard** ceremony, much mellower (and less crowded) than you'll find outside Buckingham Palace (p 21, ❸). 🕓 *45 min. Horse Guards Rd. Household Cavalry Museum:* ☎ *020/7930-3070. www.householdcavalrymuseum.co.uk. £8 adults, £6 children 5–16. Daily 10am–5pm (Apr–Oct 'til 6pm).*

❹ **The Mall.** This red-gravel thoroughfare—running east from Buckingham Palace (p 21, ❸) to Trafalgar Square (p 22, ❺)—was created in 1660 as a venue for St. James's gallants to play the popular game of *paille maille* (a precursor to croquet). In the early 18th century it was a fashionable promenade for the beau monde, and in 1903 it was redesigned as a processional route for royal occasions. When foreign heads of state visit the queen, the Mall is decked out in the Union Jack and the flag of the visitor's country. *Between Buckingham Palace & Admiralty Arch.*

❺ ★ **Admiralty Arch.** Built in 1910, this quintuple-arched building looks west to the grand statue of Queen Victoria in front of Buckingham Palace. The central gates are for ceremonial use, opening only to let a royal procession pass. Adorable little ships sitting atop nearby street lamps are a nod to the Old Admiralty Offices that

10 Downing Street.

inhabited the arch. Its lease now sold by the government, the arch will become an opulent Waldorf Astoria hotel, opening in 2022.

6 ★★★ Banqueting House. All that remains of Whitehall Palace is this grand hall, completed in 1621 by Inigo Jones. The city's first Renaissance-style construction was inspired by the Italian architecture of Palladio, but is best known for its glorious Rubens-painted ceiling—commissioned by Charles I (1600–49), who used the building for elaborate parties called "masques" and for greeting foreign delegations (not actually for banqueting). The allegorical painting, equating the Stuart kings with the gods, may have gone to Charles's head: His stubborn belief in the divine right of kings led directly to the English Civil Wars and ultimately his execution for treason, right outside the hall. *Whitehall.* ⏲ *30 min.* ☎ *020/3166-6155. www.hrp.org.uk/banquetinghouse. £5.50 adults, free children 15 & under. Daily 10am–5pm.*

7 Horse Guards, Whitehall Entrance. Just across from the Banqueting House is another entrance to Horse Guards Parade, guarded by mounted soldiers in ceremonial garb who provide good photo opportunities for visitors. Walk through the gates and have a look through the arched tunnel, framing a beautiful view of St. James's Park.

8 10 Downing Street. The home address of Britain's prime minister since 1732 is set in a quiet cul-de-sac blocked off by iron gates for security reasons. There's not much to see now except a lot of police giving you the evil eye, though there is a *frisson* of excitement to be had while standing near so much power.

Of the many pubs in Whitehall, one of the best is the 9 **Silver Cross,** which, despite its faux ye olde England decor, is genuinely old (it was granted a brothel license in 1674). It offers filling fish and chips, lots of seating, and its own ghost—a young girl in Tudor dress. *33 Whitehall.* ☎ *020/7930-8350. £–££.* ●

4 The Best Shopping

Shopping Best Bets

Best **Time to Shop**
During the July/August and December/January citywide sales, lasting a month or more

Best for **Last Season's Designer Threads at Big Discounts**
★★ Pandora, *16–22 Cheval Place (p 81)*

Best for the **British Look**
★★ John Smedley, *24 Brook St. (p 80);* ★★ Fred Perry, *12 Newburgh St. (p 80); or* ★ Lulu Guinness, *9 The Piazza (p 80)*

Best **Fun & Vintage Jewelry**
★★ Hirst Antiques, *59 Pembridge Rd. (p 84)*

Best for a **Sugar Rush**
★★ Artisan du Chocolat, *89 Lower Sloane St. (p 82)*

Best **Toy Store**
★ Hamleys, *189–196 Regent St. (p 86)*

Best Place to **Score Stuff from Other People's Attics**
★★★ Alfies Antique Market, *13–25 Church St. (p 78)*

Best **Foot Forward**
★ The Natural Shoe Store, *13 Neal St. (p 80)*

Best Place to **Find Out Where You Are**
★★★ Stanfords, *12–14 Long Acre (p 80)*

Best **Hot-Date Lingerie**
★★ Agent Provocateur, *6 Broadwick St. (p 84)*

Best for **Foodies**
★★★ Borough Market, *Southwark St. (p 82)*

Best for **Vintage Street Fashions**
★ Rokit, *101 Brick Lane (p 81)*

Best **Weekend Wandering**
★★★ Portobello Road Market, *Portobello Rd. (p 86);* or ★★ Spitalfields & Sunday UpMarket, *Brick Lane (p 85)*

Best **Everything**
★★★ Selfridges, *400 Oxford St. (p 82)*

Best **Museum Shop**
★★★ Victoria & Albert Museum, *Cromwell Rd. (p 86)*

Best **Parfumerie**
★★ Angela Flanders, *4 Artillery Passage (p 78)*

Previous page: Selfridge's Department Store. Below: Head to Borough Market for lunchtime.

Chelsea & Knightsbridge Shopping

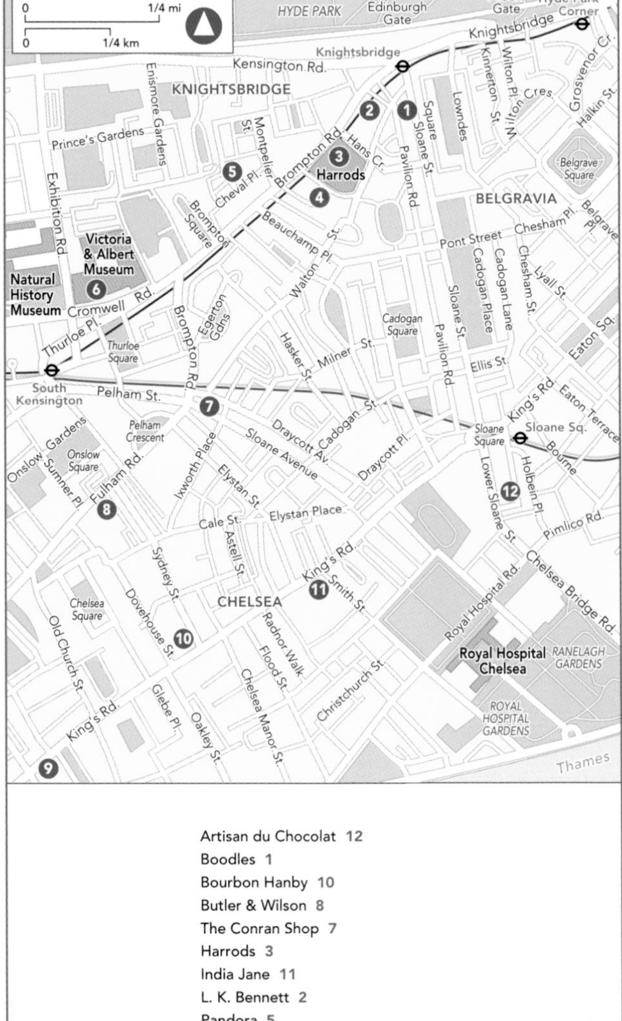

Artisan du Chocolat 12
Boodles 1
Bourbon Hanby 10
Butler & Wilson 8
The Conran Shop 7
Harrods 3
India Jane 11
L. K. Bennett 2
Pandora 5
Rigby & Peller 4
Rococo Chocolates 9
Victoria & Albert Museum 6

Central London Shopping

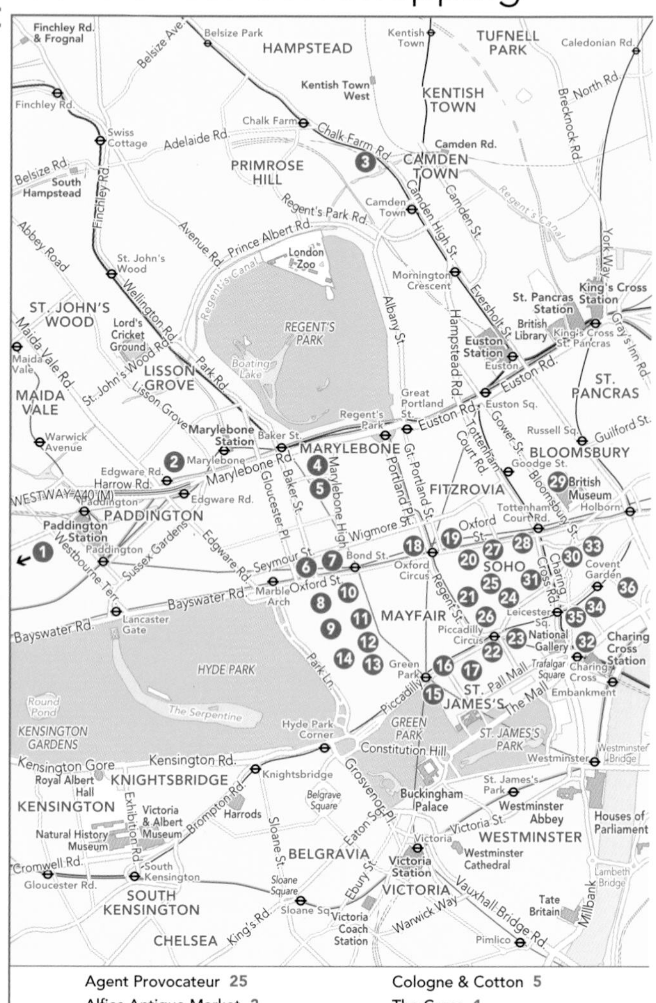

Agent Provocateur 25
Alfies Antique Market 2
Angela Flanders 40
Bermondsey Market 37
Borough Market 38
Boxpark 42
Browns 10
British Museum 29
Camden Market 3
Christie's 17
Cologne & Cotton 5
The Cross 1
Daunt Books 4
Fortnum & Mason 16
Foyles 31
Fred Perry 26
Geo. F. Trumper 13
Gosh! 24
Graham & Green 1
Grays Antique Market 8

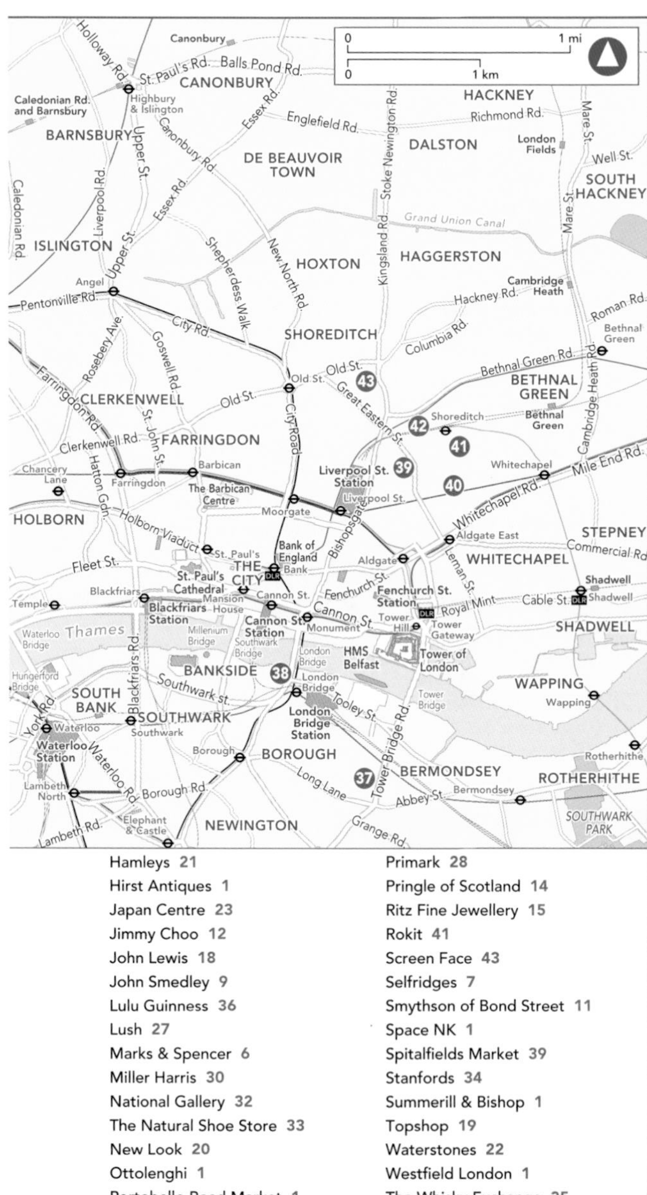
CANONBURY
HACKNEY
BARNSBURY
DE BEAUVOIR TOWN
DALSTON
SOUTH HACKNEY
ISLINGTON
HOXTON
HAGGERSTON
SHOREDITCH
CLERKENWELL
FARRINGDON
BETHNAL GREEN
HOLBORN
THE CITY
STEPNEY
WHITECHAPEL
SHADWELL
BANKSIDE
WAPPING
SOUTH BANK
SOUTHWARK
BOROUGH
BERMONDSEY
ROTHERHITHE
NEWINGTON
Thames
Grand Union Canal

London Shopping A to Z

Antiques & Auctions

★★★ Alfies Antique Market MARYLEBONE The city's largest indoor antique and vintage market—four floors of secondhand knickknacks, plus old fabrics and dresses. *13–25 Church St.* ☎ *020/7723-6066. www.alfiesantiques.com. Some dealers take credit cards. Tube: Marylebone. Map p 76.*

★ Bermondsey (New Caledonian) Antiques Market BERMONDSEY Join the crush of dealers fighting over the estate goods and antiques sold here from 5am every Friday. Stalls are pretty much all packed up and gone by lunchtime. *Corner of Bermondsey St. & Long Lane. https://bermondseysquare.net. Some dealers take credit cards. Tube: Bermondsey or Borough. Map p 77.*

★ Bourbon Hanby CHELSEA A rather grand arcade of antiques stalls featuring upscale estate goods, jewelry, and fine art. *151 Sydney St.* ☎ *020/7352-2106. www.bourbonhanby.com. Some dealers take credit cards. Tube: Sloane Sq. Map p 75.*

Alfies Antique Market.

★ Christie's ST. JAMES'S Don't be scared off by the cost of its serious treasures; this venerable auction house often has something unique for regular budgets. *8 King St.* ☎ *020/7839-9060. www.christies.com. AE, MC, V. Tube: Green Park. Map p 76.*

★★★ Grays Antique Market MAYFAIR Vendors across two neighboring sites sell everything from Art Deco paperweights and antique jewelry to vintage Edwardian toys. *58 Davies St.* ☎ *020/7629-7034. www.graysantiques.com. Some dealers take credit cards. Tube: Bond St. Map p 76.*

Beauty Products

★★ Angela Flanders EAST END This exclusive shop is well worth the effort it takes to find, in a passageway close to Old Spitalfields Market. Flanders' bespoke, signature scents have a devoted clientele. *4 Artillery Passage.* ☎ *020/7247-7040. www.angelaflanders-perfumer.com. AE, MC, V. Tube: Liverpool St. Map p 77.*

★★ Geo. F. Trumper MAYFAIR An essential shop for the well-groomed man, the woman who wants a great gift for her guy, or anyone interested in high-quality toiletries and shaving accessories. *9 Curzon St.* ☎ *020/7499-1850. www.trumpers.com. AE, MC, V. Tube: Green Park. Map p 76.*

★ Lush SOHO There's no missing a branch of this popular British chain—not if you have a sense of smell, anyway. The fruity, heady scents of their "cruelty free" soaps, bath oils, and cosmetics pervade the air surrounding its London flagship store. Great for portable gifts.

Daunt Books on Marylebone High Street.

175–179 Oxford St. ☎ 020/7789-0001. www.lush.co.uk. MC, V. Tube: Oxford Circus. Map p 76.

★★ **Miller Harris** COVENT GARDEN Trained in Grasse, France, Lyn Harris has created a global brand of sexy and elegant scents of the finest quality, as well as beautifully packaged lotions and candles. *14 Monmouth St. ☎ 020/7836-9378. www.millerharris.com. AE, MC, V. Tube: Covent Garden. Map p 76.*

★ **Screen Face** SHOREDITCH Even if you're not in the market for a special-effects bruise kit, you'll be knocked out by the range and variety of makeup, accessories, and skin goods at this favorite of pro makeup artists. *47 Charlotte Rd. ☎ 020/7836-3955. www.screenface.co.uk. MC, V. Tube: Old St. Map p 77.*

★ **Space NK** NOTTING HILL This upscale British chain sells many boutique lines of makeup, creams, fragrances, and decadently scented candles. *127–131 Westbourne Grove. ☎ 020/7727-8063. www.spacenk.com. MC, V. Tube: Notting Hill Gate or Bayswater. Map p 76.*

Books & Stationery

★★★ **Daunt Books** MARYLEBONE The most atmospheric branch of this small chain still has its wonderful, century-old interior intact. It has an excellent travel section and the latest U.K. fiction, with a peaceful atmosphere for browsing. *183 Marylebone High St. ☎ 020/7224-2295. www.dauntbooks.co.uk. MC, V. Tube: Baker St. Map p 76.*

★★ **Foyles** SOHO The flagship store of London's best-known independent bookseller has made its home on this street since 1906. From academic to kids' books and London guides, it's all here. *107 Charing Cross Rd. ☎ 020/7434-1574. www.foyles.co.uk. MC, V. Tube: Tottenham Court Rd. Map p 76.*

★★ **Gosh!** SOHO Arthouse comics, special editions, and mainstream graphic novels for every age and taste. Staff is superbly helpful for newbies. *1 Berwick St. ☎ 020/7437-0187. www.goshlondon.com. MC, V. Tube: Piccadilly Circus. Map p 76.*

★★ **Smythson of Bond Street** MAYFAIR This expensive and exclusive stationer caters to generations of posh Londoners, who would feel naked without a Smythson appointment diary. Also sells elegant leather travel accessories. *131–132 New Bond St. ☎ 020/3535-8009. www.smythson.com. AE, MC, V. Tube: Bond St. Map p 76.*

★★★ Stanfords COVENT GARDEN The destination for all disoriented travelers (providing you can find your way here, of course), Stanfords is London's largest guidebook and map store. If you can't find a guide to it here, it probably hasn't been discovered yet. *12–14 Long Acre. ☎ 020/7836-1321. www.stanfords.co.uk. MC, V. Tube: Covent Garden or Leicester Sq. Map p 76.*

★★ Waterstones PICCADILLY The flagship branch of the U.K.'s leading book chain takes up six floors, making it Europe's largest bookstore. The choice is enormous. The top floor has a bar/restaurant and stunning views of London. *203–206 Piccadilly. ☎ 020/7851-2400. www.waterstones.com. MC, V. Tube: Piccadilly Circus. Map p 76.*

Clothing & Shoes

★ Browns MAYFAIR The best place in town for up-to-the-minute fashions, including a discriminating selection of hip high-end designers. It's expensive, so keep your eyes peeled for sales. *23–27 S. Moulton St. ☎ 020/7514-0016. www.brownsfashion.com. AE, MC, V. Tube: Bond St. Map p 76.*

★★ The Cross NOTTING HILL Fashionistas in the know come here for Missoni, Johnny Loves Rosie, Alice Lee, and lots of up-and-coming designers. You'll also find housewares and witty children's gifts. *141 Portland Rd. ☎ 020/7727-6760. www.thecrossshop.co.uk. AE, MC, V. Tube: Holland Park. Map p 76.*

★★ Fred Perry SOHO Petite home of the famous Laurel Wreath logo and the twin-tipped polos for men and women. A 20th-century style icon that still says Made in England. *12 Newburgh St. ☎ 020/7734-4494. www.fredperry.com. AE, MC, V. Tube: Oxford Circus. Map p 76. Also at: Units 6–7 Thomas Neal's, Seven Dials.*

★★ Jimmy Choo MAYFAIR The London-based global brand pops up on the well-tended feet of Oscar contenders and one-percenters. You'll pay dearly for a pair. *27 New Bond St. ☎ 020/7493-5858. www.jimmychoo.com. AE, MC, V. Tube: Bond St. Map p 76.*

★★ John Smedley MAYFAIR Fashion-forward Merino woolens and cashmere with Swinging Sixties cachet. Contemporary and classic lines are always on show. *24 Brook St. ☎ 020/7495-2222. www.johnsmedley.com. AE, MC, V. Tube: Bond St. Map p 76.*

★ L.K. Bennett KNIGHTSBRIDGE Leave the clothes on the rack, but do step into the shoes. Boots are plentiful, and there are plenty of dressy flats and come-hither pumps for the demure-shoe freak. *39–41 Brompton Rd. ☎ 020/7225-1916. www.lkbennett.com. AE, MC, V. Tube: Knightsbridge. Map p 75.*

★ Lulu Guinness COVENT GARDEN The celebrated Brit bag designer has been turning out bags and purses in a range of funky styles and shapes for two decades now. *9 The Piazza. ☎ 020/7240-2537. www.luluguinness.com. AE, MC, V. Tube: Covent Garden. Map p 76.*

★ The Natural Shoe Store COVENT GARDEN Come here for the best of Birkenstock, Trippen, Arche, and other comfortable, ethical hippie styles now totally in vogue. *70 Neal St. ☎ 020/7240-2783. www.thenaturalshoestore.com. AE, MC, V. Tube: Covent Garden. Map p 76. Also at: 325 King's Rd., Chelsea.*

★ New Look SOHO One of the giants of the affordable women's and girls' fashion scene, New Look's strength is its dependability. The clothes may be cheap, but they're always durable enough to last the season—or beyond—unlike those of many competitors. *203 Oxford St.* ☎ *020/7851-7360. www.newlook.com. AE, MC, V. Tube: Oxford Circus. Map p 76.*

★★ **Pandora** KNIGHTSBRIDGE A big, well-organized shop featuring gems from big designer names, shoes, and accessories previously owned by fashionable Knightsbridge clotheshorses. Expect Celine, Louis Vuitton, and the like. *16–22 Cheval Place.* ☎ *020/7589-5289. www.pandoradressagency.com. AE, MC, V. Tube: Knightsbridge. Map p 75.*

★★ **Primark** SOHO A four-floor flagship megastore for the U.K.'s leading cost-conscious fashion retailer. Menswear, womenswear, kids' clothes, travel accessories, and seasonal ranges. Usually open till 10pm. *14–28 Oxford St.* ☎ *020/7580-5510. www.primark.com. MC, V. Tube: Tottenham Court Rd. Map p 76.*

★ **Pringle of Scotland** MAYFAIR Its reputation for cheesy golf cardigans left far behind, this luxury retailer now sells an assortment of dressy casual-wear and woolens that are up to the minute. *94 Mount St.* ☎ *020/3011-0031. www.pringlescotland.com. AE, MC, V. Tube: Bond St. Map p 76.*

★ **Rokit** EAST END Hipster vintage for the London look. Everything from blouses and dungarees to classic sunglasses, fridge magnets, and even vintage bridal wear. *101 Brick Lane.* ☎ *020/7375-3864. www.rokit.co.uk. MC, V. Tube: Aldgate East or Liverpool St. Map p 77.*

★★★ **Topshop** MARYLEBONE An absolute must-go for the younger generation, but even older women find something to love in this mecca of street fashion at decent prices. The flagship shop on Oxford Circus is a madhouse, but it's got the widest range of items, including experimental lines available nowhere else. *Oxford Circus.* ☎ *0344/848-7487. www.topshop.com. AE, MC, V. Tube: Oxford Circus. Map p 76.*

Department Stores

★ **Harrods** KNIGHTSBRIDGE From its food halls to its home entertainment centers, Harrods is a London institution—as well as overhyped and overpriced. *87–135 Brompton Rd.* ☎ *020/7730-234. www.harrods.com. AE, MC, V. Tube: Knightsbridge. Map p 75.*

Harrods, purveyor of luxury goods.

★★★ **John Lewis** MARYLEBONE This is *the* place to find homey necessities such as sewing notions, fabrics, and kitchenwares, plus lighting and beauty lines. Londoners can't live without it. *300 Oxford St.* ☎ *020/7629-7711. www.johnlewis.com. AE, MC, V. Tube: Oxford Circus. Map p 76.*

★★★ **Selfridges** MARYLEBONE Inside and out, this grand old department store (opened by a Wisconsiner) is the best in town. The food halls are great, as are the fashions; it even offers piercing. *400 Oxford St.* ☎ *0800/123-400. www.selfridges.com. AE, MC, V. Tube: Marble Arch. Map p 76.*

Food & Drink

★★ **Artisan du Chocolat** CHELSEA This award-winning shop creates quirky and delicious flavored chocolates and truffles for the connoisseur. Try the lavender chocolate—close your eyes, and you're in Provence. *89 Lower Sloane St.* ☎ *0845/270-6996. www.artisanduchocolat.com. AE, MC, V. Tube: Sloane Sq. Map p 75.*

★★★ **Borough Market** BANKSIDE This is a gourmet's paradise, stalls piled high with free-range meats, cheeses, fruits and veggies, craft beers, and many, many homemade treats. But London's finest food market can be both mouthwateringly delicious and eyewateringly expensive—unless you restrict yourself to free samples. Open Wednesday to Saturday. *Southwark St.* ☎ *020/7407-1002. www.boroughmarket.org.uk. Tube: London Bridge. Map p 77.*

★★ **Fortnum & Mason** MAYFAIR The city's ultimate grocer stocks goodies fit for the queen—or friends back home—plus gourmet picnic fare and specialty teas. *181 Piccadilly.* ☎ *020/7734-8040. www.fortnumandmason.com. AE, DC, MC, V. Tube: Green Park. Map p 76.*

★★ **Harrods Food Halls** KNIGHTSBRIDGE Harrods sells loads of tasty edible gifts branded with its famous name; be sure to ogle the remarkable ceilings in the produce and meat sections. *87–135 Brompton Rd.* ☎ *020/7730-1234. www.harrods.com. AE, MC, V. Tube: Knightsbridge. Map p 75.*

★ **Japan Centre** ST. JAMES'S Opened in 2017, this basement food hall is a Japanophile's dream, stuffed with groceries, teas, sake,

Royal fare at Fortnum & Mason.

Beautifully wrapped Rococo Chocolates.

and shochu. There's also a sashimi bar and a small ramen kitchen. *35b Panton St. ☎ 020/3405-1246. www.japancentre.com. MC, V. Tube: Piccadilly Circus or Leicester Sq. Map p 76.*

★★★ Ottolenghi NOTTING HILL This small shop is filled with exquisite European desserts—English puddings, French gâteaux, Italian *torta*, German *bundt*—in every form and flavor. They also serve a delicious breakfast and lunch. *63 Ledbury Rd. ☎ 020/7727-1121. www.ottolenghi.co.uk. MC, V. Tube: Notting Hill Gate or Westbourne Park. Map p 76.*

★★ Rococo Chocolates CHELSEA Chocoholics love this fine store, which stocks wittily shaped, high-cocoa-content designer confections and creative flavors (Earl Grey, gingerbread, and more). *321 King's Rd. ☎ 020/7352-5857. www.rococochocolates.com. MC, V. Tube: Fulham Broadway. Map p 75.*

★ The Whisky Exchange COVENT GARDEN Fine and rare Scotch, plus a huge range of boutique liquors to take (or ship) home. *2 Bedford St. ☎ 020/7100-0088. www.thewhiskyexchange.com. AE, MC, V. Tube: Covent Garden. Map p 76.*

Home Decor

★ Cologne & Cotton MARYLEBONE Stock up here on elegant bedclothes of pure linen, Miller Harris fragrances, and cotton sheets in soothing colors and simple designs. The pillowcases are gorgeous. *88 Marylebone High St. ☎ 020/7486-0595. www.cologneandcotton.com. MC, V. Tube: Baker St. Map p 76. Also at: 39 Kensington Church St.*

★ The Conran Shop SOUTH KENSINGTON Your best bets among the large and varied selection of high-priced merchandise here are the kitchenware and bath items. *Michelin House, 81 Fulham Rd. ☎ 020/7589-7401. www.conranshop.co.uk. AE, MC, V. Tube: S. Kensington. Map p 75.*

★★ Graham & Green NOTTING HILL Lighting, stationery, and attractive home-decor whatnots fill Graham & Green's charming little shop, just off Portobello Road. *4 Elgin Crescent. ☎ 020/7243-8908. www.grahamandgreen.co.uk. AE, MC, V. Tube: Ladbroke Grove. Map p 76.*

★ India Jane CHELSEA This store gathers the best of India's modern-boho furnishings and decor, and sells well-priced portable knickknacks and bibelots. *121 King's Rd. ☎ 020/7351-9940. www.indiajane.co.uk. AE, MC, V. Tube: Sloane Sq. Map p 75.*

★★ Summerill & Bishop HOLLAND PARK Shop here for a sumptuous collection of French housewares, from efficient, humble radiator dusters to the finest table settings and cookery items. *100 Portland Rd. ☎ 020/7221-4566. www.summerillandbishop.com. AE, MC, V. Tube: Holland Park. Map p 76.*

VAT (Value Added Tax)

The U.K. levies a crushing 20% Value Added Tax (VAT) on all non-essential purchases. (By law, VAT *must* be included in the retail price tag you see instore—there's no extra to pay at the checkout.) If you live outside the E.U., you can apply to have your VAT refunded. Most shops will help you if you spend a certain amount, usually at least £75 (look for a "Tax Free Shopping" sign or sticker). Ask for VAT Form 407 when you pay and have it filled out instore; forms must be validated by the seller. When you get to the airport, present your form, passport, and purchases—do not pack them in your checked luggage—to the Customs agency for certification. Once your papers have been stamped, you can get a cash refund from one of the agencies at the airport (minus a service charge), or you can mail in the forms to get a cash or credit card refund. The process is only worth going through for high-ticket items. For more information, visit **www.gov.uk/tax-on-shopping/taxfreeshopping**.

Jewelry

★ **Boodles** KNIGHTSBRIDGE One of England's oldest jewelers (founded in 1798), Boodles has resident designers who keep its collection fresh and modern (not to mention expensive). *6 Sloane St. ☎ 020/7235-0111. www.boodles.com. AE, DC, MC, V. Tube: Knightsbridge. Map p 75. Also at: 178 New Bond St.*

★★ **Butler & Wilson** SOUTH KENSINGTON You won't have to remortgage your house to buy the beautiful costume or silver jewelry here. It's *the* best shop in town for tiaras and brooches. *189 Fulham Rd. ☎ 020/7352-3045. www.butlerandwilson.co.uk. AE, MC, V. Tube: S. Kensington. Map p 75.*

★★ **Hirst Antiques** NOTTING HILL Something of a jewelry museum, here you'll find extravagant vintage costume baubles from European catwalks of yore, plus interesting affordable and new gems. It's on Etsy, too (as TheHirstCollection). *59 Pembridge Rd. (at Portobello Rd.). ☎ 020/7727-9364. MC, V. Tube: Notting Hill Gate. Map p 76.*

★★ **Ritz Fine Jewellery** ST. JAMES'S Arguably the best hotel jewelry shop in the world, thanks to its collections of well-set semiprecious gems and serious rocks. Of course, when the hotel is the Ritz, it had better be the best. *150 Piccadilly. ☎ 020/7409-1312. www.ritzfinejewellery.com. AE, MC, V. Tube: Green Park. Map p 76.*

Lingerie

★★ **Agent Provocateur** SOHO Provocative, indeed! This store's sexy underclothes are works of art. If you've fallen off your diet, however, keep in mind that sizes are small. *6 Broadwick St. ☎ 020/7439-0229. www.agentprovocateur.com. AE, MC, V. Tube: Oxford Circus. Map p 76.*

★★ **Marks & Spencer** MARYLEBONE This beloved, reliable outlet for comfy cotton underwear for men and women has kept up with the times, offering a lot more than old-lady knickers. *458 Oxford St. ☎ 020/7935-7954. www.marksandspencer.com. AE, MC, V. Tube: Marble Arch. Map p 76.*

★ **Rigby & Peller** KNIGHTSBRIDGE The former corsetiere to the queen specializes in classy underwear, bathing suits (ask for "swimming costumes"), and finely engineered brassieres. *2 Hans Rd. ☎ 020/7225-4760. www.rigbyandpeller.com. MC, V. Tube: Knightsbridge. Map p 75.*

Malls

★★ **Boxpark** SHOREDITCH Old shipping containers turned tiny stores for urban fashions, pop-ups, one-off accessories, street food, and more. You won't find this stuff anywhere else. *2–10 Bethnal Green Rd. www.boxpark.co.uk. Overground: Shoreditch. Map p 77.*

★★ **Westfield London** SHEPHERDS BUSH Big European brands—both luxe and Main St.—all under one immaculately designed roof just west of the center. Whether you want beauty products, bags, a Bond watch, or a Bentley automobile, you can buy it here. Dining options aplenty. *Ariel Way. ☎ 020/3371-2300. http://uk.westfield.com/london. AE, MC, V. Tube/Overground: Shepherds Bush. Map p 76.*

Markets

★★★ **Camden Market** CAMDEN TOWN It may promote itself as the "capital of alternative London," but this riotous collection of venues (there's no one Camden Market, but rather several stretching along the high street), selling art, crafts, jewelry, vintage fashion, club wear, food, and more, is now one of the capital's top tourist attractions, putting it at the heart of the mainstream. Head to The Stables area for a more alt-vibe. *Camden High St. ☎ 020/3763-9900. www.camdenmarket.com. Tube: Camden Town. Map p 76.*

★★ **Spitalfields & Sunday UpMarket** EAST END Spitalfields' huge indoor market has street food, ethnic clothes, knick-knacks, handmade crafts, and a few chain stores open all week. The UpMarket is a Sunday-only vintage, clothing, and designer takeover of multiple sites along Brick Lane. *Commercial St., Brick Lane & Around. Most traders take cash only. www.sundayupmarket.co.uk. Tube: Liverpool St./Overground: Shoreditch. Map p 77.*

Camden Market.

★★★ **Portobello Road Market** NOTTING HILL Saturday is the best day to join the throngs at Portobello's famous antiques market, although you can also find fashion, secondhand goods, and fruits and vegetables. Bring cash. *Portobello Rd. ☎ 020/7361-3001. Some dealers take credit cards. www.portobelloroad.co.uk. Tube: Notting Hill Gate or Ladbroke Grove. Map p 76.*

Museum Shops

★ kids **British Museum** BLOOMSBURY The B.M. has multiple shops and product ranges, including a bookshop, a "family" shop, a "collection" shop (selling souvenirs), and a "culture" shop (stocked with luxury items, many based on items in the museum's collection). *Great Russell St. ☎ 020/7323-8000. www.britishmuseumshoponline.org. AE, MC, V. Tube: Russell Sq. Map p 76.*

★★ **National Gallery Shop** WEST END This is the city's best source for historical art-related books and stationery. An "on demand" service allows you to purchase a print of any picture in the collection in a size of your choice. *Trafalgar Sq. ☎ 020/7747-2870. www.nationalgallery.org.uk. AE, MC, V. Tube: Charing Cross. Map p 76.*

★★★ kids **Victoria & Albert Museum** SOUTH KENSINGTON This must-stop shop sells everything from postcards to jewelry inspired by the V&A collection. Cool finds include hand-painted tools and nostalgic toys. *Cromwell Rd. ☎ 020/7942-2000. www.vam.ac.uk. AE, MC, V. Tube: S. Kensington. Map p 75.*

Lego department at Hamley's.

Toys

★ kids **Hamleys** PICCADILLY London's most famous toy store has seven floors of toys, games, tricks, dolls, and more. As you enter the store, you are greeted by a giant array of (often giant-size) cuddly toys. *189–196 Regent St. ☎ 0371/704-1977. www.hamleys.com. AE, MC, V. Tube: Oxford Circus. Map p 76.*

★ kids **Harrods Toy Kingdom** KNIGHTSBRIDGE There is something here for all ages, plus kiddie-size cars and life-size stuffed animals. Be prepared for a bad case of the "gimmes" from your kids. *3rd Floor, 87–135 Brompton Rd. ☎ 020/7730-1234. www.harrods.com. AE, MC, V. Tube: Knightsbridge. Map p 75.* ●

5 The **Great Outdoors**

Hyde **Park**

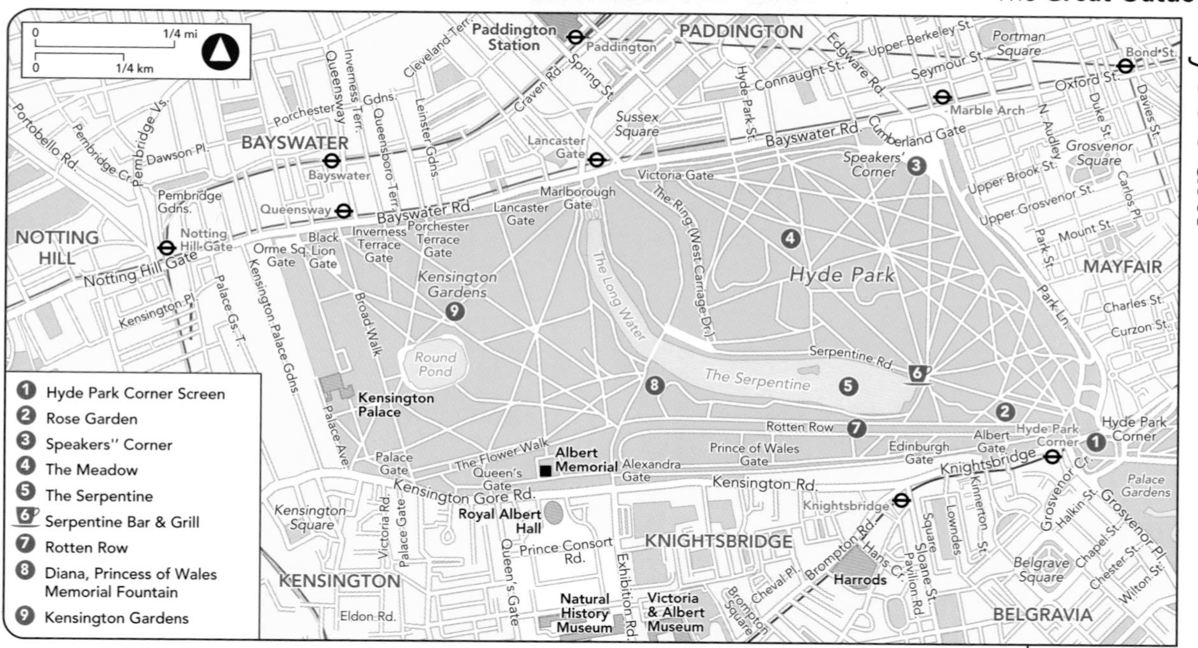

1. Hyde Park Corner Screen
2. Rose Garden
3. Speakers'' Corner
4. The Meadow
5. The Serpentine
6. Serpentine Bar & Grill
7. Rotten Row
8. Diana, Princess of Wales Memorial Fountain
9. Kensington Gardens

Previous page: Serpentine Lake in Hyde Park.

Since 1536, when Henry VIII appropriated the land from the monks of Westminster Abbey for hunting, 142-hectare (351-acre) Hyde Park has been the scene of duels, highway robbery, and sport. Today, it is a beloved oasis in the midst of London where the locals come to sunbathe, roller-blade, putter around in boats, and generally try to leave the noise of their city behind. START: **Tube to Hyde Park Corner.**

1 Hyde Park Corner Screen. Erected in 1828, this imposing park entrance (one of six) was designed by Decimus Burton, the noted architect responsible for much of Hyde Park's layout. The triple-arched screen is composed of Ionic columns, bronzed ironwork, and carved friezes inspired by the Elgin Marbles (p 27, 3). Unfortunately, it's being degraded by air pollution at this busy traffic circle. *10 min.*

2 ★ kids Rose Garden. From the Rose Garden, a riot of color in early summer, you can admire the back of Apsley House, the former home of (and currently a museum dedicated to) the Duke of Wellington. Nearby stands the Wellington Arch, topped by a majestic statue, *Winged Victory,* erected to commemorate the Iron Duke's numerous military triumphs, notably at Waterloo (1815). The garden is filled with fountains and climbing-rose trellises, both much loved by kids. Its central fountain is ringed with benches where you can sit with a picnic lunch, as hopeful sparrows flutter. *20–30 min.*

3 Speakers' Corner. The park's northeast corner provides a peculiarly British tribute to free speech. Since 1872, members of the public have been able to stand here and declaim their heartfelt opinions on whatever they choose—and anyone is allowed to answer back. In the past, you may have heard Karl Marx, the suffragettes, or George Orwell trying to convert the masses. These days, they would be on Twitter. *15 min.*

4 ★★ kids The Meadow. Amid all the neatly tended greenery is something a little more real. A 4-hectare (10-acre) section of the park has been turned into a wild meadow, filled with blooming flowers in summer and home to an

Speakers' Corner.

assortment of creatures, including songbirds, butterflies, and creepy-crawlies. Themed walks are offered in summer; check the website for details. ⏱ *30 min. www.royalparks.org.uk/parks/hyde-park.*

5 ★★★ kids The Serpentine. Queen Caroline had the Westbourne River dammed in 1730 to create the Serpentine Lake, upon which she moored two royal yachts. This lovely lake is now the premier boating spot in London for the masses. Should you venture out on the water, you can go it alone by renting a pedal boat or rowboats from the Boat House, or take it easy aboard the solar-powered ferry. ⏱ *1 hr. Bluebird Boats Ltd., Serpentine Rd. ☎ 020/7262-1989. www.solarshuttle.co.uk. Hourly rentals £12 adults, £5 children, £29 family. Mar–Oct 10am–5pm.*

6 With the best views of the Serpentine in the park, ★ kids **Serpentine Bar & Kitchen** serves hot meals, sandwiches, and drinks (wine included) that are a cut above the usual park cafeteria cuisine. You're welcome to picnic on the tables outside. *Eastern side of the Serpentine. ☎ 020/7706-8114. £.*

7 ★ kids Rotten Row. In the late 1680s, William III ordered 300 lamps to be hung from trees along this 1.5-mile riding path—whose name is an English corruption of its original appellation, *Route de Roi* ("King's Road")—in a vain attempt to stop a plague of highwaymen active in the park, and thereby creating the first artificially illuminated road in Britain. The lamps have gone, but the path is still used by riders from local stables. If you want to give it a try, contact **Ross Nye Stables,** 8 Bathurst Mews (☎ 020/7262-3791). ⏱ *1 hr. Just north of the park, behind Lancaster Gate Tube Station. 1-hr rides start at £75.*

8 ★ kids Diana, Princess of Wales Memorial Fountain. This contemporary granite fountain, on the south shore of the Serpentine, was opened by the Queen in July 2004. No less dogged by controversy than the woman who inspired it, the 700-ton, £6.5-million fountain has suffered from flooding, closures, and a slippery bottom. Children, who were meant to play happily in its cascading waters, are now restricted to toe-dipping and an occasional splash. ⏱ *20 min. Near the Lido.*

Princess Diana memorial water fountain.

9 ★★★ kids **Kensington Gardens.** Originally a part of Hyde Park, the 111-hectare (274-acre) Kensington Gardens were partitioned into an exclusive preserve of royalty in the 18th century, and only opened again to the public in the early 1800s. Originally laid out in Dutch style (emphasizing water, avenues, and topiary), these attractive gardens are especially popular with families.

Kensington Gardens Highlights

The bronze **9A** ★★ kids **Peter Pan Statue** was sculpted in 1912 by Sir George Frampton at the behest of author J. M. Barrie and is the most visited landmark in the park. A short walk north and you arrive at the **9B** ★ kids **Italian Gardens,** which followed the rage for all things Italian when they were built in 1861. Generations of children have plied model boats at the **9C** ★ kids **Round Pond,** built in 1728. Today you'll also find sophisticated models and lots of fowl. West of the pond is the **9D** **Broad Walk.** Nineteenth-century ladies and gentlemen promenaded along this tree-lined path past Kensington Palace, and flirted by the nearby bandstand. Kids will race on to the **9E** ★★ kids **Diana, Princess of Wales Memorial Playground,** centered around a huge wooden pirate ship. Finish up at Kensington Palace, restored and revamped (p 36, **7**) and a well-earned sit-down at the **9F** ★★ kids **Orangery Café,** where a good afternoon tea is served. *2–3 hr. Go in the afternoon. 020/3166-6113. www.orangerykensingtonpalace.co.uk. Tube: High St. Kensington, Queensway, or Lancaster Gate.*

Regent's **Park**

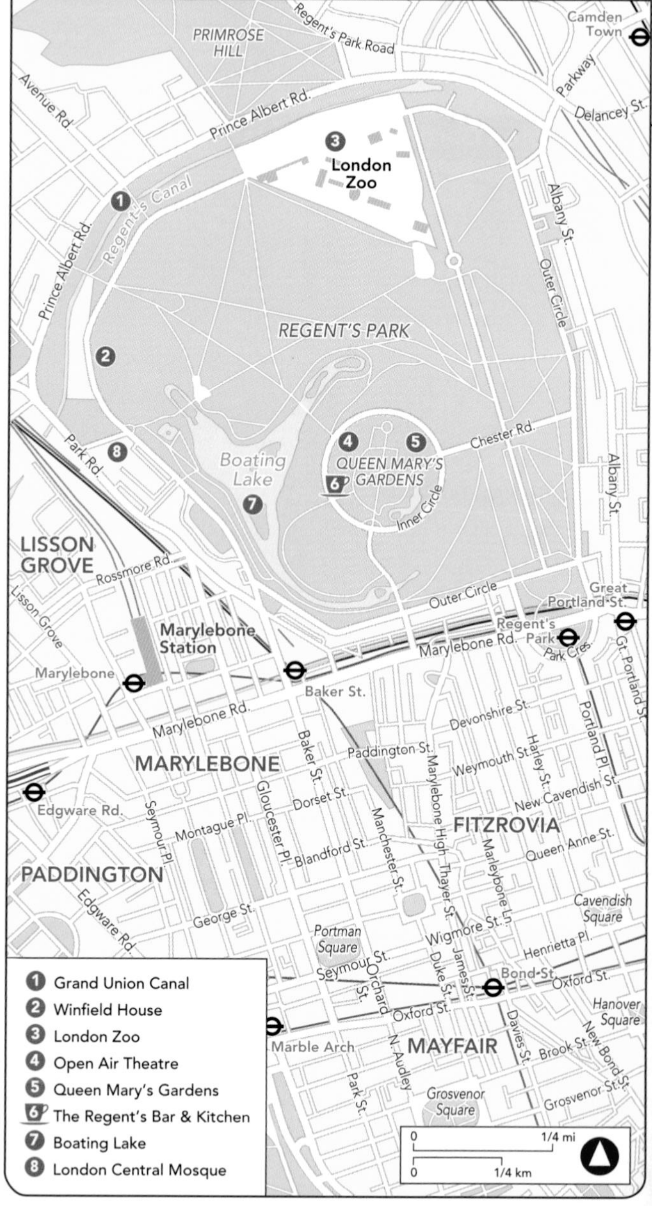

This 197-hectare (487-acre) gem started out, like so many parks, as a hunting ground for Henry VIII. It was restyled in the 19th century by John Nash (1752–1835) following the Romantic ideal of *rus in urbe* ("country in the city"). In truth, the sophistication of its flowerbeds, formal gardens with fountains, and ornamental lake make it much more *urbe* than *rus*. START: **Tube to Camden Town.**

❶ ★ kids **Grand Union Canal.** Londoners traveled the city by boat when Regent's Park was in its infancy, and this is your chance to follow in their wake. The Grand Union Canal, opened in 1814, now incorporates 137 miles of waterway connecting the River Thames with the Chiltern Hills in Oxfordshire. Water buses ply the scenic Regent's Canal section (opened in 1820), taking you from Camden Lock's market stalls through neighborhoods of colorful houseboats and grand Victorian houses on either side of the canal path to Little Venice—an area whose name is more wishful than accurate (there's just the one canal). Your final destination is the London Zoo inside Regent's Park, for which you can buy slightly discounted combo tickets before getting on the boat. ⏲ *50 min. Camden Lock.* ☎ *020/7482-2550. www.londonwaterbus.com. One-way tickets £9 adults, £7.50 children 3–15 (£25/£18 including zoo entry). Cash not accepted. Year-round, depending on the weather.*

Regent's Canal.

❷ **Winfield House.** As you sail, notice to your left some 4.6-m (15-ft.) high gates protecting a fine mansion beyond. Woolworth heiress Barbara Hutton built this Georgian pile in 1936, adding extensive gardens and trees. A year after World War II, Hutton donated the antiques-filled home to the American government for use as the official residence of the U.S. ambassador. Unfortunately, you have to be an invited guest to enter.

❸ ★★★ kids **London Zoo.** When this former zoology center opened to the public in 1847, many of its captives, such as Jumbo the Elephant (later bought by P. T. Barnum and shipped off to the U.S.), became celebrities. Visitors who complain about the high price of admission might feel differently about this venerable institution if they knew that roughly one-sixth of its 650 species (about 5,000 animals reside here) are endangered—and that the zoo's world-renowned breeding program is the only thing preventing their extinction. Highlights include "Gorilla Kingdom," a moated island resembling an African forest clearing that provides a naturalistic habitat, and "Tiger Territory." ⏲ *2 hr, longer for families. Outer Circle, Regent's Park.* ☎ *0344/225-1826. www.zsl.org/zsl-london-zoo. £25 adults, £22.50 seniors, £19.50 children 3–15 (at least 10% cheaper online). Daily 10am–5pm.*

Regent's Park Boating Lake.

❹ ★★ **Open Air Theatre.** From late May to early September, the stage features alfresco concerts and plays, notably Shakespearean comedies performed by the English Shakespeare Company. *See p 141.*

❺ ★ kids **Queen Mary's Gardens.** Laid out in the 1930s, these regal, dog-free gardens lie at the heart of the park's Inner Circle and are a place of enchanting colors, fragrances, and watery vistas. The fabulous and carefully tended Rose Gardens are especially beautiful in early summer. *30 min. Inner Circle.*

Resident giraffes at the London Zoo.

Food kiosks scattered around Regent's Park offer snacks and drinks. A less informal option is 6 **The Regent's Bar & Kitchen,** which sells hot mains, salads, and sandwiches, as well as wine and beer, which you can enjoy on a lovely terrace. *Queen Mary's Gardens, adjacent to Rose Gardens. ☎ 020/7935-5729. £.*

❼ ★★ kids **Boating Lake.** Operating on a schedule that adapts to the weather, the Boathouse rents pedal boats and rowboats you can take out on this picturesque lake. On any sunny, warm day—whatever the season—this is the ideal angle for a romantic park photo, complete with a fetching backdrop of weeping willows and reed beds. *1 hr. ☎ 020/7724-4069. Daily 11am–6pm, weather permitting. Hourly rentals £10 adults, £7 children, £28 family.*

❽ ★ **London Central Mosque.** The minaret and dome poking above the plane trees, visible from many a park vantage point, belongs to central London's main mosque and Islamic cultural center. It dates to the 1940s, when King George VI laid its first stone. *146 Park Rd. ☎ 020/7724-3363. www.iccuk.org.* ●

6 The Best Dining

Dining Best Bets

Best for **Keeping the Kids Happy**
★★ Kensington Crêperie, *2–6 Exhibition Rd. (p 106)*

Best **Pub Food**
★★ Anchor & Hope, *36 The Cut (p 103)*

Best **Business Lunch**
★★ Gaucho, *19 Swallow St. (p 104)*

Best for a **Taste of Modern Britain**
★★ Rabbit, *172 Kings Rd. (p 108)*

Best for **Beef**
★★★ Hawksmoor, *3 Yeomans Row (p 105)*

Best **Afternoon Tea**
★★★ Goring Hotel, *Beeston Place (p 105); or* ★★★ The Ritz Palm Court, *150 Piccadilly (p 108)*

Best **Menu from Centuries Past**
★★★ Dinner by Heston Blumenthal, *66 Knightsbridge (p 104)*

Best **Ramen**
★★ Shoryu, *35 Great Queen St. (p 110)*

Best **Fish & Chips**
★★★ Geales, *2 Farmer St. (p 104)*

Best **Tapas**
★★ Tapas Brindisa, *18 Southwark St. (p 110)*

Previous page: Palm Court at the Ritz.

Best for an **Olde England Vibe**
★★ Rules, *35 Maiden Lane (p 109)*

Best **View**
★★ The Portrait, *St. Martin's Lane (p 108); or* ★ Oxo Tower Brasserie, *Bargehouse St. (p 108)*

Best for **Stargazing**
★★★ The Wolseley, *160 Piccadilly (p 111)*

Best for a **Blowout**
★★★ Gordon Ramsay, *68 Royal Hospital Rd. (p 105)*

Best **Fast Food**
★★ Leon, *12 Ludgate Circus (p 107)*

Best **French Cuisine**
★★★ Le Gavroche, *43 Upper Brook St. (p 106)*

Best **Greek**
★★ Halepi, *18 Leinster Terrace (p 105)*

Best **Indian**
★★ Tamarind, *20 Queen St. (p 110)*

Best for a **Nose-to-Tail Carnivore**
★★★ St. John, *26 St. John St. (p 109)*

Best **Subterranean Dining**
★ Café in the Crypt, *Duncannon St. (p 103)*

Notting Hill Dining

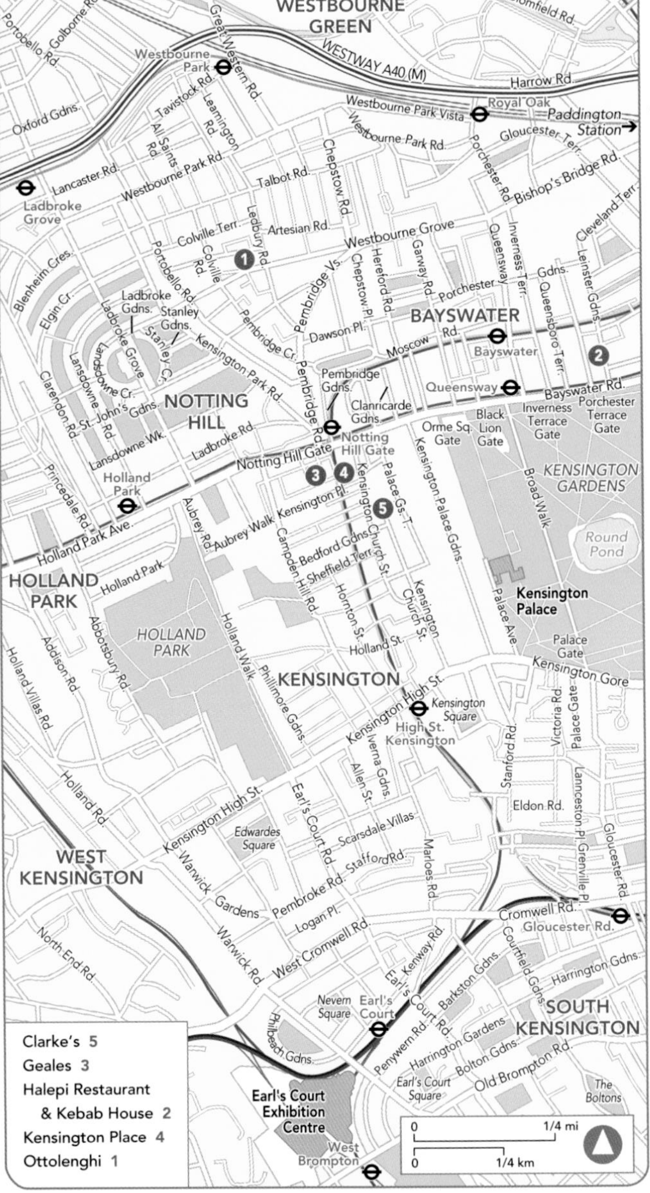

Kensington & Chelsea Dining

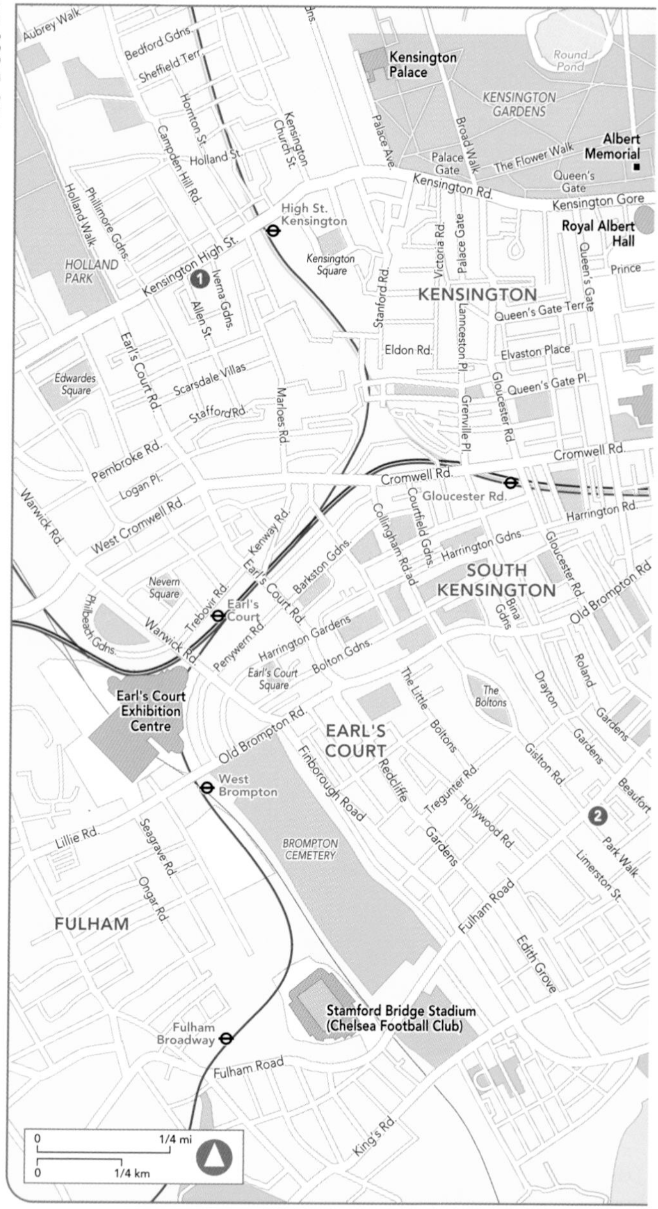

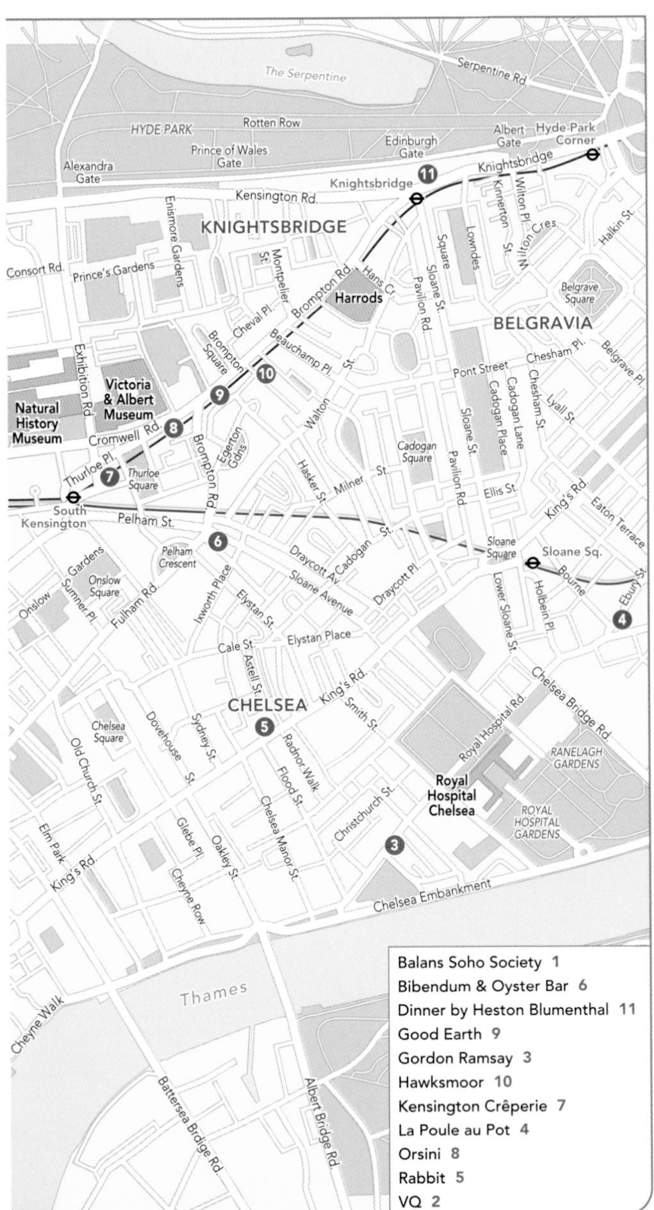

Balans Soho Society 1
Bibendum & Oyster Bar 6
Dinner by Heston Blumenthal 11
Good Earth 9
Gordon Ramsay 3
Hawksmoor 10
Kensington Crêperie 7
La Poule au Pot 4
Orsini 8
Rabbit 5
VQ 2

West End Dining

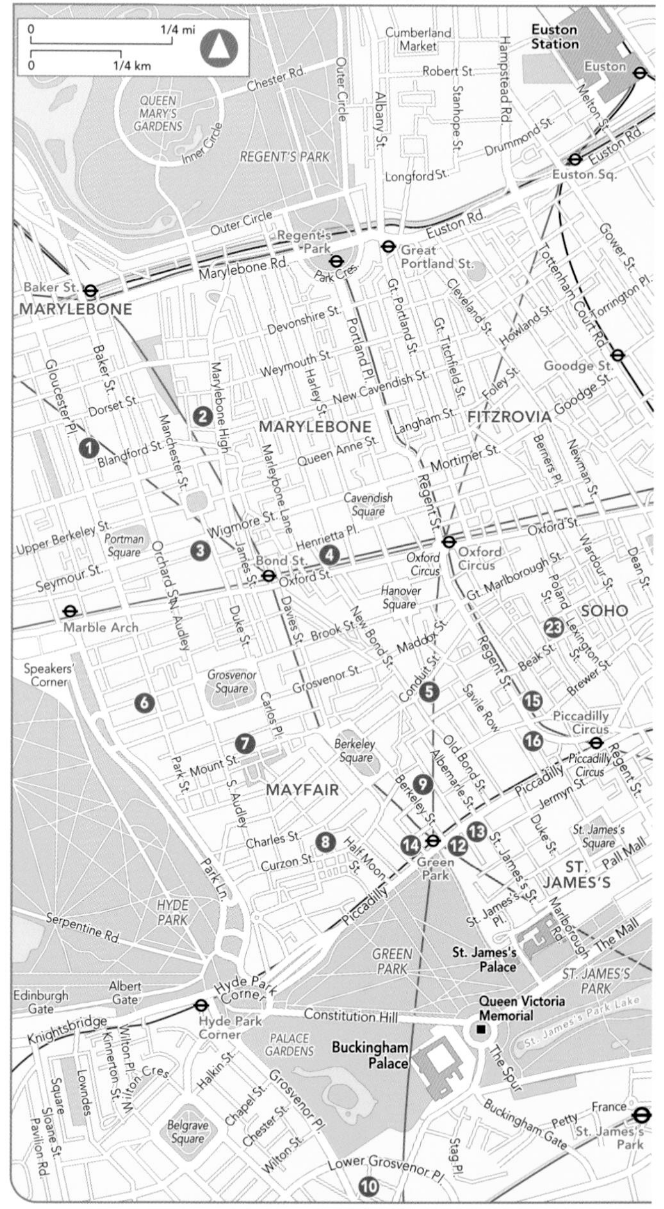

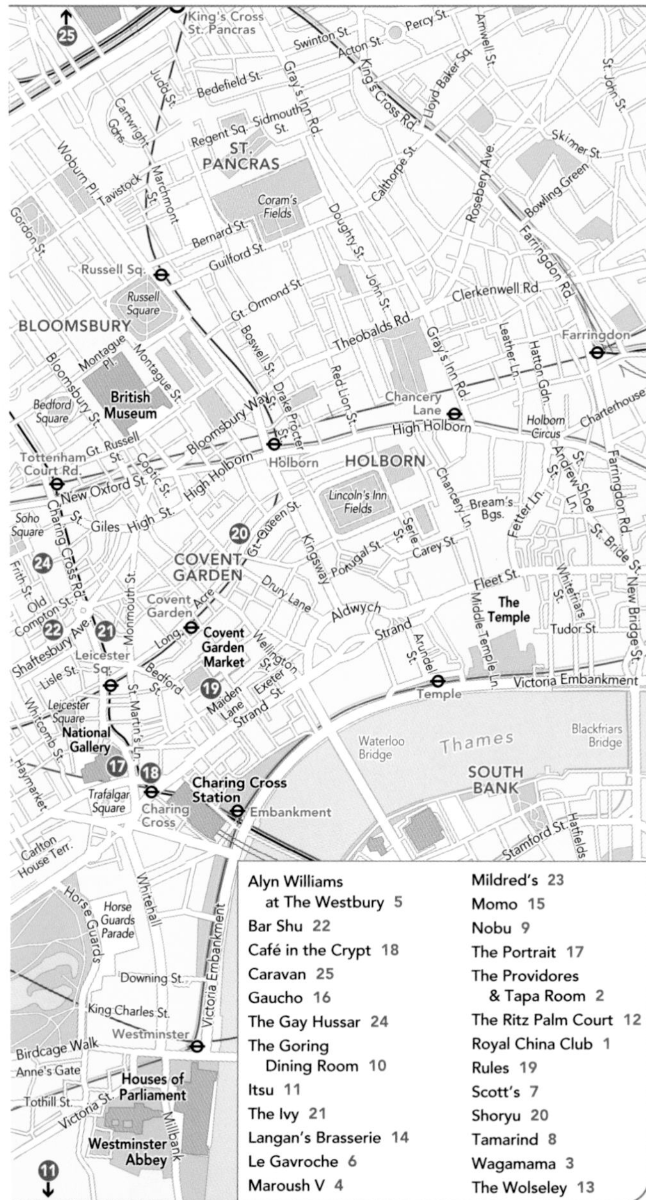
King's Cross St. Pancras
25
Swinton St.
Acton St.
Percy St.
Amwell St.
Judd St.
Bedefield St.
Gray's Inn Rd.
King's Cross Rd.
Lloyd Baker Sq.
St. John St.
Cartwright Gdns.
Regent Sq.
Sidmouth St.
ST. PANCRAS
Skinner St.
Woburn Pl.
Tavistock
Marchmont St.
Coram's Fields
Calthorpe St.
Rosebery Ave.
Bowling Green
Gordon St.
Bernard St.
Doughty St.
Farringdon Rd.
Guilford St.
Russell Sq.
Russell Square
Gt. Ormond St.
John St.
Clerkenwell Rd.
BLOOMSBURY
Theobalds Rd.
Boswell St.
Gray's Inn Rd.
Leather Ln.
Hatton Gdn.
Farringdon
Montague Pl.
Montague St.
Bloomsbury St.
Bedford Square
British Museum
Red Lion St.
Drake St.
Procter St.
Chancery Lane
Holborn Circus
Charterhouse
Bloomsbury Way
High Holborn
Tottenham Court Rd.
Gt. Russell St.
Holborn
HOLBORN
St. Andrew St.
Shoe Ln.
Farringdon Rd.
Coptic St.
New Oxford St.
High Holborn
Chancery Ln.
Lincoln's Inn Fields
Bream's Bgs.
Fetter Ln.
St. Bride St.
Soho Square
Charing Cross Rd.
St. Giles High St.
20
Gt. Queen St.
Kingsway
Serle St.
Carey St.
24
COVENT GARDEN
Portugal St.
Frith St.
Old Compton St.
Drury Lane
Fleet St.
Whitefriars St.
New Bridge St.
Covent Garden
Acre
Aldwych
Middle Temple Ln.
The Temple
22
21
Monmouth St.
Long
Covent Garden Market
Wellington St.
Strand
Arundel St.
Tudor St.
Shaftesbury Ave.
Leicester Sq.
Bedford St.
Exeter St.
Victoria Embankment
Lisle St.
19
Maiden Lane
Strand
Temple
Whitcomb St.
Leicester Square
St. Martin's Ln.
National Gallery
Waterloo Bridge
Thames
Blackfriars Bridge
Haymarket
17
18
SOUTH BANK
Trafalgar Square
Charing Cross Station
Charing Cross
Embankment
Stamford St.
Hatfields
Carlton House Terr.
Whitehall
Horse Guards
Horse Guards Parade
Victoria Embankment
Downing St.
King Charles St.
Westminster
Birdcage Walk
Anne's Gate
Houses of Parliament
Tothill St.
Victoria St.
Millbank
Westminster Abbey
11
Alyn Williams at The Westbury 5
Bar Shu 22
Café in the Crypt 18
Caravan 25
Gaucho 16
The Gay Hussar 24
The Goring Dining Room 10
Itsu 11
The Ivy 21
Langan's Brasserie 14
Le Gavroche 6
Maroush V 4
Mildred's 23
Momo 15
Nobu 9
The Portrait 17
The Providores & Tapa Room 2
The Ritz Palm Court 12
Royal China Club 1
Rules 19
Scott's 7
Shoryu 20
Tamarind 8
Wagamama 3
The Wolseley 13

City & East End Dining

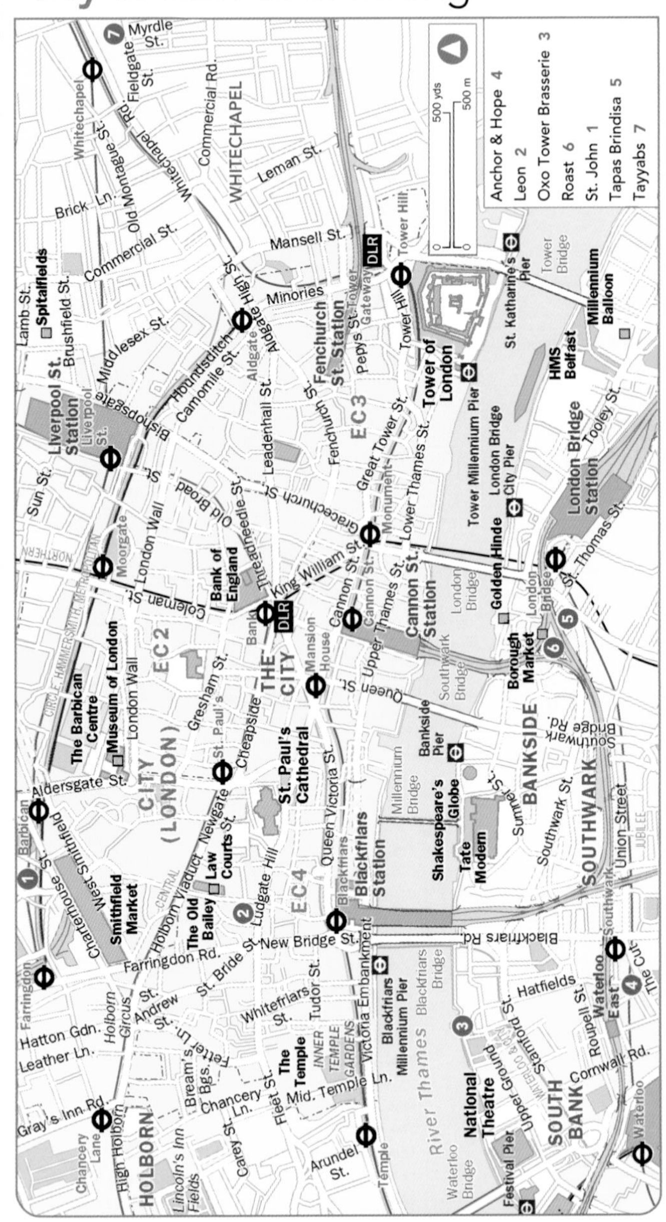

London Restaurants A to Z

★★ Alyn Williams at The Westbury MAYFAIR *MODERN EUROPEAN* Confident seasonal cooking, impeccable service, and a renowned wine list have won this place multiple fine-dining awards. Lunch menus are an excellent value. *Inside Westbury Hotel, 37 Conduit St.* ☎ *020/7183-6426. www.westbury-mayfair.com/alyn-williams. Main courses: lunch £30–£40; dinner £70–£90. AE, MC, V. Lunch & dinner Tues–Sat. Tube: Oxford Circus. Map p 100.*

★★ Anchor & Hope SOUTH BANK *MODERN BRITISH* A stripped-back pub serves British food that's stripped back to its flavors: big, bold, and modern. No reservations: Show up early and wait with a pint. *36 The Cut.* ☎ *020/7928-9898. www.anchorandhopepub.co.uk. Main courses £17–£20; set 2-course "worker's lunch" £15. MC, V. Lunch Tues–Sun, dinner Mpn–Sat. Tube: Southwark. Map p 102.*

★ kids Balans Soho Society KENSINGTON *INTERNATIONAL* A reasonably priced and varied menu make this a reliable minichain for all-day dining and even a wide selection of cocktails. *187 Kensington High St.* ☎ *020/7376-0115. www.balans.co.uk. Main courses £10–£26. AE, MC, V. Breakfast, lunch & dinner daily. Tube: High St. Kensington. Map p 98.*

★ Bar Shu SOHO *CHINESE* Super-spicy Szechuan cooking at its best, even if some of the dishes—like dry-wok pig's intestines—may require a leap of faith from the uninitiated. It has plenty of more traditional choices, too. *28 Frith St.* ☎ *020/7287-8822. www.barshurestaurant.co.uk. Main courses £8–£31. MC, V. Lunch & dinner daily. Tube: Leicester Sq. Map p 101.*

★★ Bibendum & Oyster Bar SOUTH KENSINGTON *MODERN EUROPEAN* Reliably on-point food from award-winning chef Claude Bosi, with an emphasis on fresh fish, plus an airy location in the stylish Art Nouveau Michelin Building, make this restaurant an enduring favorite. The downstairs Oyster Bar is ideal for an informal seafood lunch. *81 Fulham Rd.* ☎ *020/7581-5817. www.bibendum.co.uk. Main courses (Bibendum) £28–£48; menus £90–£110. AE, MC, V. Bibendum: Lunch & dinner Wed–Sun. Oyster Bar: Breakfast, lunch & dinner Mon–Sat, breakfast & lunch Sun. Tube: S. Kensington. Map p 99.*

★ kids Café in the Crypt SOHO *BRITISH DINER* This subterranean cafeteria offers cheap, hearty meals, as well as a jolly good tea. There's outdoor seating in summer and weekly live jazz (prebooking recommended). *St. Martin-in-the-Fields, enter on Duncannon St.* ☎ *020/7766-1158. www.stmartin-in-the-fields.org. Main courses £9–£10. MC, V. Breakfast & lunch daily, dinner Mon–Sat. Tube: Charing Cross. Map p 101.*

★ Caravan KING'S CROSS *MODERN EUROPEAN* The industrial interior of a former grain warehouse serves an all-day menu of creative small plates (molasses beets with goat's curd); pizzas; and its own house-roasted coffee. *1 Granary Sq.* ☎ *020/7101-7661. www.caravanrestaurants.co.uk. Main courses £9–£19. AE, MC, V. Breakfast & lunch daily, dinner Mon–Sat. Tube: King's Cross. Map p 101.*

★★★ Clarke's KENSINGTON *MODERN EUROPEAN* Chef Sally Clarke gratifies taste buds in her charming dining room, with a focus on the freshest produce in ingredient-led, ever-changing dishes. There's an onsite shop and bakery. *124 Kensington Church St.* ☎ *020/7221-9225. www.sallyclarke.com/restaurant. Main courses £25–£39. AE, MC, V. Breakfast, lunch & dinner Mon–Sat. Tube: Notting Hill Gate. Map p 97.*

★★★ **Dinner by Heston Blumenthal** KNIGHTSBRIDGE *CONTEMPORARY BRITISH* When Britain's "culinary scientist" Heston Blumenthal serves up traditional fare, he really means it, with recipes scoured from the history books and reinvented. Tuck into the charmingly named "Rice & Flesh" (actually calf tail, saffron, and red wine), from 1390, nettle porridge from 1660, or spiced pigeon from 1780. Book online and well ahead. *Inside Mandarin Oriental Hyde Park, 66 Knightsbridge.* ☎ *020/7201-3833. www.dinnerbyheston.com. Main courses £37–£49. AE, DC, MC, V. Lunch & dinner daily. Tube: Knightsbridge. Map p 99.*

★★ kids **Gaucho** WEST END *ARGENTINEAN* Among the best Argentinean dining in Europe, with an emphasis (of course) on meat: grilled beef every which way, ribs, tamales, and more. Look for a good selection of South American wines. Now a minichain with multiple London locations, it's also a banker for a business lunch. *25 Swallow St.* ☎ *020/7734-4040. www.gauchorestaurants.co.uk. Main courses £17–£40. AE, DC, MC, V. Lunch & dinner daily. Tube: Piccadilly Circus. Map p 100.*

★ **The Gay Hussar** SOHO *HUNGARIAN* Since 1953, this tiny dining room has served tasty goulashes, blinis, and other East European comfort food to loyal locals and tourists. In summer, try the *hideg meggyleves* (chilled wild-cherry soup). *2 Greek St.* ☎ *020/7437-0973. www.gayhussar.co.uk. Main courses £13–£23. MC, V. Lunch & dinner Mon–Sat. Tube: Tottenham Court Rd. Map p 101.*

★★★ **Geales** NOTTING HILL *SEAFOOD* Yes, it's got tempura crab, lobster linguine, fresh flowers, linen tablecloths, and other posh touches, but go for the humble fish and chips, among the best in London, or the classic fish pie. The weekday 2-course lunch (£10) is a steal. *2 Farmer St.* ☎ *020/7727-7528. www.geales.com. Main courses £13–£26. AE, MC, V. Lunch Tues–Sun, dinner daily. Tube: Notting Hill Gate. Map p 97.*

Poached halibut with Atlantic king crab, cauliflower couscous, finger lime, and ras el hanout–infused broth at Gordon Ramsay.

★ kids **Good Earth** KNIGHTSBRIDGE *CHINESE* More elegant than your usual Chinese restaurant, with prices to match, this Knightsbridge favorite does a great Beijing duck. It's good for vegetarians, too. *233 Brompton Rd. ☎ 020/7584-3658. www.goodearthgroup.co.uk. Main courses £10–£19. AE, MC, V. Lunch & dinner daily. Tube: Knightsbridge or S. Kensington. Map p 99.*

★★★ **Gordon Ramsay** CHELSEA *FRENCH* It's easy to forget, amid the TV shows, cookbooks, and business empire, that the foul-mouthed chef is also a culinary colossus. His flagship eatery still has three Michelin stars and remains one of London's ultimate dining destinations. *68 Royal Hospital Rd. ☎ 020/7352-4441. www.gordonramsayrestaurants.com. 3-course lunch £65; 3-course dinner £110. AE, DC, MC, V. Lunch & dinner Mon–Fri. Tube: Sloane Sq. Map p 99.*

★★★ **The Goring Dining Room** VICTORIA *BRITISH* Mutton broth, potted shrimp, roast grouse, salt marsh lamb, Cornish fish galore, and rice pudding: You can't get more English than the menu at the Goring, a hotel whose restaurant recalls Edwardian elegance at its finest. Afternoon tea is done just right. *15 Beeston Place. ☎ 020/7396-9000. www.thegoring.com. 3-course lunch £52; 3-course dinner £64; afternoon tea £49–£69. AE, DC, MC, V. Breakfast & dinner daily; lunch Sun–Fri. Tube: Victoria. Map p 100.*

★★ kids **Halepi Restaurant & Kebab House** BAYSWATER *GREEK* Bring the whole family to share classic home-style Greek taverna dishes and simple Mediterranean grilled fish and meat. The baklava is the best around. *18 Leinster Terrace. ☎ 020/7262-1070. www.halepi-restaurant.co.uk. Main courses £14–£26. AE, MC, V. Lunch & dinner daily. Tube: Bayswater or Queensway. Map p 97.*

The Ivy restaurant.

★★★ **Hawksmoor** KNIGHTSBRIDGE *STEAKHOUSE* London's best steaks—from rump to premium cuts—are joined by a supporting cast of grilled fish, classic sides, and well-crafted cocktails. *3 Yeomans Row. ☎ 020/7590-9290. www.thehawksmoor.com. Main courses £20–£36. MC, V. Lunch & dinner daily. Tube: S. Kensington or Knightsbridge. Map p 99.*

★ kids **Itsu** WESTMINSTER *ASIAN* One of the larger branches of this fun, garishly colored chain, where diners choose from small, reasonably priced dishes that roll by on a conveyor belt. Sushi and salad takeouts are dependable, healthy, and good value. *16 Great Peter St. ☎ 020/7222-6846. www.itsu.com. Main courses £5–£12. MC, V. Lunch & dinner daily. Tube: St. James's Park. Map p 101.*

★ **The Ivy** COVENT GARDEN *MODERN BRITISH* The menu is surprisingly diverse (from caviar to fishcakes to irresistible puddings) at this exclusive haunt of British celebs. For a fancy place, it's not

Moneysaving Restaurant Deals

To bag a really top meal at an affordable price, check a restaurant's website for set-price deals, usually on a weekday lunchtime or the pre- and post-theatre slot. (You'll then need iron discipline to avoid being sucked into à la carte and/or celebrating your thrift with a signature house cocktail.) London's daily newspaper, the **Evening Standard** (www.standard.co.uk), runs regular restaurant promotions. Booking app **OpenTable** (www.opentable.com) posts specials, and **Lastminute.com** has an updated section on afternoon tea deals. And it's always worth checking **TimeOut** (www.timeout.com/London/deals/restaurants); subscribing to weekly e-mail newsletters from **Travelzoo.com;** and bookmarking **Secret London** (https://secretldn.com) and **The Handbook** (www.thehandbook.com) for the skinny on openings.

overpriced, especially the set menu (2 courses, £23.50). *1–5 West St.* ☎ *020/7836-4751. www.the-ivy.co.uk. Main courses £17–£34. AE, DC, MC, V. Lunch & dinner daily. Tube: Leicester Sq. Map p 101.*

★★ kids **Kensington Crêperie** SOUTH KENSINGTON *FRENCH* With its sidewalk seating and picture windows, this place has an almost continental feel—appropriate for a French crêperie serving sweet and savory crêpes or galettes, fresh waffles, and indulgent ice cream. Ideally located for hungry museum hoppers. *2–6 Exhibition Rd.* ☎ *020/7589-3184. www.kensingtoncreperie.com. Main courses £8–£12. MC, V. Breakfast, lunch & dinner daily. Tube: S. Kensington. Map p 99.*

★ **Kensington Place** KENSINGTON *MODERN BRITISH/SEAFOOD* Come for classic brasserie fish dishes served up fresh in a buzzing, modern dining room. *201 Kensington Church St.* ☎ *020/7727-3184. www.kensingtonplace-restaurant.co.uk. Main courses £14–£26. AE, MC, V. Lunch & dinner daily. Tube: Notting Hill Gate. Map p 97.*

★★ **Langan's Brasserie** MAYFAIR *BRASSERIE* A big, upscale brasserie with two noisy floors of dining, serving French-influenced British standards, from spinach soufflé and confit duck to fish and chips. *Stratton St.* ☎ *020/7491-8822. www.langansbrasserie.com. Main courses £16–£24. AE, DC, MC, V. Lunch & dinner Mon–Sat. Tube: Green Park. Map p 100.*

★★ **La Poule au Pot** CHELSEA *FRENCH* This chic retro French bistro, much-loved by Londoners, brings a slice of rural France to posh Chelsea. The romantic atmosphere, friendly staff, and rustic dishes always make eating here a joy. House wines are very moreish. *231 Ebury St.* ☎ *020/7730-7763. www.pouleaupot.co.uk. Main courses £19–£32. AE, MC, V. Lunch & dinner daily. Tube: Sloane Sq. Map p 99.*

★★★ **Le Gavroche** MAYFAIR *FRENCH* Internationally famed Michel Roux Jr. is the chef *patron* of his two-star Michelin extravaganza serving classic French haute cuisine in a clubby, elegant dining room. Smart dress required. *43 Upper Brook St.* ☎ *020/7408-0881.*

www.le-gavroche.co.uk. Lunch menu £69, dinner menu £170. AE, DC, MC, V. Lunch Wed–Fri, dinner Tues–Sat. Tube: Marble Arch. Map p 100.

★★ kids **Leon** THE CITY *FAST FOOD* This fast-growing, Mediterranean-inspired chain combines two seemingly incompatible aims—speedy service and fresh seasonal ingredients—with great success. Top choices include a grilled halloumi wrap, Moroccan meatballs, and the crushed-pea side. Staff is food-intolerance-savvy. *12 Ludgate Circus.* ☎ *020/7485-1575. www.leonrestaurants.co.uk. Main courses £5–£8. MC, V. Breakfast, lunch & dinner Mon–Fri; 11am–5pm Sat. Tube: St. Paul's or Blackfriars. Map p 102.*

★ kids **Maroush V** MARYLEBONE *LEBANESE* This branch of a popular group of restaurants, known for good value, offers a big menu that includes freshly squeezed juices and excellent falafel. Open late. *4 Vere St.* ☎ *020/7493-5050. www.maroush.com. Main courses £14–£17. AE, MC, V. Lunch & dinner daily. Tube: Bond St. Map p 100.*

★ kids **Mildred's** SOHO *VEGETARIAN* A vegan and vegetarian institution, with affordable international dishes including stir-fries, burgers, salads, and juices. Don't skip the tasty desserts. *45 Lexington St.* ☎ *020/7494-1634. www.mildreds.co.uk. Main courses £7–£12. MC, V. Lunch & dinner Mon–Sat. Tube: Piccadilly Circus or Oxford Circus. Map p 100.*

★★ kids **Momo** MAYFAIR *MOROCCAN* Decorated in Arabian Nights splendor, this West End success story is a wonderful spot for a taste of exotic *tagines* (Moroccan spiced stews) *25 Heddon St.* ☎ *020/7434-4040. www.momoresto.com. Main courses £14–£30. AE, MC, V. Lunch & dinner daily. Tube: Piccadilly Circus. Map p 100.*

★★★ **Nobu** MAYFAIR *JAPANESE/FUSION* Famous for its glamour, celebrity customers, and creative modern sushi. *19 Old Park Lane.* ☎ *020/7447-4747. www.noburestaurants.com. Main courses £10–£36. AE, MC, V. Tube: Hyde Park Corner. Map p 100.*

★ kids **Orsini** SOUTH KENSINGTON *ITALIAN* Opposite the V&A, this cafe right out of Naples features great daily specials, perfectly prepared pastas, and super cappuccino. *8a Thurloe Place.* ☎ *020/7581-5553. www.orsinicaffe.*

Outdoor seating at Oxo Tower Brasserie.

com. Main courses £9–£19. AE, MC, V. Lunch & dinner daily. Tube: S. Kensington. Map p 99.

★★★ **Ottolenghi** NOTTING HILL *MEDITERRANEAN* One of four Ottolenghis strewn across town, this cafe and deli has a new, Eastern Mediterranean–inspired menu daily. The food is based around healthy and imaginatively prepared salads and light, flavorsome cakes. There's one communal table—but this is probably London's best takeout box lunch. *63 Ledbury Rd. ☎ 020/7727-1121. www.ottolenghi.co.uk. Lunch menu (2–4 dishes) £16.50–£22.50. MC, V. Breakfast & lunch daily. Tube: Bayswater or Notting Hill Gate. Map p 97.*

★ **Oxo Tower Brasserie** SOUTH BANK *INTERNATIONAL* Enjoy the best river views in London while sampling dishes that combine Mediterranean, French, and Asian ingredients. The vegetarian and vegan selection exceeds the norm. Dine on the balcony in summer. *Oxo Tower Wharf, Bargehouse St. ☎ 020/7803-3888. www.oxotowerrestaurant.com. Main courses £17–£30. AE, MC, V. Lunch & dinner daily. Tube: Blackfriars. Map p 102.*

★★ **The Portrait** SOHO *MODERN BRITISH* There's a gorgeous view over Trafalgar Square, and the food—from pan-fried scallops and *parmentier* potato to an elegant afternoon tea (£27.50)—is tasty, too. *3rd Floor, National Portrait Gallery, St. Martin's Lane. ☎ 020/7312-2490. www.npg.org.uk/portraitrestaurant. Main courses £18–£28. AE, MC, V. Breakfast, lunch & afternoon tea daily, dinner Thurs–Sat. Tube: Charing Cross. Map p 101.*

★ kids **The Providores & Tapa Room** MARYLEBONE *PACIFIC/INTERNATIONAL* The Tapa Room serves up savory breakfasts and a casual, all-day menu (no

The Providores.

reservations). Head upstairs to the restaurant for interesting twists on global favorites. New Zealand wines are a specialty. *109 Marylebone High St. ☎ 020/7935-6175. www.theprovidores.co.uk. Main courses £11–£28. AE, MC, V. Tapa Room: Breakfast, lunch & dinner daily. Providores: Lunch & dinner daily. Tube: Bond St. or Baker St. Map p 100.*

★★ **Rabbit** CHELSEA *CONTEMPORARY BRITISH* Come for the snug banquette seating and genuine farm-to-table credentials: Most of the meat comes from the owners' family farm. You'll be back for the creative food, such as venison liver salad with pickled raisins. *172 Kings Rd. ☎ 020/375-00172. www.rabbit-restaurant.com. Tapas £6.50–£13 (Sun lunch menu £19). MC, V. Lunch Tues–Sun, dinner Mon–Sat. Tube: Sloane Sq. Map p 99.*

★★★ **The Ritz Palm Court** ST. JAMES'S *ENGLISH TEA* Ladies, wear your best dress to London's most famous, very deluxe (and pricey!) tea, served in a Versailles-like setting. Book well in advance. *150 Piccadilly. ☎ 020/7300-2345. www.theritzlondon.com/tea. £57*

London Dining: The Lowdown

All restaurants and cafes are required to display the prices of their food and drink in a place visible from outside. Charges for service, as well as any minimums or cover charges, must also be made clear. The prices shown include 20% VAT, the so-called "value-added" tax. Most restaurants also add a 12% to 15% service charge to your bill, but check to make sure. If nothing has been added, leave a 10% to 15% tip. ***Insider tip:*** By law, restaurants must charge you a higher tax rate if you eat on premises, so takeaway is always cheaper. Doggy bags are frowned upon, however, and most restaurants expect you to give up your table after 90 minutes to 2 hours.

adults, £35 children. AE, DC, MC, V. Afternoon tea daily 11:30am–7:30pm. Tube: Green Park. Map p 100.

★★ kids **Roast** BANKSIDE *BRITISH* Explore Borough Market, then retreat upstairs for views of St. Paul's. Classic British dishes are made from local, seasonal produce, as are the inventive vegetarian and vegan dishes. Contemporary decor adds a twist to the splendor of this Victorian market architecture. *Floral Hall, Borough Market, Stoney St. ☎ 020/300-66111. www.roast-restaurant.com. Main courses £16–£35. AE, MC, V. Breakfast & dinner Mon–Sat, lunch daily. Tube: London Bridge. Map p 102.*

★ kids **Royal China Club** MARYLEBONE *CHINESE* This is the real deal for dim sum, with the choice and quality you'd find in Hong Kong. *40–42 Baker St. ☎ 020/7486-3898. www.theroyalchina.co.uk. Main courses £15–£40 (dim sum £5–£12). AE, MC, V. Lunch & dinner daily. Tube: Baker St. Map p 100.*

★★ **Rules** COVENT GARDEN *TRADITIONAL ENGLISH* The most traditional Olde English restaurant in London, Rules dates back to 1798, and is a must for Anglophile lovers of game, Scottish salmon, steak and kidney pies, and traditional English puddings. The cozy Upstairs bar serves classic

The elegant dining room at Tamarind.

Transporting Teatimes in London

Afternoon tea is an overpriced tourist's pursuit, to be sure, but that doesn't mean it's not delightful to pass the time pretending to be fancy. Arrive hungry and you'll be served a never-ending banquet of scones, clotted cream, pastry, light sandwiches, and a bottomless brewed torrent. Dress up, if you please, and be discreet about photos. Among the most transporting, legendary, and best-located teatimes, consider **Brown's Hotel** (www.roccofortehotels.com; ☎ 020/7518-4155; noon–6:30pm; £55), a Mayfair institution, open since 1837; the **Goring** (www.thegoring.com; ☎ 020/7396-9000; 3–4pm; from £49), near Buckingham Palace and serving on its own bespoke canary-yellow china; the **Houses of Parliament** (www.parliament.uk/visiting; ☎ 020/7219-4114; generally 2pm and 3:45pm; £29 plus price of tour), where you sip tea overlooking the Thames in the modern Terrace Pavilion rooms; the **Lanesborough** (lanesborough.com; ☎ 020/7259-5599; weekdays 2:30pm–4:30pm, weekends 3pm–4:30pm; £48), dazzling in every way, from the delicacy of the pastry to the Regency frills of the conservatory glass overhead; or the **Ritz** (www.theritzlondon.com; ☎ 020/7300-2345; five seatings 11:30am–7:30pm; £54 adults, £30 children), perhaps the only way most of us can afford the hotel's formal gilding, mirrors, and boisterous floral arrangements—but be sure to book 6 to 8 weeks ahead.

—Jason Cochran

predinner cocktails. *35 Maiden Lane. ☎ 020/7836-5314. www.rules.co.uk. Main courses £20–£34. AE, MC, V. Lunch & dinner daily. Tube: Covent Garden or Leicester Sq. Map p 101.*

★★ **St. John** CLERKENWELL *MODERN BRITISH* Inside a former smokehouse, just a hoof's throw from Smithfield Meat Market, this is a carnivore's delight—founder chef Fergus Henderson is famed for using every part of the animal (aka "nose-to-tail" eating). Dishes like ox tongue may not be for the squeamish, but food writers have been raving since 1994. *26 St. John St. ☎ 020/7251-0848. www.stjohnrestaurant.com. Main courses £15–£25. MC, V. Lunch Mon–Fri & Sun, dinner Mon–Sat. Tube: Farringdon. Map p 102.*

★★ **Scott's** MAYFAIR *SEAFOOD* With a shimmering, show-stopping Busby Berkeley arrangement of crustaceans as its centerpiece, this is one of London's finest fish restaurants. Menu highlights include octopus carpaccio, smoked haddock with colcannon, and beluga caviar blini with crème fraiche (a mere £210 for 30g/1 oz). *20 Mount St. ☎ 020/7495-7309. www.scotts-restaurant.com. Main courses £20–£36. AE, MC, V. Lunch & dinner daily. Tube: Bond St. Map p 100.*

★★ **Shoryu** COVENT GARDEN *JAPANESE* It's grown from one restaurant to ten on the silky strength of the tonkotsu ramen. Book ahead at dinner—or wait in line. *35 Great Queen St. No phone. www.shoryuramen.com. Ramen*

Cheese plate at Tapas Brindisa.

£12–£14. MC, V. Lunch & dinner daily. Tube: Sloane Sq. Map p 101.

★★ **Tamarind** MAYFAIR *INDIAN* Everyone from business execs to couples appreciates an imaginative menu that takes Indian cooking way beyond the usual curries. *20 Queen St. ☎ 020/7629-3561. www.tamarindrestaurant.com. Main courses £18–£35. AE, DC, MC, V. Lunch & dinner daily. Tube: Green Park. Map p 100.*

★★ **Tapas Brindisa** BANKSIDE *SPANISH* A top candidate for the best tapas in London, Brindisa is owned by a Spanish food importer—which gives them an edge. There's a "no reservations" policy and it can get crowded on weekends, but grab a seat at the bar and wait your turn—the contemporary tapas are worth it. *18–20 Southwark St. ☎ 020/7357-8880. www.brindisarestaurants.com. Dishes £5.50–£12. AE, MC, V. Lunch & dinner daily, breakfast Sat & Sun. Tube: London Bridge. Map p 102.*

Chicken Curry at Wagamama

★ **Tayyabs** EAST END *PUNJABI* A little off the beaten track, but ferociously popular, with peak-time lines. Londoners are drawn by expertly spiced curries at keen prices. Decor is a little ragged in places, but this place is about flavor, not frills. *83–89 Fieldgate St. ☎ 020/7247-6400. www.tayyabs.co.uk. Main courses £10–£15. MC, V. Lunch & dinner daily. Tube: Whitechapel. Map p 102.*

★ kids **VQ** CHELSEA *DINER* The best reason to come to this busy diner is that it's always open, serving comfort food and tasty brasserie staples to jet-lagged insomniacs and after-hours clubbers. No reservations. *325 Fulham Rd. ☎ 020/7376-7224. www.vqrestaurants.com. Main courses £8–£15. MC, V. Open 24 hr. Tube: S. Kensington or Fulham Broadway. Map p 98.*

Quail eggs in hollandaise sauce at The Wolseley.

★ kids **Wagamama** MARYLEBONE *JAPANESE/ASIAN* You sit at large communal tables where the noise level is considerable, but this popular, family-friendly chain is tops for consistently tasty, well-priced Asian food. *101a Wigmore St. ☎ 020/7409-0111. www.wagamama.com. Main courses £9–£14. AE, MC, V. Lunch & dinner daily. Tube: Bond St. Map p 100.*

★★★ **The Wolseley** ST. JAMES'S *EUROPEAN* This lively, atmospheric restaurant on Piccadilly has a high-ceilinged Art Deco dining room, serves up regular celeb sightings, and offers an extensive menu of British and European classics at decent value. Plus it does breakfast and afternoon tea. *160 Piccadilly. ☎ 020/7499-6996. www.thewolseley.com. Main courses £15–£32. AE, DC, MC, V. Breakfast, lunch, afternoon tea & dinner daily. Tube: Green Park. Map p 100.* ●

Tea treats at the Lanesborough.

7 The Best Nightlife

Nightlife Best Bets

Best **Dance Club**
★★★ Fabric, *77a Charterhouse St. (p 124)*

Best **Wine Bar**
★★ Gordon's, *47 Villiers St. (p 122)*

Best **Jazz Club**
★★★ Ronnie Scott's, *47 Frith St. (p 125)*

Most **Wacky Decor**
★★ Callooh Callay, *65 Rivington St. (p 122)*

Most **Unpretentious Clubbing**
★ 93 Feet East, *150 Brick Lane (p 124)*

Best for **Secret Drinking**
★★★ The Lamb, *98 Lamb's Conduit St. (p 127)*

Best **Views**
★★★ Vertigo 42, *25 Old Broad St. (p 123); or* ★★ Sky Garden, *1 Sky Garden Walk (p 123)*

Most **Historic Pub**
★★★ Ye Olde Cheshire Cheese, *145 Fleet St. (p 131)*

Best for **Blues**
★★ Ain't Nothin' But…, *20 Kingly St. (p 121)*

Best **West End Pub**
★★★ The Harp, *47 Chandos Place (p 127)*

Best **City Pub**
★★★ The Counting House, *50 Cornhill (p 132); or* ★★★ The Black Friar, *174 Queen Victoria St. (p 132)*

Best for **Watching the Game**
★ Bar Kick, *127 Shoreditch High St. (p 121)*

Best **Pub Singalong**
★★ Coach & Horses, *29 Greek St. (p 126)*

Best **Gay Venue**
★★ Heaven, *Villiers St. (p 124)*

Most **Refined Cocktail Lounge**
★★ Blue Bar, *Berkeley Hotel, Wilton Place (p 121)*

Best **Hotel Bar**
★★★ The Connaught Bar, *Connaught Hotel, Carlos Place (p 122)*

Best **Cocktails**
★★ 69 Colebrooke Row, *69 Colebrooke Row (p 121)*

Best for **Craft Beer Lovers**
★★ Craft Beer Co., *168 High Holborn (p 122); or* ★★ The Rake, 14 Winchester Walk *(p 123)*

Best **Sound System**
★★★ Ministry of Sound, *103 Gaunt St. (p 125); or* ★★ Spiritland, *9–10 Stable St. (p 123)*

Best **Club to Wear Your Bathing Suit To**
★ Aquarium, *256 Old St. (p124)*

Previous page: Cocktails at the Connaught Bar.

Notting Hill & Kensington Nightlife

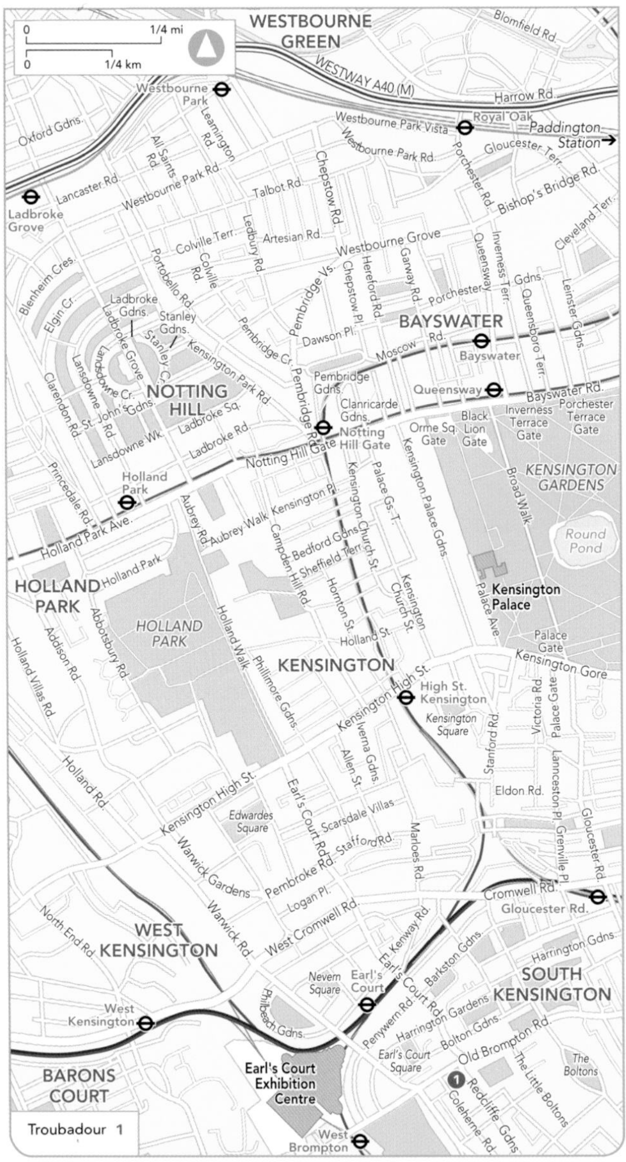

West End Nightlife

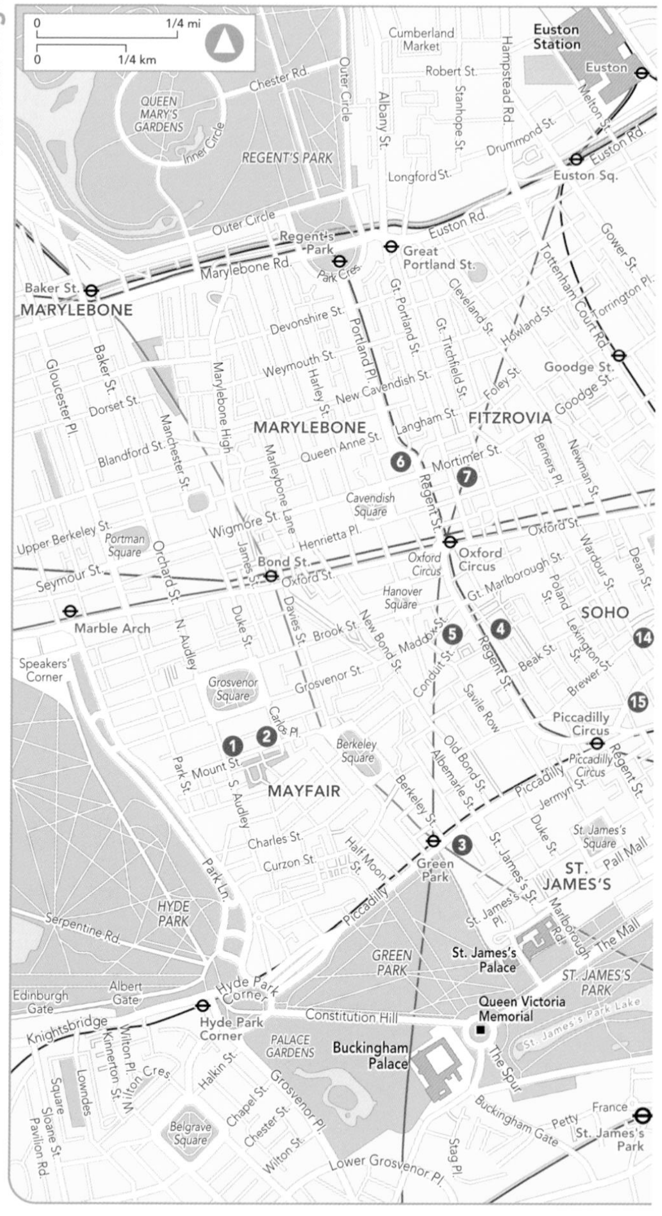

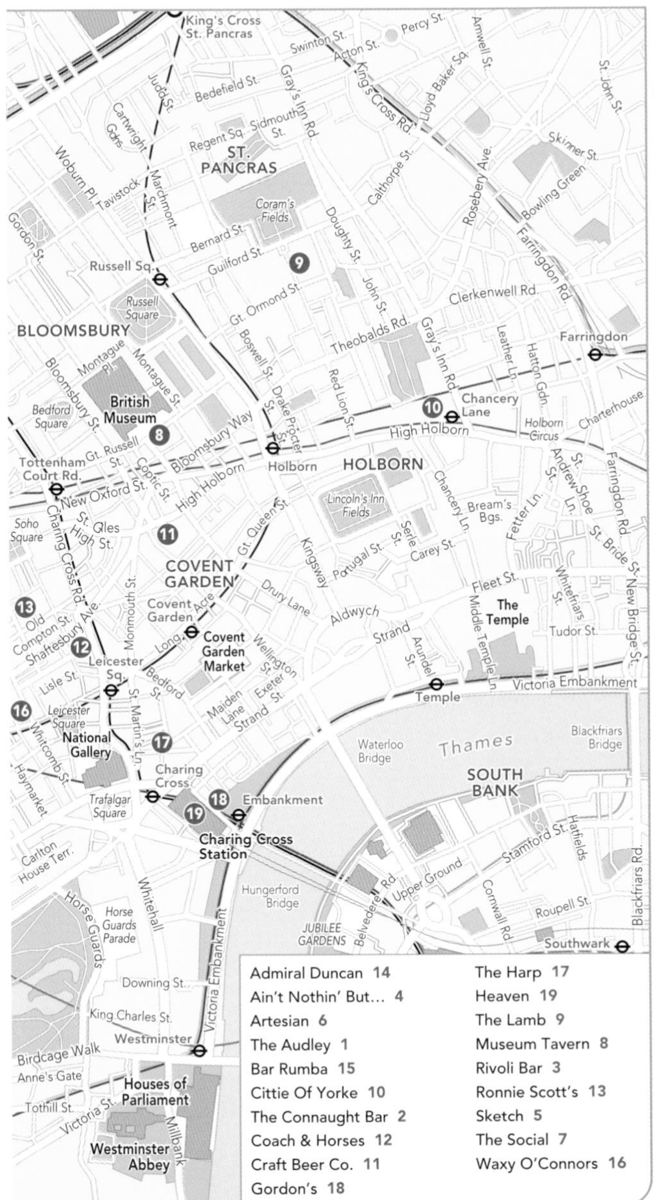
King's Cross St. Pancras
ST. PANCRAS
BLOOMSBURY
British Museum
Russell Square
Russell Sq.
Coram's Fields
Tottenham Court Rd.
Holborn
HOLBORN
Chancery Lane
Farringdon
Lincoln's Inn Fields
COVENT GARDEN
Covent Garden
Covent Garden Market
Leicester Sq.
Leicester Square
National Gallery
Charing Cross
Trafalgar Square
Embankment
Charing Cross Station
Temple
The Temple
Thames
Waterloo Bridge
Blackfriars Bridge
SOUTH BANK
Hungerford Bridge
JUBILEE GARDENS
Southwark
Horse Guards Parade
Westminster
Houses of Parliament
Westminster Abbey
Soho Square
Bedford Square
Admiral Duncan 14
Ain't Nothin' But… 4
Artesian 6
The Audley 1
Bar Rumba 15
Cittie Of Yorke 10
The Connaught Bar 2
Coach & Horses 12
Craft Beer Co. 11
Gordon's 18
The Harp 17
Heaven 19
The Lamb 9
Museum Tavern 8
Rivoli Bar 3
Ronnie Scott's 13
Sketch 5
The Social 7
Waxy O'Connors 16

City & East End Nightlife

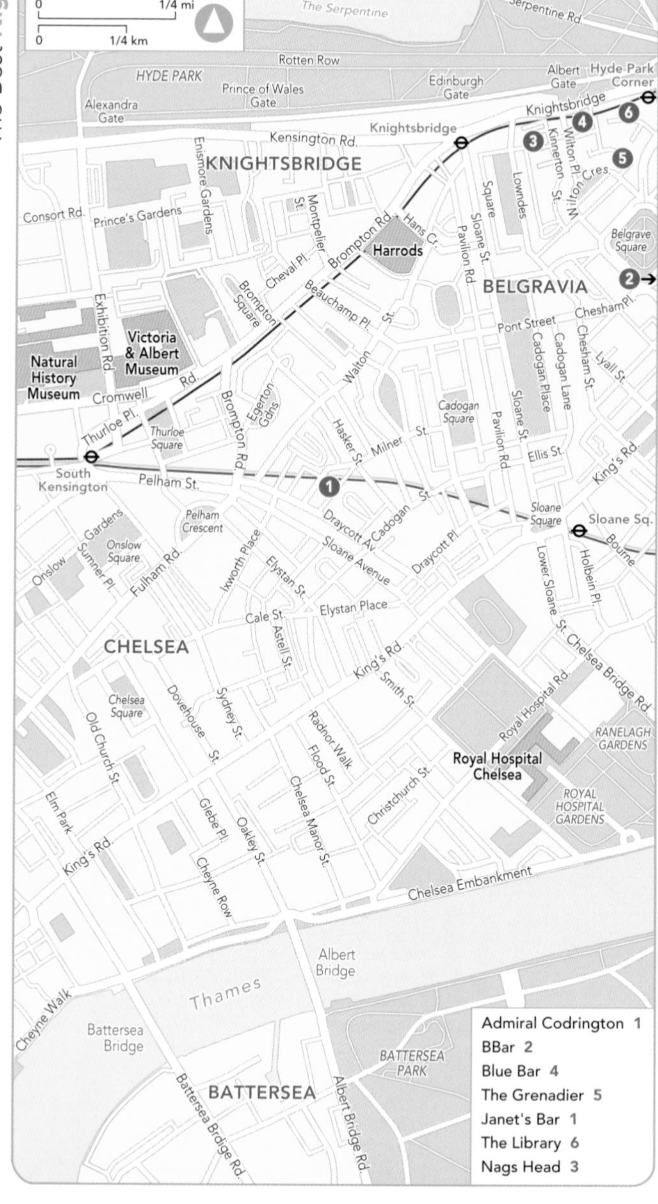

Nightlife in Knightsbridge & Chelsea

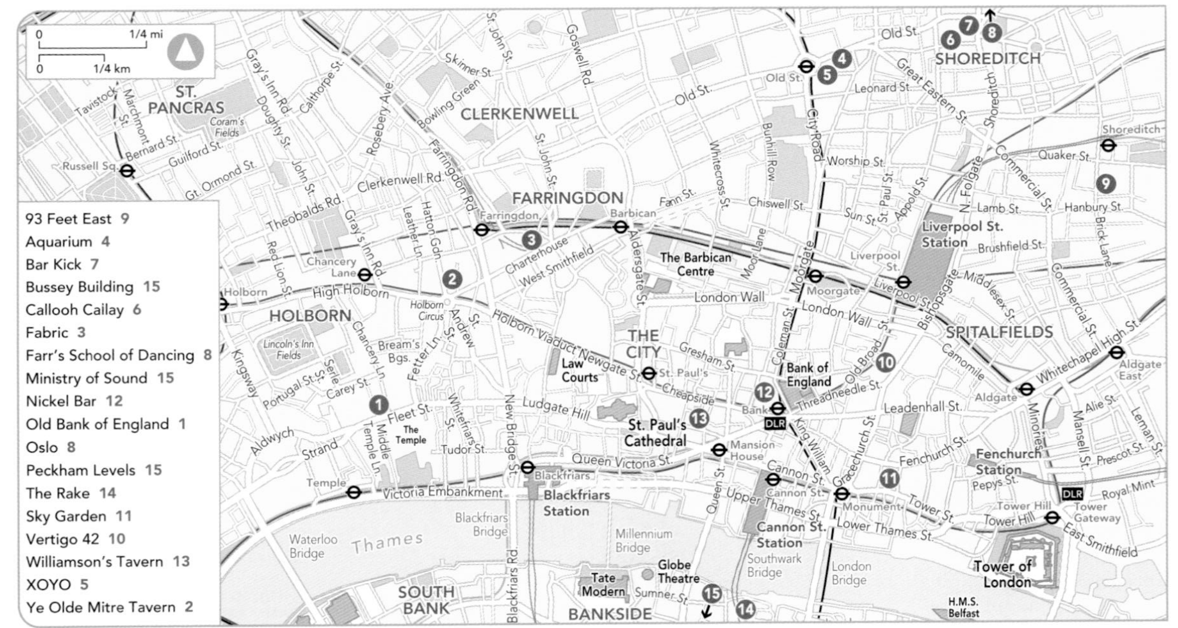

Camden Nightlife

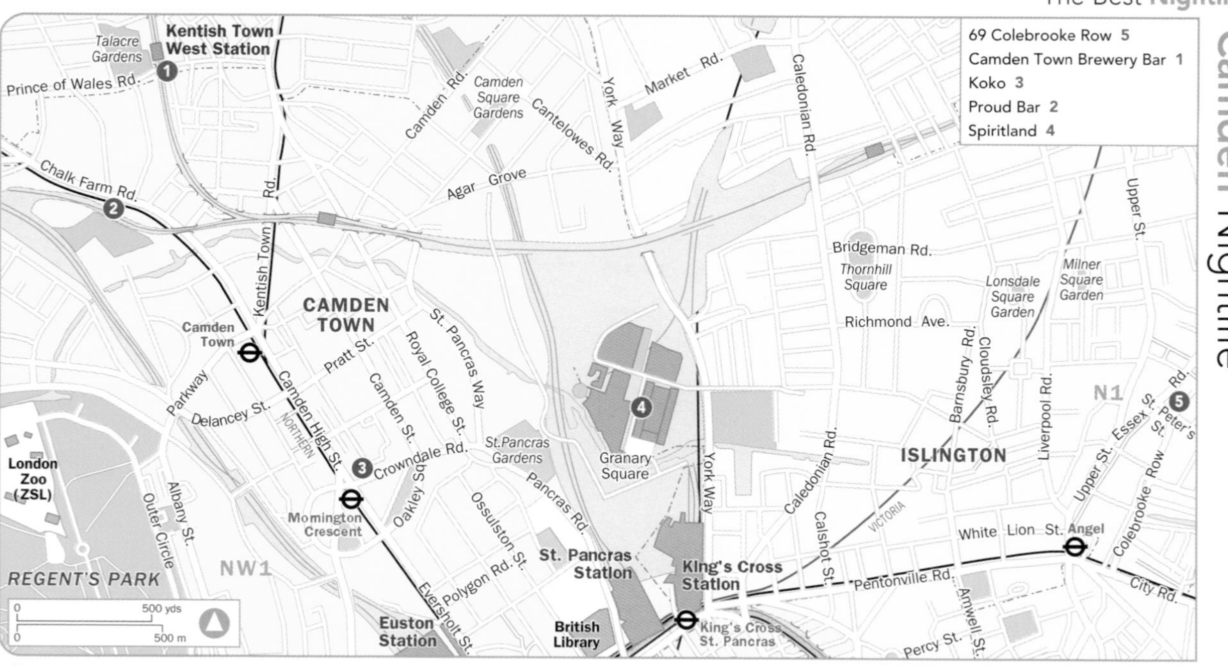

London Nightlife A to Z

Bars

★★ 69 Colebrooke Row ISLINGTON Billed as "The Bar with No Name," this place has an on-trend speakeasy ambience, with jazz-era piano tinkling, low lighting, and limited capacity—just 30 seats. Cocktails are award-winning and the vibe just the right side of illicit. *69 Colebrooke Row. ☎ 07540/528-593. www.69colebrookerow.com. Tube: Angel. Map p 120.*

★★ Ain't Nothin' But... SOHO This tiny joint plucked straight from the bayou may not be Bourbon Street, but it offers live blues every night of the week. *20 Kingly St. ☎ 020/7287-0514. www.aintnothinbut.co.uk. Tube: Piccadilly Circus or Oxford Circus. Map p 116.*

★★ Artesian MARYLEBONE Terribly swanky and expensive, Artesian has some of the most opulent decor this side of royalty; the interior is a riot of silver-leaf mirrors and huge chandeliers. Take plenty of money and make your cocktails last—the special, denser, long-lasting ice cubes will help. *Langham Hotel, 1c Portland Pl. ☎ 020/7636-1000. www.artesian-bar.co.uk. Tube: Oxford Circus. Map p 116.*

★ Bar Kick SHOREDITCH Every bar needs to stand out from the crowd. Bar Kick's theme is, appropriately enough, kicking things. The interior is filled with table football, and TVs show live soccer matches. Don't go expecting a rowdy pub, however. *127 Shoreditch High St. ☎ 020/7739-8700. www.cafekick.co.uk. Overground: Shoreditch. Map p 119.*

★ BBar VICTORIA This trendy bar with South African–inspired decor serves all kinds of cocktails—classic, skinny, mocktail, and show-stopping vapor cocktails. There's a good wine cellar, strong on South African labels, and a fusion menu of appetizing nosh. *43 Buckingham Palace Rd. ☎ 020/7958-7000. www.bbarlondon.com. Tube: Victoria. Map p 118.*

★★ Blue Bar KNIGHTSBRIDGE In the lovely Berkeley Hotel, this tiny (50-person) and, yes, blue (Luytens Blue, to be exact) bar serves more than 50 varieties of whisky, refined cocktails, and tapas-type snacks to a very upscale crowd. No reservations. *Wilton Place. ☎ 020/7235-6000. www.the-berkeley.co.uk. Tube: Hyde Park Corner. Map p 118.*

Ain't Nothing But...blues bar in Soho.

Bar Kick.

★★ Callooh Callay SHOREDITCH It's very Shoreditch, with plenty of wacky touches—gramophone punch bowls, a wardrobe linking the two bars, crazy mismatched decor—but this long-running bar is also plenty of fun, attracting a young, hip crowd with its adventurous cocktails. The name is derived from *Jabberwocky*, the Lewis Carroll nonsense poem, in case you were wondering. *65 Rivington St. ☎ 020/7739-4781. www.calloohcallaybar.com. Tube: Old St. Map p 119.*

★★★ The Connaught Bar MAYFAIR The Connaught Bar is where guests at this most traditional, old-style hotel go to let off a little steam in fin-de-siecle surrounds. Immaculate service and mixology. The dress is smart-casual. *Carlos Place. ☎ 020/7314-3419. www.the-connaught.co.uk. Tube: Bond St. Map p 116.*

★★ Craft Beer Co. COVENT GARDEN ILocal minichain (8 venues so far) that delivers exactly what you expect: a long line of pumps, fridges heaving with small-batch bottles, and a friendly crowd of beer geeks. *168 High Holborn. ☎ 020/7240-0431. www.thecraftbeerco.com. Tube: Covent Garden. Map p 117.*

★★ Gordon's COVENT GARDEN Gordon's first began serving drinks back in 1890, and if the decor has changed since then it's news to us. This gloomy, subterranean place is an absolute institution, with an eclectic modern wine list that includes lots of New World and organic labels. Other bars may be swankier, but few can compete for atmosphere. *47 Villiers St. ☎ 020/7930-1408. www.gordonswinebar.com. Tube: Embankment. Map p 117.*

★★ The Library KNIGHTSBRIDGE Business execs on expense accounts sip cocktails and cognac at this sophisticated bar inside the Lanesborough Hotel. A roaring fire and tinkling piano complete the picture. *1 Lanesborough Place. ☎ 020/7259-5599. www.lanesborough.com. Tube: Hyde Park Corner. Map p 118.*

★★ Nickel Bar THE CITY Opened in 2017, this American bar serves classic cocktails inside a grand former bank (now luxe hotel) in the financial center. There's nightly live jazz and bags of atmosphere. *The Ned Hotel, 27 Poultry. ☎ 020/3828-2000. www.thened.com. Tube: Bank. Map p 119.*

★★ Proud Bar CAMDEN Inside a 200-year-old horse hospital, this immense bar, photo gallery, and music venue is visually stunning. The gig room hosts big-name stars, while the roof terrace is perfect in summer (and heated in winter). *Stables Market, Chalk Farm Rd.* ☎ *020/7482-3867. www.proudcamden.com. Tube: Chalk Farm. Map p 120.*

★★ The Rake BANKSIDE Just around the corner from Borough Market, this tiny bar serves, by way of contrast, one of the capital's most diverse selections of independent beers. There are usually more than 140, way more than there ever are people. There's also an equally small garden. *14 Winchester Walk.* ☎ *020/7407-0557. www.utobeer.co.uk/the-rake. Tube: London Bridge. Map p 119.*

★★★ Rivoli Bar WEST END The Ritz Hotel's restored Art Deco bar offers all the atmosphere you would expect from this bastion of over-the-top swank, as well as a drinks menu with surprisingly modern cocktails. A strict dress code keeps the young at bay. *150 Piccadilly.* ☎ *020/7493-8181. www.theritzlondon.com. Tube: Green Park. Map p 116.*

The Blue Bar at The Berkeley.

★★ Sky Garden THE CITY You have a choice of two bars amid the greenery on top of London's best-named skyscraper, the "Walkie-Talkie." Expect classic and seasonal cocktails, sharing platters, and a stunning view through the picture windows. You can also enjoy the view for free by prebooking online. *1 Sky Garden Walk, Fenchurch St.* ☎ *0333/772-0020. https://sky garden.london. Tube: Monument. Map p 119.*

★★ Spiritland KING'S CROSS An audiophile's dream of a bar: The whole place is the inside of a bespoke sound system, with speakers everywhere. Cocktails and beers aren't bad, either. *9–10 Stable St.* ☎ *020/3319-0050. www.spiritland.com. Tube: King's Cross. Map p 120.*

★★ Troubadour EARL'S COURT Yes, it's a restaurant, but it's also a pub, a wine bar, a nightclub, and a bohemian hangout. Its warren of small rooms holds poetry readings, live music, and singer-songwriter nights. *265 Old Brompton Rd.* ☎ *020/7341-6333. www.troubadour.co.uk. Tube: Earl's Court. Map p 115.*

★★★ Vertigo 42 THE CITY On the 42nd floor of the City's fourth-tallest skyscraper, Britain's highest Champagne bar features splendid (and rare for London) views. It's the perfect place to sip a cocktail at sunset. Reservations essential. *Tower 42, 25 Old Broad St.* ☎ *020/7877-7842. www.vertigo42.co.uk. Tube: Bank or Liverpool St. Map p 119.*

★ Waxy O'Connors SOHO This roaring Irish bar features mad Gaelic music, tipsy crowds, and a shameless sort of tourist appeal. The weird decor improves with each drink—you'll love the indoor tree. *14–16 Rupert St.* ☎ *020/7287-0255. www.waxyoconnors.co.uk. Tube: Leicester Sq. Map p 117.*

Cocktail garnished with rose petals at The Connaught Bar.

Dance Clubs & Live Music

★ **93 Feet East** EAST END Relaunched (again) in 2018, this large space has DJs spinning all kinds of eclectica—funk, hip-hop, house, disco, rock, or indie. Hit the main room for live music, or relax in one of the intimate galleries and bars. *150 Brick Lane. www.93feeteast.co.uk. Cover £5 and up. Tube: Aldgate East. Map p 119.*

★ **Aquarium** SHOREDITCH This crazy nightclub offers you the chance to shed your clothes and jump in a pool with strangers. Germaphobes may want to stick to the fully clothed drinking and dancing to mainstream house/techno and, on Saturdays, Eighties tunes. *256–260 Old St. ☎ 020/7251-6136. www.clubaquarium.co.uk. Cover around £10. Tube: Old St. Map p 119.*

★ **Bar Rumba** SOHO A big basement venue with mood lighting and leather couches. The music is a mix of unashamedly commercial dance, R&B, and party classics. Look for dating and social evenings plus comedy nights, too. *36 Shaftesbury Ave. ☎ 020/7287-6933. www.barrumbadisco.co.uk. Cover £5–£10 after 9pm. Tube: Piccadilly Circus. Map p 116.*

★★★ **Fabric** CLERKENWELL A legend among London's committed weekend partygoers and hot-off-the-press vinyl lovers, Fabric closed "forever" in 2016 only to reopen the next year. Dance till daylight to the drum & bass, electro, and techno beats on the "bodysonic" dance floor, where you can feel the vibrations through your feet. Friday to Sunday only. *77a Charterhouse St. ☎ 020/7336-8898. www.fabriclondon.com. Cover £15–£29 (cheaper in advance online). Tube: Farringdon. Map p 119.*

★★ **Heaven** COVENT GARDEN Home to G-A-Y—since the Astoria was demolished to build the Tube's new Elizabeth Line—this landmark LGBT-friendly venue, with more than 25 years of partying under its belt, is growing old disgracefully. Live-music gigs midweek. *Under the Arches, Villiers St. ☎ 020/7930-2020. www.heavennightclub-london.com. Cover around £4–£15. Tube: Embankment. Map p 117.*

★ **Koko** CAMDEN You could encounter anything from guitar bands to disco DJs to a singer-songwriter playing an acoustic set at this relaxed, anything-goes music venue. Long-running "Guilty

The Nickel Bar in the Ned Hotel.

Going Underground—By Overground

Two decades of investment in London's above-ground urban rail lines has formed the Overground network, interconnected and mostly well-integrated routes that Londoners treat like a new Tube line. It's marked in a lurid orange on most metro maps (see http://tfl.gov.uk/maps/track/overground). One happy side effect: Several non-central neighborhoods are now more accessible (especially since the line's eastern stretch, including Shoreditch, Hoxton, and Dalston, runs 24 hours). You need not roam far from your seat in a heated/air-conditioned Overground rail carriage to spend the night socializing with the locals. The **Camden Town Brewery Bar,** 55 Wilkin St. Mews (www.camdentownbrewery.com), inhabits railway arches directly below the track at Kentish Town West Station. **Oslo,** 1A Amhurst Rd. (☎ **020/3553-4831;** www.oslohackney.com), has an upstairs bar and a subterranean space for indie bands and club nights—and is right beside Hackney Central Station. Across the road from Dalston Junction Station is **Farr's School of Dancing,** 17–19 Dalston Lane (☎ **020/7923-4553;** www.farrsschoolofdancing.com)—a trendy vintage-styled pub, not a dance school—and the **Arcola Theatre** (p 141). In south London, the area around Peckham Rye Station has transformed into a lively arts hub, centered on the **Bussey Building,** the **Peckham Levels** (www.peckhamlevels.org), and the bars and coffeehouses of **Blenheim Grove,** directly below the station platforms.

Pleasures" (last Sat of month) is London's ultimate trashy music night out. *1A Camden High St.* ☎ *020/7388-3222. www.koko.uk.com. Tickets around £10–£25. Tube: Mornington Crescent. Map p 120.*

★★★ **Ministry of Sound** ELEPHANT & CASTLE This legendary venue has seen competitors come and go over almost 30 years of history, but is still going strong with multiple bars, huge dance floors, and a hefty Dolby sound system playing techno, hip-hop, funk, house, and garage. Book tickets ahead to ensure entry. *103 Gaunt St.* ☎ *020/7740-8600. www.ministryofsound.com. Tickets around £5–£26. Tube: Elephant & Castle. Map p 119.*

★★★ **Ronnie Scott's** SOHO Open since 1959, the granddaddy of London jazz clubs fully deserves its legendary reputation. The best jazz musicians in the world play this classy but relaxed venue every night. *47 Frith St.* ☎ *020/7439-0747. www.ronniescotts.co.uk. Tickets £10–£45. Tube: Leicester Sq. Map p 117.*

★ **Sketch** MAYFAIR Glitzy, glam, and riotously decorated, Sketch attracts celeb visitors and well-heeled regulars by successfully combining food, music, drinking, and art. Dress up in your most stylish party gear. *9 Conduit St.* ☎ *020/7659-4500. www.sketch.uk.com. Tube: Oxford Circus. Map p 116.*

Enjoying sunset views from the Sky Garden.

★★ The Social WEST END Civilized and unpretentious, this bar/club hosts a casual, eclectic crowd, including the occasional celeb. It's tiny, but there's an evening jukebox, late-night DJs, and fun fast food. *5 Little Portland St.* ☎ *020/7636-4992. www.thesocial.com. Tube: Oxford Circus. Map p 116.*

★ XOYO SHOREDITCH A fine addition to Shoreditch's ever-expanding range of clubs, this former print works is a place for dancing, not chilling, laying on a mix of DJ sets and live music. Up to 800 revelers gyrate away inside cavernous industrial confines. *32–37 Cowper St.* ☎ *020/7608-2878. www.xoyo.co.uk. Tickets £5–£20. Tube: Old St. Map p 119.*

The Black Friar.

Pubs

★ Admiral Codrington KNIGHTSBRIDGE "The Cod" has modern British cuisine, a well-heeled crowd, and a nice atmosphere, made all the better on summer days by the retractable glass roof. Outdoor tables handle overflow on warm evenings. *17 Mossop St.* ☎ *020/7581-0005. www.theadmiralcodringtonpub.co.uk. Tube: S. Kensington. Map p 118.*

★ Admiral Duncan SOHO This popular gay pub offers bargain shots, a good selection of wines, cabaret, and karaoke nights. LGBT or not, it's a fun and friendly place to drink. *54 Old Compton St.* ☎ *020/7437-5300. www.admiralduncan.co.uk. Tube: Leicester Sq. Map p 116.*

★★ The Audley MAYFAIR This is one of London's more beautiful old-school pubs, evocative of a Victorian-era gentlemen's club (it was built in the 1880s). Slip into a booth beneath the original chandeliers and sample traditional English grub. *41 Mount St.* ☎ *020/7499-1843. Tube: Bond St. Map p 116.*

★ Cittie of Yorke BLOOMSBURY There's been a pub on this site since 1430, and though the current building dates back "only" to the 1890s there's still a (faux) old-world vibe, and (real) ale. Check out the churchlike interior and its immense wine vats. Closed Sunday. *22 High Holborn.* ☎ *020/7242-7670. Tube: Chancery Lane. Map p 117.*

★★ Coach & Horses SOHO Perhaps the ultimate no-nonsense English pub, and the inspiration behind Keith Waterhouse's play *Jeffrey Bernard Is Unwell*. It has bags of character, vegetarian food, and a traditional singalong with the pub's pianist every Wednesday and Saturday. *29 Greek St.* ☎ *020/7437-5920. www.coachsoho.co.uk. Tube: Leicester Sq. or Tottenham Court Rd. Map p 117.*

★★ The Grenadier BELGRAVIA This charming pub, tucked away in a secluded mews, is best known for its Bloody Marys, resident ghost, and military past (the Duke of Wellington's soldiers used it as their mess hall). *18 Wilton Row.* ☎ *020/7235-3074. Tube: Knightsbridge. Map p 118.*

★★★ The Harp COVENT GARDEN This small pub off Trafalgar Square is usually packed to the rafters after work hours—justly so, because it was (and still is) a pioneer of "real ale" and craft beers long before they were cool. Comfy seats upstairs are delightful on a quiet midafternoon. *47 Chandos Place.* ☎ *020/7836-0291. www.harp-coventgarden.com. Tube: Charing Cross. Map p 117.*

The Old Bell Tavern.

Going Local: Points on Pints

Pubs have been the beating heart of British life for centuries. Your neighborhood hangout is called your **"local,"** but many of the oldest premises have been so well-loved (or so well-bombed) that their original features are gone. Most, if not all, serve food of some kind (burgers, meat pies, and the like) for at least part of the day. Pubs commonly charge around £5 for a pint of the favored serving size—about 20 American ounces—and the ABV percentage tends to be strong. A good **cask ale** is a specialty you must try while you're in England. Cask ale is not refrigerated because it's stored in the cellar, where the temperature is right for the fermentation process to continue until the drink hits your glass. Cask ale is drawn using stiff hand-pumped taps, and it only stays fresh for a short time, like bread or pastry. To find pubs that persevere in the dying art of pouring old-fashioned cask ales, visit the **Campaign for Real Ale** (www.camra.org.uk). When the bell is rung, it's last call—as early as 11pm—and the landlord *will* turf you out.

—Jason Cochran

Easy, Cheap & Daring: Pub Theaters

In the early 1970s, a new form of alternative theater swept London: the pub theater. Often just a tatty back room where you can bring your beer from the scruffy front bar, your typical theater pub is where some of the city's most affordable, idiosyncratic, let's-try-this-and-see-if-it-sticks stuff is found—which is why they launched so many megastar actors to fame. Some of the most respected fringe venues in town are pub theaters, which have just as much artistic power as many better-heeled West End palaces. Four fantastic ones, all charging £15 or less for most shows, are the **Etcetera Theatre ★** (265 Camden High St., NW1; www.etceteratheatre.com; ☎ **020/7482-4857**), a very small black box featuring odd, challenging fare; **Hen & Chickens ★** (109 St Paul's Rd., N1; www.henandchickens.com; ☎ **020/7354-8246**), home to a resident company, Unrestricted View, that showcases strong writing; the **King's Head ★★★** (115 Upper St., N1; www.kingsheadtheatre.com; ☎ **020/7226-8561**), whose alums include Kenneth Branagh, Clive Owen, Joanna Lumley, Ben Kingsley, Juliet Stevenson, Hugh Grant, and John Hurt in their younger, braver, poorer days; and **Old Red Lion ★** (418 St John St., EC1; www.oldredliontheatre.co.uk; ☎ **0844/412-4307**), a very pubby 60-seat space that hosts aspiring producers and the occasional comedy night.

—Jason Cochran

★★★ The Lamb BLOOMSBURY You'll find one of the city's few remaining "snob screens"—used to protect drinkers from prying eyes—at this Victorian pub. Those who've enjoyed the anonymity here include the Bloomsbury Group and Charles Dickens. *98 Lamb's Conduit St.* ☎ *020/7405-0713. www.thelamblondon.com. Tube: Russell Sq.* *Map p 117.*

★ Museum Tavern BLOOMSBURY This early-18th-century pub, the former Dog & Duck, changed

Wynton Marsalis at Ronnie Scott's.

The Counting House.

its name when the British Museum was built across the street in the 1760s. Old-style decor remains mostly intact. *49 Great Russell St. ☎ 020/7242-8987. Tube: Russell Sq. Map p 117.*

★ **Nags Head** BELGRAVIA This rarity, an independently owned pub, was built in the early 19th century for the posh area's workers. A "no phones" rule attempts to keep the 21st century from intruding. Beers by Suffolk brewery Adnams. *53 Kinnerton St. ☎ 020/7235-1135. Tube: Knightsbridge. Map p 118.*

★ **Old Bank of England** THE CITY This unusual pub is housed in a converted former bank branch that has retained all the majesty of a palace of finance, with a huge interior and wonderful murals. Closed Sundays. *194 Fleet St. ☎ 020/7430-2255. www.oldbankofengland.co.uk. Tube: Temple. Map p 119.*

★★ **Williamson's Tavern** THE CITY With a history that goes back to Londinium (real excavated Roman tiles decorate the fireplace), this pub lies in an alley fronted by gates that were gifts of William III and Mary II. Closed on weekends. *1 Groveland Court. ☎ 020/7248-5750. Tube: Mansion House. Map p 119.*

★★★ **Ye Olde Mitre Tavern** CLERKENWELL Good service, beamed ceilings, and the stump of a tree Queen Elizabeth I reportedly frolicked under make this historic treasure a must-see. It's hard to find, but do try. *Ely Court, off Ely Place. ☎ 020/7405-4751. www.yeoldmitreholborn.co.uk. Tube: Chancery Lane. Map p 119.*

City of London Pub Crawl

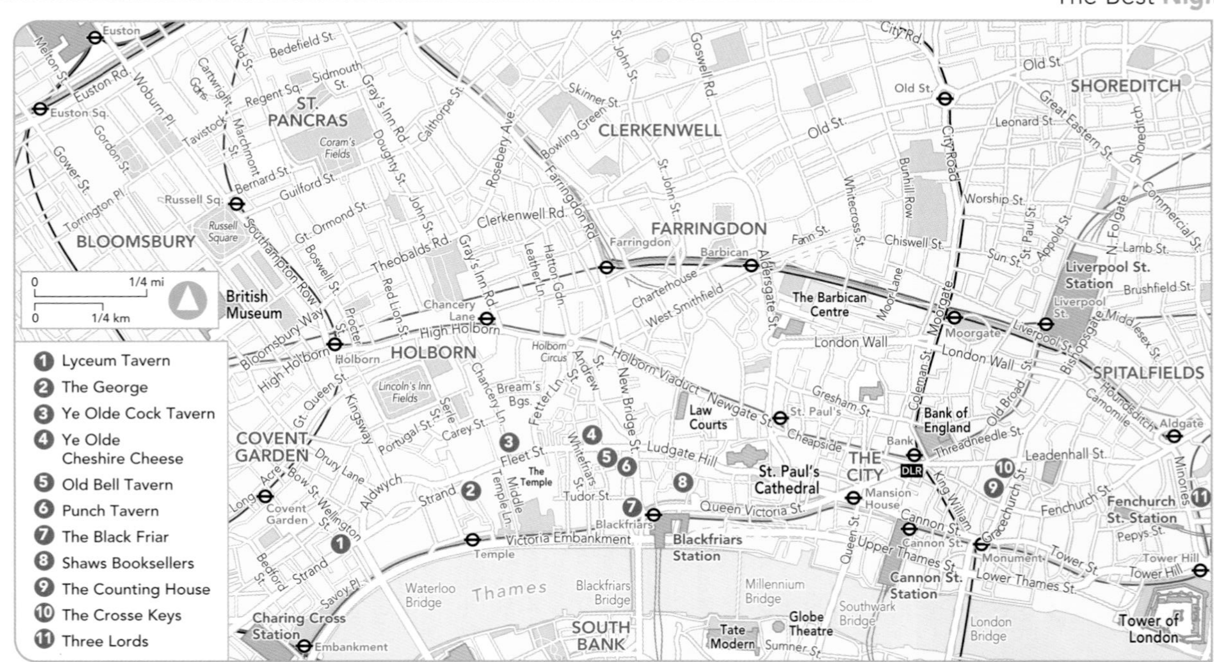

If London is, as has often been claimed, less a single, cohesive city than a collection of villages, then its pubs are the hearts of those villages. A local is a place to wind down after work, hang out with friends on the weekend, and of course, get rip-roaring drunk. This evening jaunt explores some of the best pubs in the City, London's oldest neighborhood. START: **Temple Tube Station.**

❶ ★ **Lyceum Tavern.** The two floors of this Strand stalwart have very different personalities. Downstairs it's dark and snug, the space divided into separate booths with tables and benches. The upstairs area, where food is served, is open plan, with a large window giving views of comings and goings across the Thames. It's run by Samuel Smith's Brewery, so prices are reasonable. *354 Strand.* ☎ *020/7836-7155. Map p 130.*

❷ ★ **The George.** Just across from the Royal Courts of Justice, this was a coffeehouse when it opened in 1723 and was frequented by scribblers Horace Walpole, Oliver Goldsmith, and the ubiquitous Dr. Samuel Johnson. A pub since Victorian times, it still has beautiful (if faux) medieval timbering and leaded glass. *213 Strand.* ☎ *020/7353-9638. www.georgeinthestrand.com. Map p 130.*

❸ ★ **Ye Olde Cock Tavern.** The main reason to come to this pub is its architecture: The cockerel was supposedly made by master carver Grinling Gibbons, and much of the building survived the Great Fire of London and dates back to the 16th century. It was a favorite of Dickens, Samuel Pepys, and Alfred Lord Tennyson (who mentioned it in one of his poems, a copy of which hangs near the entrance). Upstairs is a gin bar, once common in London and now making a comeback. *22 Fleet St.* ☎ *020/7353-8570. Map p 130.*

❹ ★★★ **Ye Olde Cheshire Cheese.** This wonderfully atmospheric, labyrinthine old pub was rebuilt right after the fire of 1666 and hasn't changed much since. Dr. Samuel Johnson lived around the corner, and other literary ghosts haunt the place. It's also operated by the Samuel Smith's Brewery, whose pints are probably the cheapest in the capital. *Wine Office Court, 145 Fleet St.* ☎ *020/7353-6170. Map p 130.*

❺ ★★ **Old Bell Tavern.** This cozy and authentic pub was built in the 1670s for workmen building nearby St. Bride's (the "wedding cake" church designed by Wren in 1670). It maintains an old-world ambience with its leaded windows and wainscoted walls. The pub's laidback, genial atmosphere makes it a good spot for a pint—it serves half a dozen hand-pulled ales. *95 Fleet St.* ☎ *020/7583-0216. Map p 130.*

Ye Olde Cheshire Cheese.

❻ ★★ **Punch Tavern.** Bearing the scars of an ownership feud that divided its premises in two, this Victorian pub (a former gin palace) was where the satirical magazine *Punch* was founded in 1841; look for artifacts from that publication (as well as "Punch & Judy" themed memorabilia) on the walls. The bright interior features some beautifully etched mirrors and Art Nouveau chandeliers. *99 Fleet St. ☎ 020/7353-6658. www.punchtavern.com. Map p 130.*

❼ ★★★ **The Black Friar.** The amazingly detailed interior of this wedge-shaped Arts & Crafts pub is a feast for the eyes. Magnificent carved friezes of monks remind you that the pub was built on the site of a 13th-century Dominican monastery, and under the vaulted ceiling you'll find such inscribed thoughts as WISDOM IS RARE. It's a popular after-work watering hole for the City's lawyers and business set. *174 Queen Victoria St. ☎ 020/7236-5474. Map p 130.*

❽ ★ **Shaws Booksellers.** As much a wine bar and restaurant as a pub, Shaws performs each role well. It's set in a restored paper merchant's warehouse, with an elegant curved glass bay frontage. Expect upmarket besuited clientele, beers by Fuller's, and a respectable wine list. *31–34 St. Andrew's Hill. Queen Victoria St. ☎ 020/7489-7999. www.shawsbooksellers.co.uk. Map p 130.*

❾ ★★★ **The Counting House.** A former bank, this must-see pub has a wonderfully opulent interior with a glass dome, a balcony (great for people-watching), extravagant chandeliers, gilded mirrors, and marbled walls. It's busy after work, but closed on weekends. *50 Cornhill. ☎ 020/7283-7123. www.the-counting-house.com. Map p 130.*

❿ ★★ **The Crosse Keys.** Yet another former bank is now a huge pub with separate eating rooms, a courtyard, high ceilings, wonderful wall carvings, and glass domes. It's almost too grand to be a drinking den. Part of the Wetherspoon chain, the pub offers food and drink that are very reasonably priced for the area. *9 Gracechurch St. ☎ 020/7623-4824. Map p 130.*

⓫ ★ **Three Lords.** Named after three Scottish aristocrats who were executed just down the road on Tower Hill for their part in the failed 1745 Jacobite Rebellion, this pub was first founded in the 18th century, but the current version dates back only to the 1980s. It's a pleasant mix of modern and traditional, with a wood interior and a boisterous, cheery atmosphere, particularly toward the end of the week. Closed Sundays. *27 Minories. ☎ 020/3437-0631. www.threelordsec3.co.uk. Map p 130.*

8 The Best Arts & Entertainment

Arts & Entertainment Best Bets

Best for a **Laugh**
★★★ The Comedy Store, *1a Oxendon St. (p 140)*

Best for **Opera**
★★★ Royal Opera House, *Covent Garden (p 139)*

Best **Baroque Concerts**
★ St. Martin-in-the-Fields Evening Candlelight Concerts, *Trafalgar Sq. (p 140)*

Best **Historic Concert Venue**
★★★ Royal Albert Hall, *Kensington Gore (p 139)*

Most **Atmospheric Gig Venue**
★★ The Roundhouse, *Chalk Farm Rd. (p 138)*

Best for a **Cheap Movie Date**
★★ Prince Charles Cinema, *7 Leicester Place (p 139)*

Best **Free Live-Music Performances**
★★ LSO St. Luke's, *161 Old St. (p 138)*

Best for **Independent Films**
★ Curzon Mayfair, *38 Curzon St. (p 140)*

Best **Large Pop Concert Venue**
★ O2 Arena, *Peninsula Sq. (p 138)*

Best **Outdoor Performances**
★★ Open Air Theatre, *Inner Circle, Regent's Park (p 141)*

Best for **Ballet**
★★★ Sadler's Wells, *Rosebery Ave. (p 140)*

Best **Orchestra**
★★★ London Symphony Orchestra at the Barbican Centre, *Silk St. (p 138)*

Best for **Modern Dance**
★★ The Place, *17 Duke's Rd. (p 140)*

Best for **New Playwrights**
★★ Royal Court Theatre, *Sloane Sq. (p 141)*

Best for **Shakespeare**
★★★ Shakespeare's Globe Theatre, *21 New Globe Walk (p 141)*

Best **Theatrical Repertory Company**
★★★ National Theatre, *South Bank (p 141)*

Longest-**Running Musical on the Planet**
★★ Les Misérables, *Queen's Theatre, Shaftesbury Ave. (p 144)*

Previous page: Albert Sessions, an Evening with Alison Balsom at Royal Albert Hall.

West End Theatres

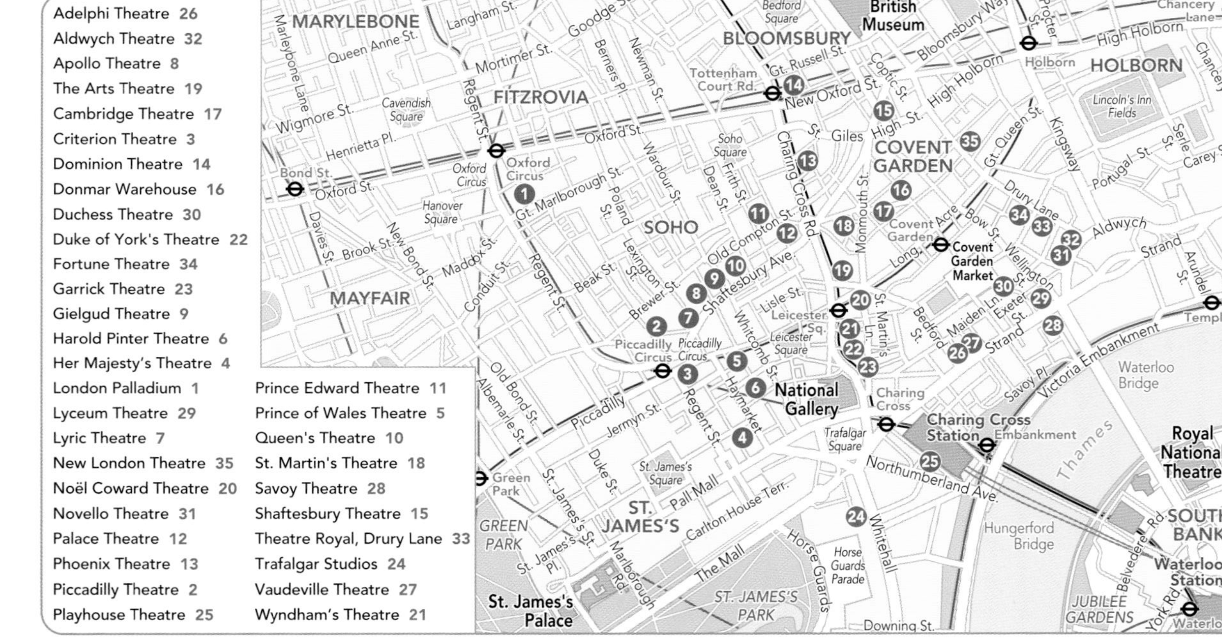

London Arts & Entertainment

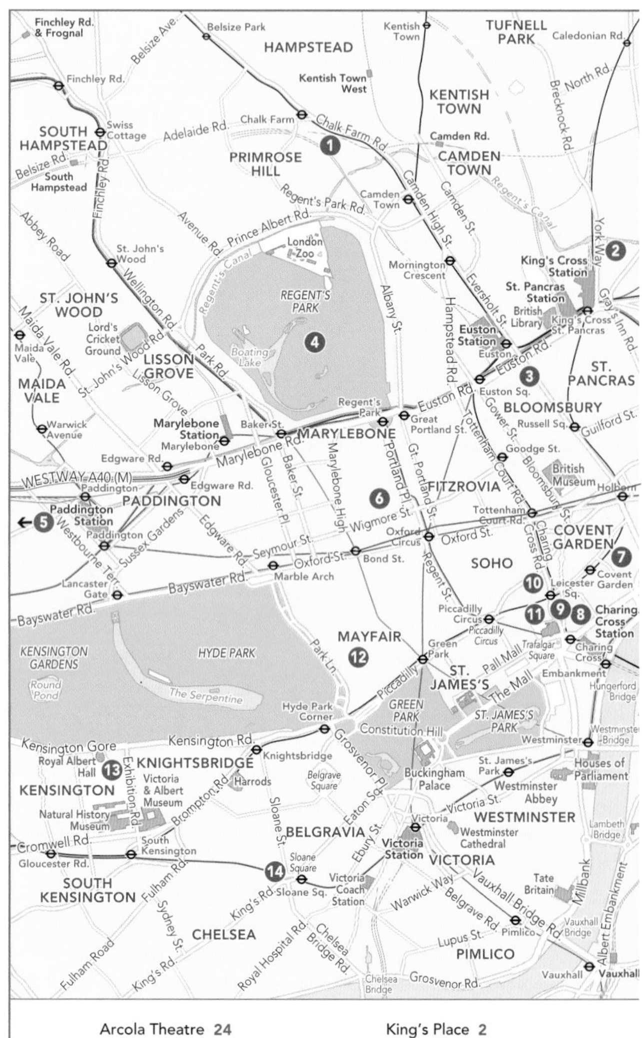

Arcola Theatre 24
Barbican Centre 20
Comedy Cafe Theatre 21
The Comedy Store 11
Curzon Mayfair 12
Electric Cinema 5

King's Place 2
London Coliseum 9
LSO St. Luke's 22
National Theatre 16
Old Vic 17
Open Air Theatre 4

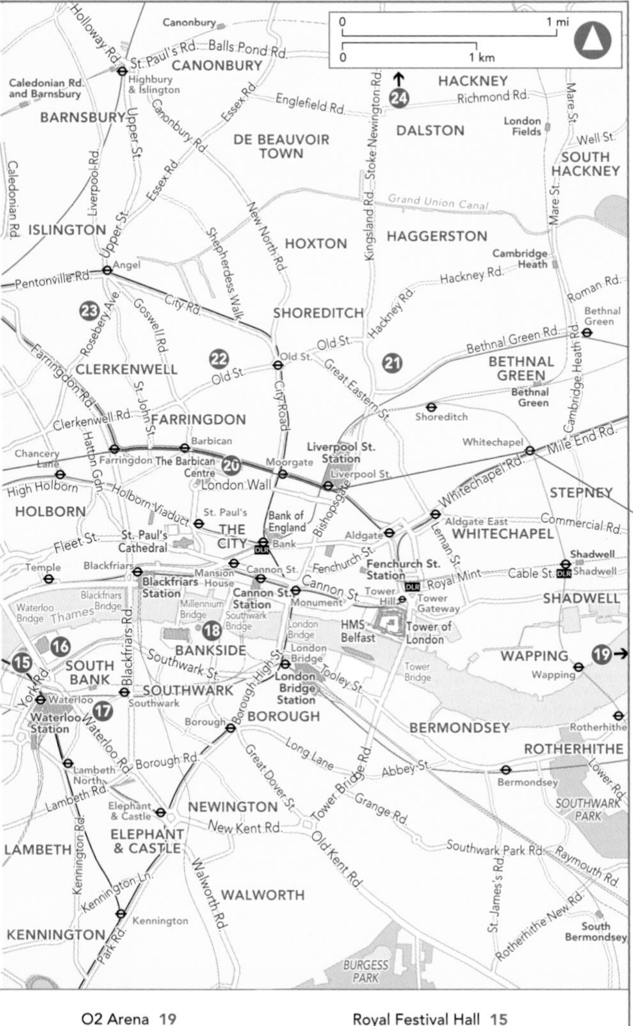

O2 Arena 19
The Place 3
Prince Charles Cinema 10
The Roundhouse 1
Royal Albert Hall 13
Royal Court Theatre 14
Royal Festival Hall 15
Royal Opera House 7
Sadler's Wells 23
St. Martin-in-the-Fields 8
Shakespeare's Globe Theatre 18
Wigmore Hall 6

London A&E A to Z

Classical, Opera & Popular Music

★★★ **Barbican Centre** THE CITY The Barbican's acoustics make it the best place for hearing music in the U.K. This gargantuan 1980s venue is home to the first-class **London Symphony Orchestra,** and puts on regular free concerts in its foyer. Performances of dance and theatre are also staged. *Silk St.* ☎ *020/7638-8891. www.barbican.org.uk. Tickets £10–£55. Tube: Barbican. Map p 137.*

★ **King's Place** KING'S CROSS London's latest major concert venue is part of the giant redevelopment around King's Cross Station. It's the home of the **London Sinfonietta** and its acoustics are notoriously precise—don't be rustling any candy wrappers unless you want a row-full of dirty looks. There are jazz and dance performances, too. *90 York Way.* ☎ *020/7520-1490. www.kingsplace.co.uk. Tickets £5–£50. Tube: King's Cross. Map p 136.*

★★ **London Coliseum** COVENT GARDEN Converted to an opera house in 1968, London's largest theatre is home to the **English National Opera.** Productions range from Verdi to Gilbert and Sullivan to challenging modern fare; most are sung in English. *St. Martin's Lane.* ☎ *020/7845-9300. www.eno.org. Tickets £10–£125. Tube: Charing Cross. Map p 136.*

★★ **LSO St. Luke's** THE CITY Designed by Hawksmoor, this deconsecrated church provides an alternative 370-seat venue for the **London Symphony Orchestra** (when it's not at the Barbican). It puts on cheap lunchtime concerts, and it is occasionally possible to watch the orchestra practice for free. *161 Old St.* ☎ *020/7638-8891. http://lso.co.uk. Tickets free–£27. Tube: Old St. Map p 137.*

★ **O2 Arena** GREENWICH The massive interior of the previously underused Millennium Dome is now the highest-profile entertainment arena in England. Alongside the 20,000-seat main venue is a smaller concert hall, **indigo at The O2**, with good acoustics and comfortable seats. *Peninsula Sq.* ☎ *020/3784-7998. www.theo2.co.uk. Tickets £10–£150. Tube: N. Greenwich. Map 137.*

★★ **The Roundhouse** CAMDEN TOWN Homegrown indie talent, transatlantic guitar bands like The National, experimental urban sounds and even a bit of baroque opera play at a former train shed whose first headline live act, in 1966, was Pink Floyd. *Chalk Farm Road.* ☎ *0300/6789-222. www.roundhouse.org.uk. Tickets £6–£90. Tube: Chalk Farm. Map p 136.*

Concert at O2 Arena.

Buying Tickets

You can buy advance tickets for most of London's entertainment venues via the theatres' websites or through **Ticketmaster** (www.ticketmaster.co.uk). Expect to pay a booking fee as high as £3.50 per ticket. Some concierges can set aside theatre tickets for hotel guests—ask when booking your room.

For same-day, half-price theatre tickets, your best bet is still the **tkts** booth (www.tkts.co.uk) on the south side of Leicester Square, which opens at 10am (11am on Sun). Boards and the website list the day's available West End shows. Blockbusters and new arrivals will likely be hard to get, but decent seats at longer-running productions should be available. Many theatres sell their own half-price standby tickets or returns at the box office about an hour before curtain time.

For a wide range of live music events, it's also worth switching on your smartphone. **Twickets** (www.twickets.live) enables theatre- and gig-goers to resell unwanted or surplus tickets ethically, at or below face value. You can set up alerts if you are waiting for something specific. **Dice** (https://dice.fm) offers smartphone ticketing, plus you can join an automated in-app waitlist for ticket returns.

★★★ **Royal Albert Hall** KENSINGTON This splendid Victorian pleasure palace is best known as the home of the city's annual **Henry Wood Promenade Concerts (the Proms)** in summer, when you'll hear orchestral classics and chamber music. Pop, rock, and jazz are offered at other times. *Kensington Gore.* ☎ *020/7589-8212. www.royalalberthall.com. Tickets £10–£120. Tube: High St. Kensington. Map p 136.*

★★★ **Royal Festival Hall** SOUTH BANK More than 150,000 hours of music have been performed at this acoustically exceptional complex since it opened in 1951. The hall's many free and low-priced concerts make it a great bet for travelers on a budget. *Belvedere Rd.* ☎ *020/3879-9555. www.southbankcentre.co.uk. Tickets £10–£65. Tube: Waterloo. Map p 137.*

★★★ **Royal Opera House** COVENT GARDEN This magnificent theatre occupies one corner of Covent Garden. Operas are sung by first-rate casts and in the original language. Get online on ticket release date if you want to grab the cheapest seats. *Covent Garden.* ☎ *020/7304-4000. www.roh.org.uk. Tickets £6–£285. Tube: Covent Garden. Map p 136.*

★ **St. Martin-in-the-Fields** WEST END You are following (allegedly) in Mozart's footsteps when you attend a concert at this atmospheric church. Admission to its popular lunchtime concerts (Mon, Tues, and Fri at 1pm) is by suggested donation (£3.50). *Trafalgar Sq.* ☎ *020/7766-1100. www.stmartin-in-the-fields.org. Tickets £9–£29. Tube: Charing Cross. Map p 136.*

★★ **Wigmore Hall** MARYLEBONE Bechstein Pianos built this

grand Renaissance-style recital hall—one of the world's finest—in 1901. The greatest names in classical music have taken advantage of the venue's fabulous acoustics. *36 Wigmore St. ☎ 020/7935-2141. www.wigmore-hall.org.uk. Tickets £10–£50. Tube: Bond St. Map p 136.*

Comedy

★ Comedy Cafe Theatre EAST END The old crowded tables and exposed walls have made way for a new space in a hip Shoreditch hotel. The raw comedy, mix of well-known and emerging comics, and heckling remain. *100 Shoreditch High St. ☎ 020/7613-9800. www.comedycafetheatre.co.uk. Tickets £10–£22. Tube: Old St. Map p 137.*

★★★ The Comedy Store WEST END In a previous incarnation, this club launched the alternative-comedy boom of the early 1980s, and it's still very much the venue where comics aspire to perform, both newbies and big names. *1a Oxendon St. ☎ 020/7024-2060. www.thecomedystore.co.uk/london. Tickets £8–£25. Tube: Piccadilly Circus. Map p 136.*

Dance

★★ The Place BLOOMSBURY Dedicated to both the teaching and the performing of dance, this small venue is the place in London to see contemporary new artists and startling modern dance. *17 Duke's Rd. ☎ 020/7121-1100. www.theplace.org.uk. Tickets £3–£17. Tube: Euston. Map p 136.*

★★★ Royal Opera House COVENT GARDEN The brilliantly restored 19th-century ROH houses the even more brilliant **Royal Ballet,** a company on a par with the world's best. You can catch any number of classics, such as *Swan Lake, Giselle,* or *Sleeping Beauty,* but you'll pay for the privilege. ***See above.***

★★★ Sadler's Wells ISLINGTON The best dance troupes in the world—from cutting edge to classical ballet—perform at this chic theatre, where they are assured of an appreciative and knowledgeable audience. *Rosebery Ave. ☎ 020/7863-8000. www.sadlerswells.com. Tickets £12–£59. Tube: Angel. Map p 137.*

Movies

★ Curzon Mayfair MAYFAIR This historic art-house theatre (dating back to 1934) is renowned for world cinema screenings. *38 Curzon St. ☎ 0330/500-1331. www.curzoncinemas.com. Tickets £10–£15. Tube: Green Park. Map p 136.*

★★ kids Electric Cinema NOTTING HILL Couches and leather seats, cocktails and yummy treats, Sunday double features, and weekly mother-and-baby screenings make this art house a destination movie theatre. Mainstream and independent films are shown. *191 Portobello Rd. ☎ 020/7908-9696. www.electriccinema.co.uk. Tickets £15–£20. Tube: Ladbroke Grove. Map p 136.*

★★ Prince Charles Cinema SOHO One of London's best movie bargains, this independent

Candlelight concert at St. Martin-in-the-Fields.

Milonga at Sadler's Wells.

theatre offers singalong sessions of classic musicals, cult hits, mainstream classics, and first-run foreign flicks. *7 Leicester Place. ☎ 020/7494-3654. www.princecharlescinema.com. Tickets £4.50–£12.50. Tube: Leicester Sq. Map p 136.*

Theatre

★ Arcola Theatre DALSTON Edgy new plays, remastered classics, and even some reinterpreted (and new) opera attract a young, politically aware East London crowd. *24 Ashwin St. ☎ 020/7503-1646. www.arcolatheatre.com. Tickets £8–£20. Overground: Dalston Junction.*

★★★ National Theatre SOUTH BANK Home to one of the world's greatest stage companies, the National presents the finest in world theatre, from classic drama to new plays, comedies, and musicals. *South Bank. ☎ 020/7452-3000. www.nationaltheatre.org.uk. Tickets £15–£67. Tube: Waterloo or Charing Cross. Map p 137.*

★★★ Old Vic SOUTH BANK Except for a few wartime interruptions, this venerable theatre has been in continuous operation since 1818. The repertory troupe at "the actors' theatre" has been a who's who of thespians over the years, including Sir Laurence Olivier and Dame Maggie Smith. *The Cut. ☎ 0844/871-7628. www.oldvictheatre.com. Tickets £12–£57.50. Tube: Waterloo. Map p 137.*

★★ Open Air Theatre MARYLEBONE The setting is idyllic, and the seating and acoustics are excellent at this Regent's Park venue. Presentations are often of Shakespeare's plays or other English classics, regularly in period costume. The season runs from May to mid-September. *Inner Circle, Regent's Park. ☎ 0844/826-4242. www.openairtheatre.com. Tickets £25–£55. Tube: Baker St. Map p 136.*

★★ Royal Court Theatre CHELSEA This leader in cutting-edge theatre is home to the English Stage Company, formed to promote serious drama. *Sloane Sq. ☎ 020/7565-5000. www.royalcourttheatre.com. Tickets £12–£45. Tube: Sloane Sq. Map p 136.*

★★★ Shakespeare's Globe Theatre SOUTH BANK This outdoor theatre is a replica of the Elizabethan original. You can choose either to sit on wooden benches (you can rent a cushion) or stand in front of the stage as a "groundling," just as theatre-goers did in the Bard's day. *21 New Globe Walk, Bankside. ☎ 020/7902-1400. www.shakespearesglobe.com. Tickets £10 groundlings, £15–£48 gallery seats. Tube: London Bridge. Map p 137.*

West End Theatres

Adelphi Theatre, 409 Strand. ☎ 020/3725-7060

Aldwych Theatre, 49 Aldwych. ☎ 0845/200-7981

Apollo Theatre, 39 Shaftesbury Ave. ☎ 0330/333-4809

The Arts Theatre, 6–7 Great Newport St. ☎ 020/7836-8463

Cambridge Theatre, Earlham St. ☎ 020/7087-7745

Criterion Theatre, Piccadilly Circus. ☎ 0844/815-6131

Dominion Theatre, 268–269 Tottenham Court Rd. ☎ 0845/200-7982

Donmar Warehouse, 41 Earlham St. ☎ 020/3282-3808

Duchess Theatre, Catherine St. ☎ 0330/333-4810

Duke of York's Theatre, St. Martin's Lane. ☎ 020/7206-1182

Fortune Theatre, Russell St. ☎ 020/7206-1182

Garrick Theatre, 2 Charing Cross Rd. ☎ 0330/333-4811

Gielgud Theatre, Shaftesbury Ave. ☎ 0844/482-5130

Harold Pinter Theatre, Panton St., ☎ 020/7206-1182

Her Majesty's Theatre, Haymarket. ☎ 020/7087-7762

London Palladium, 8 Argyll St. ☎ 020/7087-7747

Lyceum Theatre, 21 Wellington St. ☎ 020/7206-1182

Lyric Theatre, Shaftesbury Ave. ☎ 0330/333-4812

New London Theatre, 166 Drury Lane. ☎ 020/7087-7750

Noël Coward Theatre, 85 St. Martin's Lane. ☎ 0844/482-5141

Novello Theatre, Aldwych. ☎ 0844/482-5170

Palace Theatre, 109–113 Shaftesbury Ave. ☎ 0330/333-4813

Phoenix Theatre, 110 Charing Cross. ☎ 020/7206-1182

Piccadilly Theatre, 16 Denman St. ☎ 020/7206-1182

Playhouse Theatre, Northumberland Ave. ☎ 020/7206-1182

Prince Edward Theatre, Old Compton St. ☎ 0844/482-5151

Prince of Wales Theatre, Coventry St. ☎ 0844/482-5115

Queen's Theatre, Shaftesbury Ave. ☎ 0844/482-5160

St. Martin's Theatre, West St. ☎ 020/7836-1443

Savoy Theatre, Savoy Court, Strand. ☎ 020/7206-1182

Shaftesbury Theatre, 210 Shaftesbury Ave. ☎ 020/7379-5399

Theatre Royal, Drury Lane. ☎ 020/7087-7760

Trafalgar Studios, 14 Whitehall. ☎ 020/7206-1182

Vaudeville Theatre, 404 Strand. ☎ 0330/333-4814

Wyndham's Theatre, Charing Cross Rd. ☎ 0844/482-5120 ●

9 The Best **Hotels**

Hotel Best Bets

Best for an **Olde England Vibe**
★★★ Batty Langley's, *12 Folgate St., E1 (p 152)*

Best **Hotel for Families**
★★★ Haymarket Hotel, *1 Suffolk Place, SW1 (p 154)*

Best **Budget Choice in the Center**
★★★ Luna Simone Hotel, *47–49 Belgrave Rd., SW1 (p 155)*

Best **Hotel for Victoriana**
★★ The Gore, *189 Queen's Gate, SW7 (p 154)*

Best **Hotel for Clubbers**
★★ The Hoxton, *81 Gt. Eastern St., EC2 (p 155)*

Best **Luxury Hotel**
★★★ Claridge's, *Brook St., W1 (p 153)*

Best **Hotel for Royal Watching**
★★ The Rubens at the Palace, *39 Buckingham Palace Rd., SW1 (p 157)*

Best **Base for Kensington Museum-Hopping**
★ Number Sixteen, *16 Sumner Place, SW7 (p 156)*

Best for **Views of the Thames without Breaking the Bank**
★★ Park Plaza County Hall Hotel, *1 Addington St., SE1 (p 156)*

Best **Chance to Bag a Value Package Deal**
★ The Rembrandt, *11 Thurloe Place, SW7 (p 157)*

Previous page: The lobby of Claridge's Hotel.

Best **Bedrooms in East London**
★★ Town Hall Hotel, *Patriot Sq., E2 (p 158)*

Best **Hotel for Afternoon Tea**
★★ The Goring, *Beeston Place, SW1 (p 154)*

Best **Value for Money**
★★ Mowbray Court Hotel, *28–32 Penywern Rd., SW5 (p 156)*

Most **Romantic Hotel**
★★★ San Domenico House, *29–31 Draycott Place, SW3 (p 157)*

Best **Budget Chain**
Premier Inn *(p 153)*

Grandest **Bathrooms**
★★★ The Dorchester, *53 Park Lane, W1 (p 154)*

Best **Business Hotel**
★★ citizenM Tower of London, *40 Trinity Sq., EC3 (p 152); or* ★★★ The Zetter, *St. John's Sq., EC1 (p 158)*

Best for **Theatre Buffs**
★★★ Covent Garden Hotel, *10 Monmouth St., WC2 (p 153)*

Most **Refined Upscale Atmosphere**
★★★ The Connaught, *Carlos Place, W1 (p 153)*

East End & City Hotels

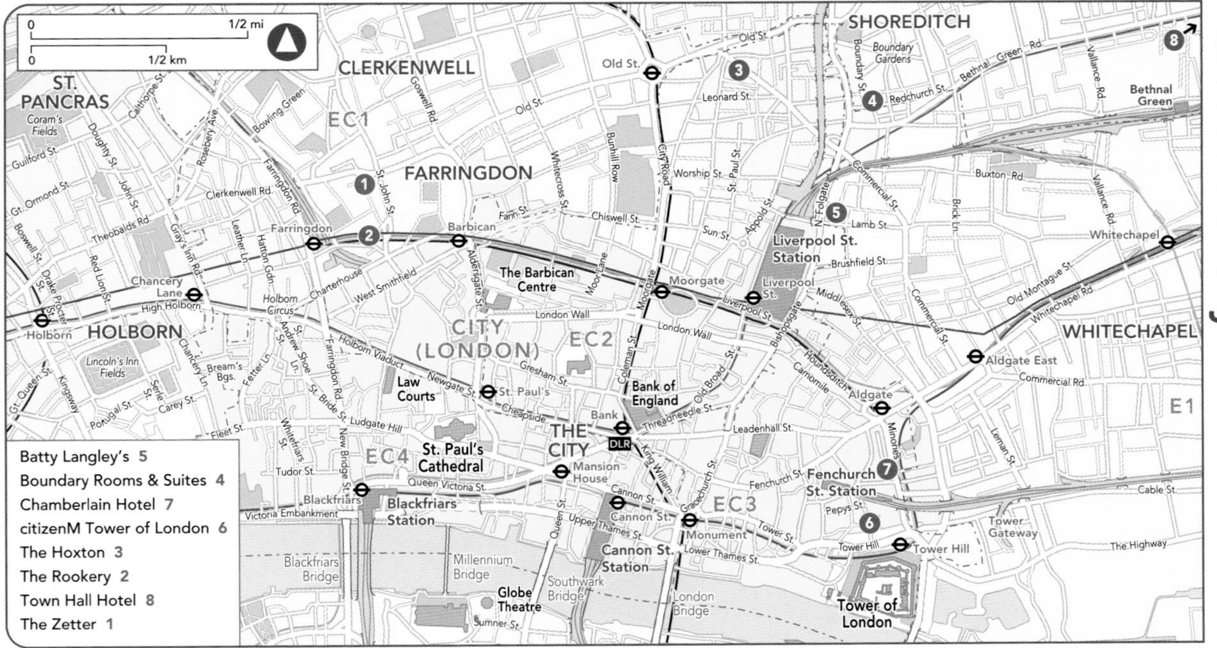

Kensington & Chelsea Hotels

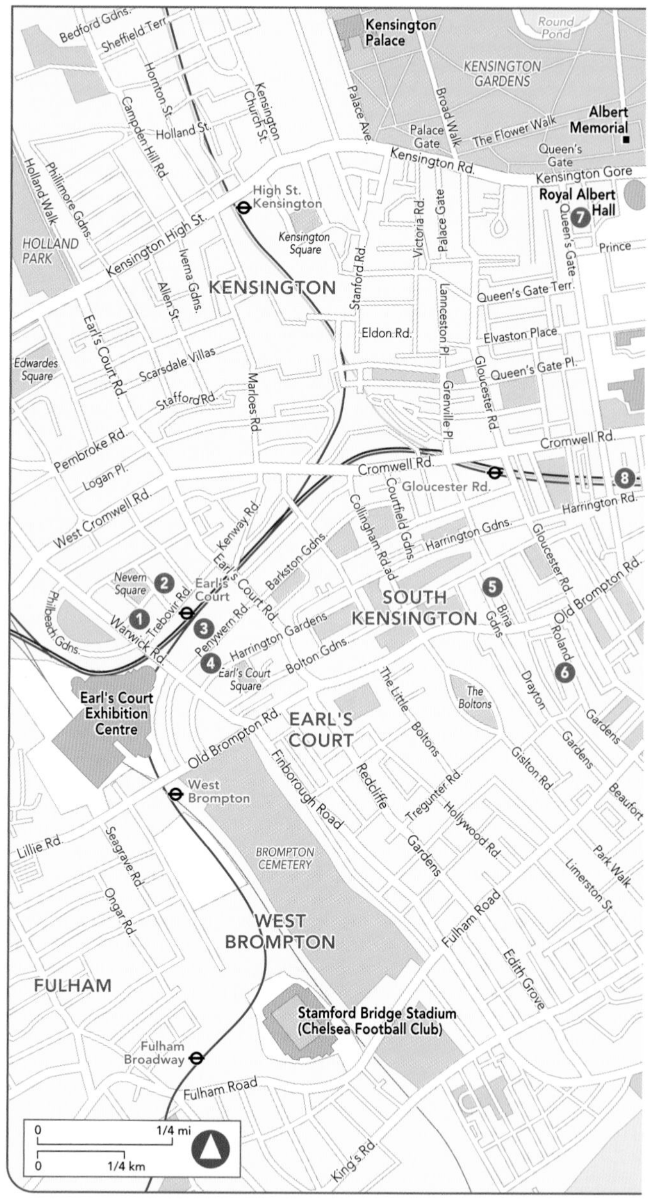

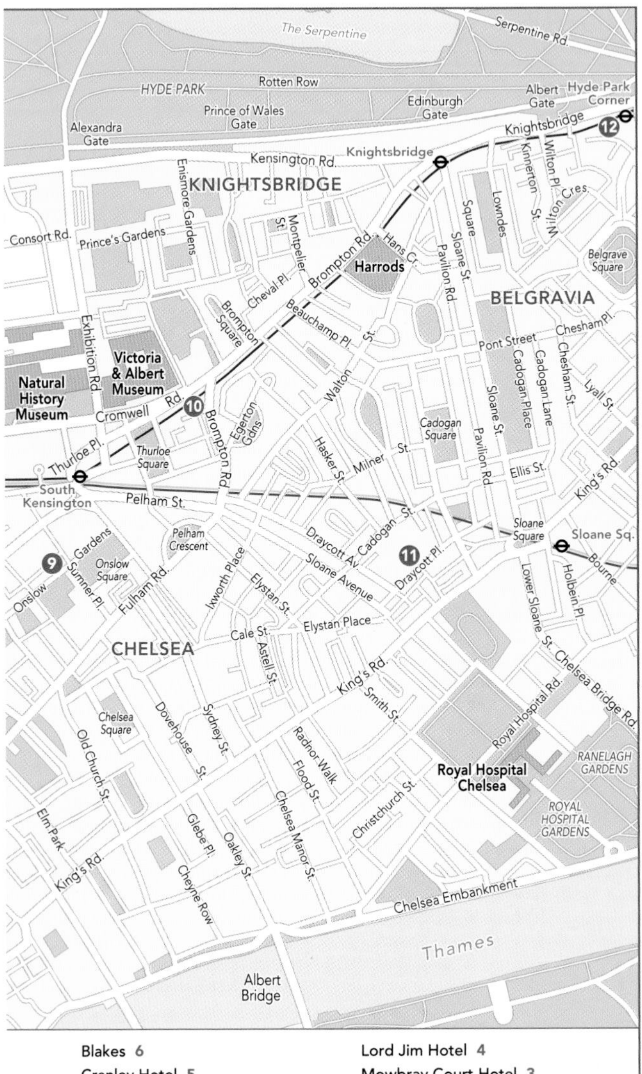

Blakes 6
Cranley Hotel 5
The Gainsborough 8
The Gore 7
K+K Hotel George 2
The Lanesborough 12
Lord Jim Hotel 4
Mowbray Court Hotel 3
Number Sixteen 9
The Rembrandt 10
San Domenico House 11
Twenty Nevern Square 1

Notting Hill & Marylebone Hotels

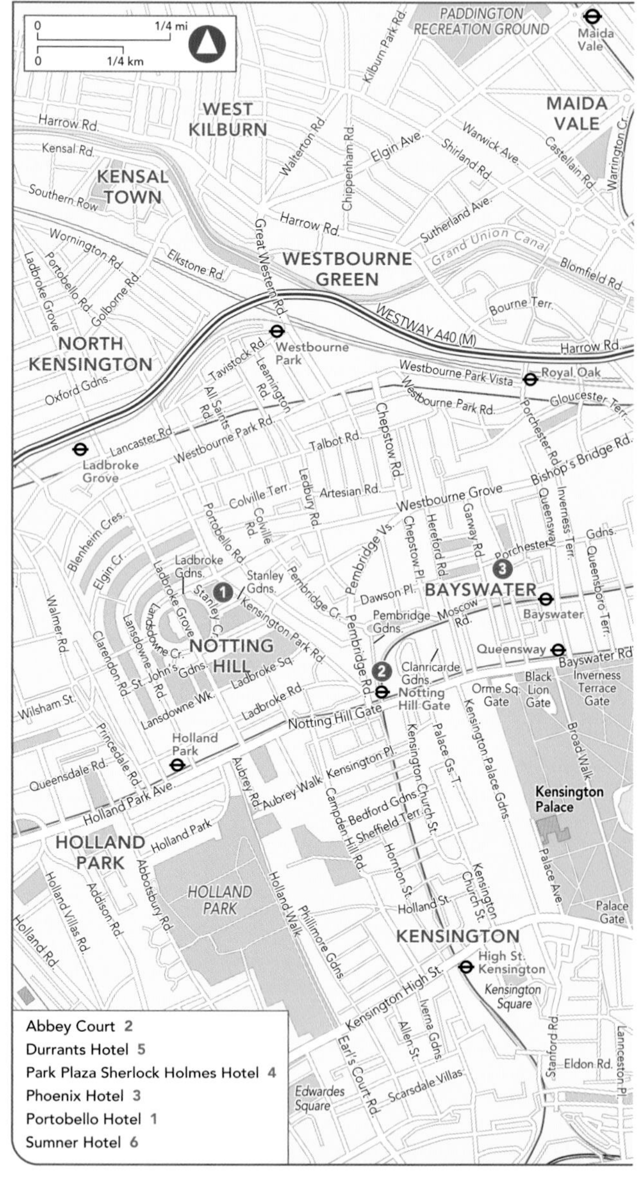

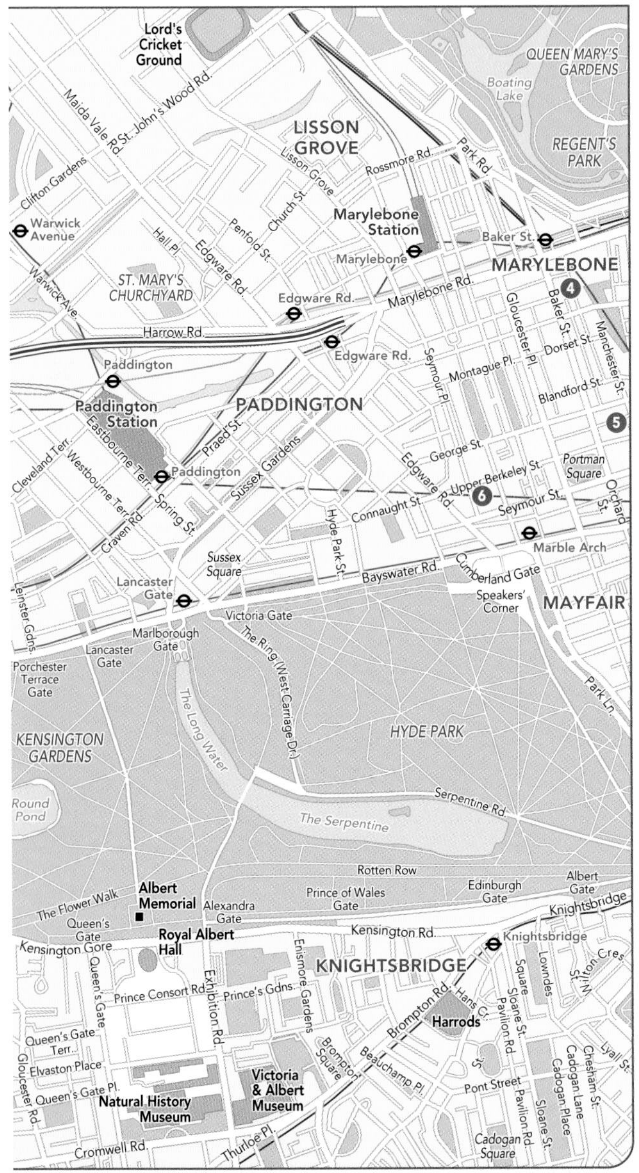
Lord's Cricket Ground
St. John's Wood Rd.
Maida Vale Rd.
LISSON GROVE
QUEEN MARY'S GARDENS
Boating Lake
REGENT'S PARK
Park Rd.
Rossmore Rd.
Lisson Grove
Clifton Gardens
Church St.
Penfold St.
Warwick Avenue
Marylebone Station
Baker St.
Marylebone
MARYLEBONE
Hall Pl.
Edgware Rd.
Warwick Ave.
ST. MARY'S CHURCHYARD
Edgware Rd.
Marylebone Rd.
Gloucester Pl.
Baker St.
Manchester St.
Harrow Rd.
Edgware Rd.
Dorset St.
Paddington
Seymour Pl.
Montague Pl.
Blandford St.
Paddington Station
PADDINGTON
Eastbourne Terr.
Praed St.
Cleveland Terr.
Westbourne Terr.
Paddington
Sussex Gardens
George St.
Portman Square
Edgware Rd.
Upper Berkeley St.
Orchard St.
Spring St.
Craven Rd.
Hyde Park St.
Connaught St.
Seymour St.
Marble Arch
Sussex Square
Bayswater Rd.
Cumberland Gate
Lancaster Gate
Speakers' Corner
MAYFAIR
Leinster Gdns.
Victoria Gate
Marlborough Gate
The Ring (West Carriage Dr.)
Lancaster Gate
Porchester Terrace Gate
Park Ln.
The Long Water
KENSINGTON GARDENS
HYDE PARK
Round Pond
Serpentine Rd.
The Serpentine
Rotten Row
Albert Memorial
The Flower Walk
Prince of Wales Gate
Edinburgh Gate
Albert Gate
Alexandra Gate
Knightsbridge
Queen's Gate
Royal Albert Hall
Kensington Rd.
Knightsbridge
Kensington Gore
Enismore Gardens
KNIGHTSBRIDGE
Queen's Gate
Exhibition Rd.
Prince Consort Rd.
Prince's Gdns.
Lowndes Square
Wilton Cres.
Brompton Rd.
Hans Cr.
Harrods
Sloane St.
Pavilion Rd.
Queen's Gate Terr.
Gloucester Rd.
Elvaston Place
Brompton Square
Beauchamp Pl.
Lyall St.
Chesham St.
Cadogan Lane
Cadogan Place
Queen's Gate Pl.
Victoria & Albert Museum
Natural History Museum
Pont Street
Pavilion Rd.
Sloane St.
Thurloe Pl.
Cromwell Rd.
Cadogan Square
4
5
6

West End & South Bank Hotels

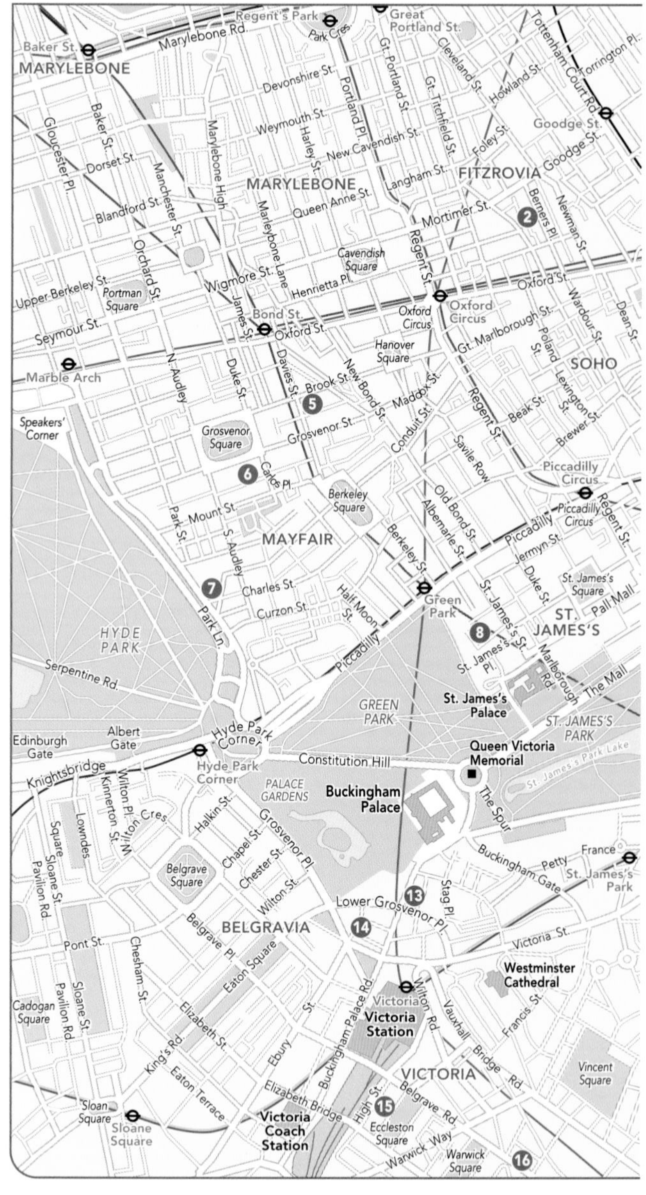

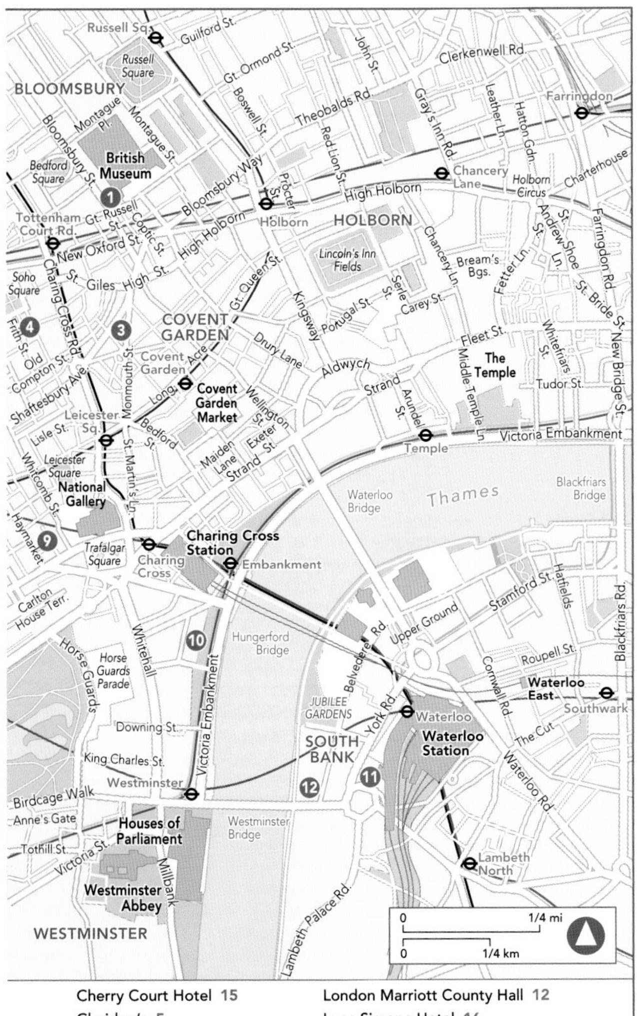

Cherry Court Hotel 15
Claridge's 5
The Connaught 6
Covent Garden Hotel 3
The Dorchester 7
The Goring 14
Haymarket Hotel 9
Hazlitt's 1718 4
London Marriott County Hall 12
Luna Simone Hotel 16
Morgan Hotel 1
Park Plaza County Hall Hotel 11
The Royal Horseguards 10
The Rubens at the Palace 13
Sanderson London 2
The Stafford London 8

London Hotels A to Z

★ kids **Abbey Court** NOTTING HILL This four-floor Victorian town house has considerable charms, if you can get along without an elevator. *20 Pembridge Gardens, W2. ☎ 020/7221-7518. www.abbeycourthotel.co.uk. 22 units. Doubles £118–£196. AE, DC, MC, V. Tube: Notting Hill Gate. Map p 148.*

★★★ **Batty Langley's** THE CITY A historic 1724 row-house immaculately converted into a luxe hotel in the shadow of 21st-century skyscrapers. East London's buzzing weekend markets are on the doorstep. *12 Folgate St., E1. ☎ 020/7377-4390. www.battylangleys.com. 29 units. Doubles £165–£339. AE, DC, MC, V. Tube: Liverpool St. Map p 145.*

★★ **Blakes** SOUTH KENSINGTON Still on-trend after all these years, and still celebrated for its exotic and lavish decor. Alas, the prices do seem to get a little harder to swallow. *33 Roland Gardens, SW7. ☎ 020/7370-6701. www.blakeshotels.com. 47 units. Doubles £325–£395. AE, DC, MC, V. Tube: Gloucester Rd. Map p 146.*

★★ **Boundary Rooms & Suites** EAST END Sir Terence Conran, always up with the latest trends, joined the great London push eastward with the opening of this hotel in a converted warehouse. The decor is as modernist as you'd expect, plus there's a roof conservatory and a destination restaurant. *2–4 Boundary St., E2. ☎ 020/7729-1051. www.boundary.london. 17 units. Doubles £170–£270. AE, DC, MC, V. Overground: Shoreditch High St. Map p 145.*

★ kids **Chamberlain Hotel** THE CITY Business travelers enjoy easy access to the City, and Tower of London sightseers couldn't be happier with the location of this modern hotel in a converted Georgian building with a pub. *130–135 Minories, EC3. ☎ 020/7680-1500. www.thechamberlainhotel.co.uk. 64 units. Doubles £90–£157. AE, MC, V. Tube: Tower Hill. Map p 145.*

★★ kids **Cherry Court Hotel** PIMLICO They don't come much cheaper than this pleasant hotel, at least not with ensuite rooms and the same degree of cleanliness and comfort. No elevator. *23 Hugh St., SW1. ☎ 020/7828-2840. www.cherrycourthotel.co.uk. 12 units. Doubles £75–£110. Add 5% for credit cards. AE, MC, V. Tube: Victoria. Map p 150.*

★★ **citizenM Tower of London** THE CITY "No-frills luxury," contemporary styling, super bar-with-a-view and outstanding value for a room with picture window overlooking the Tower. *40 Trinity Sq., EC3. ☎ 020/3519-4830. www.citizenm.com. 370 units. Doubles £104–£270. AE, MC, V. Tube: Tower Hill. Map p 145.*

The Connaught's Coburg Bar.

Chain Savings

Faced with room rates showing no sign of falling, cost-conscious travelers to London increasingly turn to budget or family-oriented U.K. and international hotel brands for an affordable stay. These chains have upped their game in recent years, with savvier design, more central locations, easy online booking, keen prices (especially if you reserve ahead), and improved service standards. On the downside, the hotel buildings themselves are often architecturally plain and functional, rather than beautiful or "historic."

Premier Inn (www.premierinn.com) has well-maintained, affordable, modern hotels in the City, King's Cross, Kensington, and along the South Bank, as well as in trendy neighborhoods such as Dalston and Brixton. The same company operates **hub by Premier Inn** (www.hubhotels.co.uk), pod-style hotels for one or two travelers where everything is controlled by a smartphone app. Hub hotels lie close to Covent Garden, Tower Bridge, and Westminster Abbey.

Another budget chain, **Travelodge** (www.travelodge.co.uk) has properties in the City, Waterloo, and King's Cross—as well as several outlying boroughs including Greenwich—plus Covent Garden. French-owned **Ibis** (www.ibis.com) has branded hotels close to Borough Market and in the East End.

Cost for any of these is £70 to £140 per night for a double room.

★★★ kids **Claridge's** MAYFAIR This redoubtable London institution, close to Bond Street's shopping, has been the final word in Art Deco elegance for decades. Rooms are spacious and service is impeccable. *Brook St., W1 (at Davies St.). ☎ 020/7629-8860. www.claridges.co.uk. 203 units. Doubles £400–£660. AE, DC, MC, V. Tube: Bond St. Map p 150.*

★★★ **The Connaught** MAYFAIR With all the stately grandeur of an old-style gentlemen's club, the Connaught is as gloriously dignified as the neighborhood around it. A major refurbishment has added modern touches. Go for tea (£50) if you can't afford the steep rates. *Carlos Place, W1. ☎ 020/7499-7070. www.the-connaught.co.uk. 123 units. Doubles £400–£680. AE, DC, MC, V. Tube: Bond St. Map p 150.*

★★★ kids **Covent Garden Hotel** SOHO Big beds, relatively large rooms, and deft English decor make this popular hotel one of the best near Soho. The downside: The neighborhood gets as rowdy at night as it is touristy by day. *10 Monmouth St., WC2. ☎ 020/7806-1000. www.firmdalehotels.com. 58 units. Doubles £310–£480. AE, DC, MC, V. Tube: Covent Garden. Map p 151.*

★★ kids **Cranley Hotel** SOUTH KENSINGTON Very romantic (the classic decor is laid over gorgeous period details), this hotel boasts a rooftop terrace, complimentary aperitifs, and free Wi-Fi in every bedroom—all in a quiet but convenient location. *10–12 Bina Gardens, SW5. ☎ 020/7373-0123. www.cranleyhotel.com. 39 units. Doubles £150–£220. AE, MC, V. Tube: Gloucester Rd. Map p 146.*

Elegant sitting room at the Covent Garden Hotel.

★★★ **The Dorchester** MAYFAIR This opulent gem welcomes kings and commoners with equal panache (so long as all have the requisite stash of cash, of course). Elegant decor, first-rate amenities, and to-die-for bathrooms. *53 Park Lane, W1. 020/7629-8888. www.dorchestercollection.com. 250 units. Doubles £408–£670. AE, DC, MC, V. Tube: Hyde Park Corner. Map p 150.*

★★ kids **Durrants Hotel** MARYLEBONE This clubby hotel offers good value and a great location close to Oxford Street shopping and the Wallace Collection. *George St., W1. ☎ 020/7935-8131. www.durrantshotel.co.uk. 92 units. Doubles £165–£210. AE, MC, V. Tube: Bond St. Map p 149.*

★ kids **The Gainsborough** SOUTH KENSINGTON A stone's throw from the Natural History Museum (p 44), this hotel offers comfortable chintz rooms at a decent price. *7–11 Queensberry Place, SW7. ☎ 020/7838-1700. www.hotelgainsborough.co.uk. 44 units. Doubles £135–£159. AE, DC, MC, V. Tube: S. Kensington. Map p 146.*

★★ kids **The Gore** SOUTH KENSINGTON Every room inside this gorgeous re-creation of an early Victorian hotel is individually decorated with fine antiques. *190 Queen's Gate, SW7. ☎ 020/7584-6601. www.gorehotel.co.uk. 50 units. Doubles £152–£370. AE, MC, V. Tube: Gloucester Rd. Map p 146.*

★★★ kids **The Goring** BELGRAVIA Although it is near Victoria Station, this hotel has the feel of a country house, with a big walled garden, charming public spaces, and refined afternoon teas. *15 Beeston Place, SW1. ☎ 020/7396-9000. www.thegoring.com. 71 units. Doubles £330–£760. AE, DC, MC, V. Tube: Victoria. Map p 150.*

★★★ kids **Haymarket Hotel** WEST END The Haymarket's location is perfect for West End fun, and the decor is worth dropping by to gawk at. It's not cheap, but neither is putting in a fabulous pool in central London. *1 Suffolk Place, SW1. ☎ 020/7470-4000. www.firmdalehotels.com. 50 units. Doubles £290–£470. AE, MC, V. Tube: Charing Cross. Map p 151.*

★★ **Hazlitt's 1718** SOHO Favored by the literary set, the 18th-century-flavored Hazlitt's feels more like a noble Georgian boardinghouse than a hotel. There's no elevator. *6 Frith St., W1. ☎ 020/7434-1771. www.hazlittshotel.com. 23 units. Doubles £219–£330. AE, DC, MC, V. Tube: Tottenham Court Rd. Map p 151.*

★★ **The Hoxton** SHOREDITCH Right at the heart of the Hoxton/Shoreditch nightlife scene, this does a roaring trade with clubbers who don't want to (or can't) drag themselves home at the end of the evening. The rooms are simple, clean, and honestly priced, and it has a fun vibe. *81 Great Eastern St., London EC2. ☎ 020/7550-1000. www.thehoxton.com. 210 units. Doubles £69–£239. AE, MC, V. Tube: Old St. Map p 145.*

★★ kids **K + K Hotel George** KENSINGTON Part of a popular European chain, this is a good bet for elegance and convenience at an affordable rate (depending on the season). Enjoy the garden when weather permits. *1–15 Templeton Place, SW5. ☎ 020/7598-8700. www.kkhotels.com. 154 units. Doubles £85–£235. AE, DC, MC, V. Tube: Earl's Court. Map p 146.*

★★★ kids **The Lanesborough** KNIGHTSBRIDGE Housed in a former hospital building, this grand Regency-style hotel features state-of-the-art amenities—and your very own butler. *Hyde Park Corner, SW1. ☎ 020/7259-5599. www.lanesborough.com. 95 units. Doubles £489–£740. AE, DC, MC, V. Tube: Hyde Park Corner. Map p 147.*

★ kids **London Marriott County Hall** SOUTH BANK You can't beat the views of Big Ben and Parliament from the rooms, though prices can be steep if you catch the wrong week. *County Hall, SE1. ☎ 020/7928-5200. www.marriotthotels.com. 200 units. Doubles £216–£425. AE, DC, MC, V. Tube: Waterloo. Map p 151.*

★ kids **Lord Jim Hotel** EARL'S COURT Known for its attractive package deals, this budget hotel offers plainly but pleasantly decorated rooms; families will fit easily inside the bigger ones. *23–25 Penywern Rd., SW5. ☎ 020/7370-6071. www.lordjimhotel.co.uk. 50 units. Doubles £45–£135. AE, MC, V. Tube: Earl's Court. Map p 147.*

★★★ kids **Luna Simone Hotel** VICTORIA Amid the great swamp of cheap accommodation around Victoria Station, the Luna Simone stands head and shoulders above its rivals. The rooms are bijou, but everything within is neat and tidy and the staff is supremely friendly. Refurbished in 2018. *47–49 Belgrave Rd., SW1. ☎ 020/7834-5897. www.lunasimonehotel.com. 36 units. Doubles £104–£155. AE, DC, MC, V. Tube: Victoria. Map p 150.*

★ kids **Morgan Hotel** BLOOMSBURY The family-run Morgan features well-kept Georgian-style rooms. It's an old favorite of Anglophiles who can't get enough of the

The Harlequin Suite at The Dorchester.

nearby British Museum (p 26). *24 Bloomsbury St., WC1. ☎ 020/7636-3735. www.morganhotel.co.uk. 17 units. Doubles £145. MC, V. Tube: Tottenham Court Rd. Map p 151.*

★★ kids **Mowbray Court Hotel** EARL'S COURT This spotless budget hotel features bright, air-conditioned rooms with modern furniture, all refurbished in 2016. Discounts for multinight stays. *28–32 Penywern Rd., SW5. ☎ 020/7373-8285. www.mowbraycourt.com. 90 units. Doubles £67–£135. AE, DC, MC, V. Tube: Earl's Court. Map p 146.*

★ kids **Number Sixteen** SOUTH KENSINGTON This Victorian townhouse hotel with contemporary styling is popular with Americans, quiet, and in a fun neighborhood. *16 Sumner Place, SW7. ☎ 020/7589-5232. www.firmdalehotels.com. 41 units. Doubles £276–£396. AE, DC, MC, V. Tube: S. Kensington. Map p 147.*

★★ kids **Park Plaza County Hall Hotel** SOUTH BANK The cheaper alternative to the Marriott (see above) if you want to stay in the superbly well-located County Hall buildings on the South Bank. Rooms are a good size, and there are plenty of amenities. *1 Addington St., SE1. ☎ 020/7034-4820. www.parkplazacountyhall.com. 399 units. Doubles £104–£205. AE, DC, MC, V. Tube: Waterloo. Map p 151.*

★ kids **Park Plaza Sherlock Holmes Hotel** MARYLEBONE This modern hotel is on Baker Street near the (imaginary) home of the fictional sleuth, but it's hardly Sherlockian in decor. It's a short walk to Regent's Park and Oxford Street. *108 Baker St., W1. ☎ 0844/415-6742. www.parkplazasherlockholmes.com. 119 units. Doubles £111–£237. AE, DC, MC, V. Tube: Baker St. Map p 149.*

★ kids **Phoenix Hotel** BAYSWATER Unshowy convenience, with a good level of business comfort and decor. Location is the major SP: It's a very short walk from the transport links of Paddington and the green open spaces of Hyde Park. *1–8 Kensington Gardens Sq., W2. ☎ 020/7229-2494. www.phoenixhotel.co.uk. 125 units. Doubles £132–£165. AE, MC, V. Tube: Bayswater. Map p 148.*

★★ **Portobello Hotel** NOTTING HILL Sumptuously decorated guest rooms are the hallmark of this small, trendy hotel—a long-standing hit with the music and

The Silk Room at The Goring.

Afternoon tea at The Lanesborough.

modeling set—located near Portobello Road Market. *22 Stanley Gardens, W11. ☎ 020/7727-2777. www.portobellohotel.com. 21 units. Doubles £171–£285. AE, DC, MC, V. Tube: Notting Hill Gate. Map p 148.*

★ kids **The Rembrandt** SOUTH KENSINGTON This solid tourist hotel across from the V&A (p 30) is popular with travelers for its package deals, location, and the free smartphone rental with your room. *11 Thurloe Place, SW7. ☎ 020/7589-8100. www.sarova-rembrandthotel.com. 194 units. Doubles £142–£215. AE, DC, MC, V. Tube: S. Kensington. Map p 147.*

★★ **The Rookery** THE CITY A sure-footed evocation of a grandiose era, the Rookery is set in fashionable Clerkenwell, on the edge of the financial district. Each room is individually decorated with wood panels and rare antiques. *Peter's Lane, Cowcross St., EC1. ☎ 020/7336-0931. www.rookeryhotel.com. 33 units. Doubles £141–£281. AE, DC, MC, V. Tube: Farringdon. Map p 145.*

★★ kids **The Royal Horseguards** WESTMINSTER Right in the heart of royal London, this may be Westminster's best-located hotel. It's less stuffy than you might think—rooms are modern and rather snazzy-looking—but still makes for a quintessentially English experience. *2 Whitehall Court, SW1. ☎ 020/7523-5062. www.guoman.com/theroyalhorseguards. 281 units. Doubles £164–£372. AE, DC, MC, V. Tube: Embankment. Map p 151.*

★★ kids **The Rubens at the Palace** BELGRAVIA Traditional English hospitality combined with the latest creature comforts, just across the road from the Royal Mews. Royal Rooms have richer fabrics and the most atmosphere. *39 Buckingham Palace Rd., SW1. ☎ 020/7834-6600. www.rubenshotel.com. 161 units. Doubles £170–£299. AE, DC, MC, V. Tube: Victoria. Map p 150.*

★★ **Sanderson London** WEST END If glam is your thing, this is the hotel for you. Inside it's all polished steel, lip-shaped sofas, and Philippe Starck furniture. It has a bit of a party vibe, but the rooms are large, quiet, and luxurious, with plenty of opportunities to relax at the spa or Courtyard Garden. *50 Berners St., W1. ☎ 020/7300-1400. www.sandersonlondon.com. 150 units. Doubles £247–£405. AE, MC, V. Tube: Goodge St. Map p 150.*

★★★ **San Domenico House** CHELSEA An exquisite small hotel delivering divine Italian period luxury at its most romantic and English-accented. *29–31 Draycott Place, SW3. ☎ 020/7581-5757. www.sandomenicohouse.com. 19 units. Doubles £179–£244. AE, DC, MC, V. Tube: Sloane Sq. Map p 147.*

★★ kids **The Stafford London** MAYFAIR This gorgeous 18th-century hotel, in the traditional neighborhood of royal tailors, combines English country style with modern amenities. *16–18 St.*

The reception lounge at The Zetter.

James's Place, SW1. ☎ 020/7493-0111. www.thestaffordlondon.com. 81 units. Doubles £296–£505. AE, DC, MC, V. Tube: Green Park. Map p 150.

★★ **Sumner Hotel** MARBLE ARCH One of the West End's best remaining small, reasonably priced hotels, the Sumner is well-loved by clued-in shoppers. *54 Upper Berkeley St., W1. ☎ 020/7723-2244. www.thesumner.com. 20 units. Doubles £105–£242. AE, DC, MC, V. Tube: Marble Arch. Map p 149.*

★★ **Town Hall Hotel** BETHNAL GREEN The opening of this design-tastic place in a former 1910 City Hall further confirmed the East End's status as London's most up-and-coming area. It's as swanky and cool as anything in central London, with Art Deco detailing, a spa and pool, and always one of the hottest restaurants around. *Patriot Sq., E2. ☎ 020/7871-0460. www.townhallhotel.com. 98 units. Doubles £132–£215. AE, MC, V. Tube: Bethnal Green. Map p 145.*

★★ **Twenty Nevern Square** EARL'S COURT Quirky Euro–Asian decor, a full range of amenities, and a garden make this one of London's most appealing and elegant B&Bs. *20 Nevern Sq., SW5. ☎ 020/7565-9555. www.20nevernsquare.mayflowercollection.com. 24 units. Doubles £76–£154. AE, MC, V. Tube: Earl's Court. Map p 146.*

★★★ **The Zetter** CLERKENWELL A great addition to the City's lodging range, the Zetter is artsy and funky—not business-y and dull. The most basic rooms inside this five-story converted Victorian warehouse are a little small, but every unit is tastefully done. Those at the top have panoramic skyline views. *St. John's Sq., 86–88 Clerkenwell Rd., EC1. ☎ 020/7324-4567. www.thezetter.com. 59 units. Doubles £120–£306. AE, MC, V. Tube: Farringdon. Map p 145.* ●

The Savvy Traveler

Before You Go

Tourist Information

Two online-only resources to check before you leave home are Britain's national tourism agency, **VisitBritain** (**www.visitbritain.com**), and London's official visitor guide, **VisitLondon** (**www.visitlondon.com**). You can download PDF brochures, the official Welcome to London Guide and transport maps at **www.visitlondon.com/contact-us**. The **London Official City Guide** is also available free from Android and Apple app stores. The app is constantly updated with offers, including 2-for-1 ticket deals, the latest exhibitions and arts events, and more ideas.

In London, the only official information bureau with a public office is opposite the south side of St. Paul's Cathedral: The **City of London Information Centre** (www.visitthecity.co.uk; ☎ **020/7332-1456**) sells attractions tickets and Oyster cards, runs tours, supplies brochures and walking-tour maps, and offers multilongual travel advice. It's open Monday to Saturday 9:30am to 5:30pm and Sunday 10am to 4pm.

The Best Time to Go

Although prices are highest in spring and summer, the weather is best then (though you should be prepared for showers at any time). Sunny and warm August is a sensible time to visit because that's when many Londoners go on vacation and London's notorious traffic lightens up (slightly). The only problem? All those extra tourists. Fares are cheapest between November and March, Christmas and New Year excepted. The city's museum and theatre scenes are still in full swing in winter, but the city can get dark, chilly, and bleak. September and early October can be gray and rainy, too, but most gardens are still in bloom.

Previous Page: Big Ben.

Festivals & Special Events

JANUARY. The **New Year's Day Parade** (☎ **020/3275-0190;** www.londonparade.co.uk) sees an estimated 10,000 performers march, dance, and play their way through London's streets, from Parliament Square to Green Park, to celebrate the start of the year with what may seem to many inappropriate enthusiasm (particularly if they're still recovering from the night before).

FEBRUARY. **Chinese New Year** is celebrated in Soho's Chinatown with the requisite dancing lions and red confetti. The **Great Spitalfields Pancake Race** (www.alternativearts.co.uk/events) on Shrove Tuesday (called Pancake Day in the U.K.) is a bizarre old tradition that combines tossed pancakes and teams of runners.

MARCH. One of the month's best-loved events is the **Oxford & Cambridge Boat Race** from Putney Bridge to Mortlake (www.theboatrace.org). There are a number of good pubs and vantage points along the 4-mile route, but Hammersmith and Putney bridges are the best places to watch. March also sees London's large Irish community celebrate **St. Patrick's Day** with floats, musicians, plenty of Guinness, and a nonstop party from Hyde Park to Trafalgar Square.

APRIL. Tens of thousands of people compete in the **London Marathon** (www.virginmoneylondonmarathon.com) every year. The 26-mile course runs from Greenwich Park to St.

James's Park. The best views are from Victoria Embankment.

MAY. A difficult ticket to get hold of, the **Chelsea Flower Show** (☎ **020/3176-5800;** www.rhs.org.uk) is a wonderful spectacle, packed with creative garden displays.

JUNE. The **Royal Academy Summer Exhibition** (www.royalacademy.org.uk), the world's largest public art display, showcases the works of artists of every genre and caliber. It runs through mid-August. **The Queen's Official Birthday** (Elizabeth II was actually born in April) is honored with a carriage ride, a gun salute, and **Trooping the Colour** at Horse Guards Parade (www.royal.uk/queens-birthday). On **London Open Weekend** (www.opensquares.org), a number of gardens usually available only to private key-holders are opened to an envious public. **Royal Ascot** (www.ascot.co.uk/royal-ascot) is the big social horse event of the year, a time when the upper classes dust off their chapeaus and take part in the old tradition of betting on horses while dressed to the nines. The **Lawn Tennis Championships at Wimbledon** (☎ **020/8971-2473;** www.wimbledon.com) need no introduction, but you will require a very-hard-to-get ticket (see "Spectator Sports," later in this chapter).

JULY. **The Proms** (☎ **020/7589-8212;** www.bbc.co.uk/proms), formally known as the BBC Sir Henry Wood Promenade Concerts, held in and outside the Royal Albert Hall, are the annual joy of London's classical music lovers. The season runs mid-July to mid-September. **Pride Parades** are now held across the country, but the capital's version, held on the first or second Sunday in July, is still the biggest event in the gay party calendar. The flamboyant procession heads from Baker Street to Trafalgar Square (www.prideinlondon.org).

AUGUST. The **Notting Hill Carnival** (www.thelondonnottinghillcarnival.com), the largest street festival in Europe, is held in and around Portobello Road. Expect crowds, beer, music, and spicy Caribbean cuisine.

SEPTEMBER. During the 2-day **Open House** (www.openhouselondon.org.uk), hundreds of usually inaccessible architectural gems are opened to the public. At the 125-year-old **Pearly Kings & Queens Harvest Festival** (www.pearlysociety.co.uk), the descendants of London's cockney costermongers (market traders) dress in costumes covered with pearly buttons and gather at a church service at St. Paul's Covent Garden for charity—and to show off their button-sewing prowess. Floats and carriages make their way from Mansion House to the Royal Courts of Justice and back again during the **Lord Mayor's Show** (www.lordmayorsshow.london).

NOVEMBER. **Guy Fawkes Night** commemorates the thwarted destruction of Parliament with bonfires and fireworks all over London. Book a couple of spins on the London Eye (p 11, ❺) after dark so you can see London's sky lit up from near and far.

DECEMBER. For the horse-mad, there is no better fun than the **International Show-jumping Championships** (☎ **0115/896-1532;** www.olympiahorseshow.com) in Kensington. Thousands of Londoners see in the **New Year** by finding vantage points for the spectacular fireworks display that takes place on and around the London Eye as Big Ben's bongs sound. The closest spots, including Westminster and Waterloo bridges, require a ticket; buy yours online at **www.london.gov.uk/events**.

LONDON'S AVERAGE TEMPERATURE & RAINFALL

	JAN	FEB	MAR	APR	MAY	JUNE
Daily Temp (°F)	43	44	50	55	63	68
Daily Temp (°C)	6	7	10	13	17	20
Avg.Rainfall (in./mm)	3/54	1.5/40	1.5/37	1.5/37	1.8/46	1.8/45
	JULY	**AUG**	**SEPT**	**OCT**	**NOV**	**DEC**
Daily Temp (°F)	72	70	66	57	50	44
Daily Temp (°C)	22	21	19	14	10	7
Avg. Rainfall (in./mm)	2.2/57	2.3/59	1.9/49	2.2/57	2.5/64	1.9/48

The Weather

London's notorious (man-made) pea-soup fogs have long been eradicated, but a tendency toward showers and gray skies is ever-present—particularly November through March, when the sun shows its face only briefly. The weather can be fickle, and experiencing all four seasons in the span of a single day is common in all seasons except winter. The general climate is relatively mild, never going much above 75°F (24°C) or below 40°F (4°C). There are no great extremes, except for a few unpleasant dog days in summer (when a temperature of 80°F/27°C is considered a heat wave) and a snowfall or two during the short, dark days of a bleak midwinter.

For the local London forecast, go to **uk.weather.com** for up-to-date weather information.

Useful Websites

- **www.londontown.com**: Offers specials on hotels, sells theater tickets, and has lots of good information.
- **www.royal.uk**: If you're a royal watcher, or are just looking for information, trivia, or anything else about the British royal family, direct your browser to this site.
- **www.tfl.gov.uk**: London Transport's website is the source of information on London's public transportation system, including the Tube, buses, and ferries.
- **www.standard.co.uk**: The London *Evening Standard*'s website is a good source of current entertainment and restaurant reviews.
- **www.timeout.com/london**: The weekly magazine has cultural event listings, as well as information on entertainment, restaurants, and nightlife.
- **www.visitbritain.com**: Great Britain's official tourist website features lots of helpful information and trip-planning advice.
- **www.visitlondon.com**: London's official website features loads of information and lets you book hotels, buy discount passes, and more.

Cellphones

If you have a GSM phone, you can make and receive calls in London, though you will accrue whopping roaming charges.

International visitors can buy a pay-as-you-go cellphone (or, if you have an unlocked GSM phone, a SIM-only tariff) at any phone store in London. This gives you a local number and minutes that can be topped up with phone cards purchased at news agents. EE and Vodafone are probably the best service networks.

Your hotel may be able to rent you a cellphone while in London, though it won't be cheap; inquire before you arrive. North Americans can rent one before leaving home from **InTouch USA** (☎ **800/872-7626;** www.intouchusa.us).

Car Rentals

In a word: Don't. Driving in London is a royal pain and I strongly recommend against it. You're far better off sticking to public transportation, when you take into account the congestion fee (a charge of £11.50 for entering a large area of the city from 7am–6pm), the dreadful traffic, the dearth of street parking, and the astronomical price of fuel. If you still want to rent a vehicle, all major car-rental companies operate in the U.K., and cars can be picked up at any of London's airports.

Getting There

By Plane

Air Canada, American, British Airways, Continental, Delta, Northwest, United, and Virgin Atlantic Airways offer nonstop service from various locations in the U.S. and Canada to London's major airports. Qantas offers a daily service to London from Sydney and Melbourne.

London is served by five airports. **London Heathrow Airport** (☎ **020/3368-8968;** www.heathrow.com), located 15 miles west of London, is the largest. The fastest way into town is the **Heathrow Express** train (☎ www.heathrowexpress.com) to Paddington Station (15 min.; £27, £22–£25 if booked online in advance). The **Heathrow Connect** train (www.heathrowconnect.com) also goes to Paddington. It's slower (30 min.) and less frequent, but much cheaper (£11). You can take an even cheaper ride on the **Tube**'s Piccadilly Line into Central London (50 min.; £5). Black taxi cabs cost roughly £50 to £80 to the city center. Ride services including **Uber** are allowed to operate at London airports, including Heathrow, but must pick up from designated zones.

The city's second airport, **Gatwick** (www.gatwickairport.com) is 25 miles south of London. The fastest way to get to the city is via the **Gatwick Express** train (www.gatwickexpress.com) to Victoria Station (30 min.; £20, £18 online in advance). The slower but cheaper **ThamesLink** train (www.thameslinkrailway.com; 40–50 min.; £11) connects with London Bridge and St. Pancras Stations. The cheapest but slowest connection is the **Easy-Bus** (www.easybus.com; 1¼ hr.; £2–£6) to West Brompton Station. A **taxi ride** into London usually takes an hour, and can cost more than £125.

Stansted (www.stanstedairport.com) and **Luton** (www.london-luton.co.uk) airports handle mostly short-hop flights on bargain airlines (often easyJet and Ryanair) from European and U.K. destinations. Both are more than 30 miles from London. To get from Stansted to the city, take a **Stansted Express** train (www.stanstedexpress.com) to Liverpool Street Station (45 min.; £17). From Luton, take **Greenline bus no. 757** (☎ **0344/801-7261;** www.greenline.co.uk) to Victoria Station (1–1½ hr.; £11). **National Express** (www.nationalexpress.com) operates a similar Luton service.

The fifth and final airport, **London City** (☎ **020/7646-0088;** www.londoncityairport.com) is by far the smallest and the only one actually in Greater London. It services mainly business travelers. **DLR** trains run every 8 to 10 minutes to Bank Tube Station (22 min.; £3–£5). A taxi to the center of town costs around £30 to £40.

By Train

The **Eurostar** provides direct train services between Paris (2¼ hr.) or Brussels (2 hr.) and London's St. Pancras Station in King's Cross. In London, make reservations for Eurostar at ☎ **0343/218-6186.** (From outside the U.K., call +44 1777/777-879.) You can make advance train reservations from any country at **www.eurostar.com**. King's Cross/St. Pancras has six Tube line connections (Piccadilly, Circle, Hammersmith & City, Metropolitan, Northern, and Victoria), as well as overland trains connecting to the north and Scotland. Buses and taxis are readily available just outside the station.

National Rail trains (☎ **03457/48-49-50;** www.nationalrail.co.uk) connect just about every major city in the U.K. to one of London's major rail stations (Charing Cross, Liverpool Street, Paddington, Victoria, King's Cross, Waterloo, London Bridge, and Euston). All major train stations in Central London have Tube stations and offer easy access to buses and taxis.

By Bus

Bus connections to Britain from the Continent, using the Channel Tunnel (Chunnel) or ferry services, are generally not very comfortable and take as long as 8 hours, but you can get a round-trip to Paris for as little as £38. Do check ahead to make sure your bus has a bathroom onboard; some do not. The long-haul buses of **National Express** (☎ **0871/781-8178;** www.nationalexpress.com) traveling within the U.K. and to the Continent generally use centrally located Victoria Coach Station as their terminus. The bus station is on the corner of Buckingham Palace Road and Elizabeth Street, a few minutes' walk from the main Victoria Station, serviced by Sputhern, Southeastern, Gatwick Express, and London Underground trains, and a stop on the Underground's District and Circle lines. Victoria Station has a taxi stand and is the terminus for many local city buses.

Getting Around

Discounted Travel

Explaining the prices and passes for London's public transport is a Byzantine exercise worthy of a *Monty Python* skit. Sorting through prices for 1-day and 7-day passes, the rules for different ages of children, prices with and without museum discount passes, peak and off-peak travel time, and the different costs of tickets among the outer travel zones in London is exceedingly complicated. Worse, the system is always trying new "improvements" in the vain hope of softening the blow of a basic £4.90 one-way paper Tube ticket in central Zones 1 and 2, even while plotting the latest fare increase. If you want the very latest news, and the opportunity to grasp the latest twist in pricing and discounted travel, settle in for a long read at the excellent **Transport for London** website at **www.tfl.gov.uk**.

Fortunately, however, you can cut right through all these variables with the efficient and penny-wise

Oyster, a prepaid, reusable, refillable smartcard that deducts the cost of a trip each time you touch your card to the yellow card reader found on all public transportation, including trams and buses, the Docklands Light Railway (DLR), Overground rail lines (marked in orange on a map), and regular rail. You pay a one-time, refundable charge of £5 for the plastic Oyster card. They can be purchased at any Tube station (including Heathrow Airport stations) or ordered online. It is not necessary to register the card. To retrieve the £5 card deposit plus any money left on it, simply present it at any Tube station and they will refund your money on the spot. Alternatively, you can pay for your travel with Apple Pay or Android Pay, or a contactless credit or debit card, including American Express. Prices are identical to using the physical Oyster card. You swipe your card or NFC-enabled phone on the yellow reader in the exact same way.

With Oyster's discounted fares, you save from your very first trip: £2.40 for a one-way, off-peak Tube trip in Zones 1 and 2, rising to £3.10 for travel between Zones 1 and 6.

Another nice feature is that paying by Oyster, smartphone, or contactless card tops out each day at a set maximum price: The cap on Oyster charges per day on buses is £4.50; on Tube trips in Zones 1–2 it's £6.80 (Zones 1–4 caps out at £9.80). For more information, check out **https://oyster.tfl.gov.uk**.

You can top up the balance on an Oyster Card at machines (using cash or credit cards) in Underground stations or at any small store displaying the blue Oyster logo in the window or by the checkout.

Under almost every circumstance, **there is no need to buy a 1- or 7-day paper Travelcard.** Use an Oyster or another form of contactless/NFC payment device—card or smartphone—instead. It's easier and much cheaper.

Tickets for Kids

There are no "family tickets" on London public transportation. However, there are many discounts and lots of free travel available for kids. Children 4 and under travel free everywhere. Up to four children aged 5 to 10 accompanied by a paying adult travel free on bus, Tube, DLR, Overground, some regular rail, and all tram services.

With children ages 11 to 15, make ensure their Oyster card has the **Young Visitor discount** activated. Tube station ticket-window staff and TfL Visitor Centre staff can do this free of charge. The Young Visitor discount ensures that your 11 to 15s pay half-fare on pretty much everything, and also have daily fare caps fixed at half the adult rate. The Young Visitor discount remains active for 14 days. For more details, see **www.tfl.gov.uk/fares-and-payments**.

By Underground (Tube)

The world's first subterranean train system (known today as the Underground or **Tube**) was born in London in 1863. Stifling, overpopulated cars, sudden mysterious stops, and arbitrary line closures make the Tube the sacred monster of London's commuters. Love it or loathe it, it's the lifeblood of the city, and its 11 lines (plus the Docklands Light Railway to Greenwich and the London Overground network covering much of eastern and southern suburbia) are usually the quickest way to get from A to B.

All Tube stations are clearly marked with a red circle and blue crossbar. Routes are color-coded. The Tube runs daily, except Christmas Day, from around 5:30am to

12:30am (until around 11:30pm Sun), except on Friday and Saturday when a limited **Night Tube** service runs on some lines. At time of writing, services were operating every 10 to 20 minutes through the night on the Jubilee, Victoria, Central, and Piccadilly lines, as well as the London Overground through East London, including nightlife hotspots Shoreditch and Dalston. For other routes, you must take a night bus or taxi (see below).

Tube fares start at £4.90 for a single journey without an Oyster card in Zones 1 and 2 (the ones most frequented by tourists). The same journey costs £2.40 if you pay via Oyster, contactless card, or Apple/Android Pay. You can buy a ticket or Oyster from a machine inside the Tube station (most take credit cards) or from a clerk at a ticket window. Insert your ticket it into the turnstile, and then retrieve it and hold onto it—it must be reinserted into the turnstile or presented to a clerk when you exit the station at your destination or you'll pay a fine of £20; repeat offenders can get hit with as much as a £1,000 fine. Oyster, contactless card, or smartphone travelers should touch the yellow reader to open the gate, and always touch the card as they leave the station (even if there is no gate) or the maximum charge may be applied.

Study a Tube map (available online and at most major Tube stations), or even consult the paper *London A to Z* street atlas (still at any London bookstore or newsstand), to find the stop nearest your destination. Note that you may have to switch lines in order to get from one destination to another. The **Citymapper** smartphone app is indispensable for plotting the most efficient route. For more information on the Tube, check out **www.tfl.gov.uk**.

By Bus

The city's bus system has many advantages over the Tube: With the bus lanes and the (slight) reduction in traffic from the city's congestion, above-ground travel is almost as efficient as the Underground. It also costs about half as much as the Tube for adults—particularly as it's a flat fare right across town—and is completely free for children under 16 (provided they have the appropriate card; see above), offering the potential for big savings for large family groups. And, it has to be said, you get far better views of the city from buses than from Tubes. The city's red double-decker buses are a tourist attraction in their own right. Route maps are available at major Tube stations (Euston, Victoria, and Piccadilly Circus, to name a few) or online at **www.tfl.gov.uk**.

Fares are a flat-rate £1.50 per adult per journey, regardless of its length, but you **must** pay with an Oyster, contactless card, smartphone, or Travelcard. You touch your card or phone against the reader when you board the bus, but not when you disembark. You can also change buses once within 1 hour without paying extra (you still touch the reader on the second bus, but you won't be charged). Remember to touch your card or phone to one of the yellow card readers on the bus, or you may be fined £20. Inspectors often board buses to catch fare evaders.

Buses are cashless and there are no single tickets or ticket machines. A full day of bus fares caps out at £4.50, no matter how many rides you take. Most children ride free; see "Tickets for Kids," above.

Night buses are the only way to get to most of the city by public transport after the Tube stops operating. Be sure there is an "N" bus listed on your bus stop's route or you'll wait in vain until morning.

The **London Bus Checker** app is an essential tool for bus travel, with route planning and real-time departure updates for all London bus stops.

By Taxi or Ride Service

All airports and train stations have well-marked areas for London's legendary black cabs, many of which are now colored with advertising but still the same distinctive model that holds five people. You can hail a licensed taxi anywhere, on any street, except in certain no-stopping zones marked by red lines along the curb. Available taxis will have a lit sign on top of the cab. Taxis can also be requested by phone or app (**MyTaxi** and **Gett** both offer up licensed taxis).

Only black cabs, whose drivers have undergone rigorous training known as "the Knowledge," are allowed to cruise the streets for fares. Don't get into cruising minicabs, which can legally pick up only those passengers who have booked them by telephone. Black cabs have metered fares (the minimum fare is £2.60, even though the average fare is now likely at least £15), and surcharges are assessed after 8pm and on weekends. Minicab charges should be negotiated in advance.

To book a black cab by phone, call **Dial-a-Cab** (☎ **020/7253-5000;** www.dialacab.co.uk). For a licensed minicab, a popular choice is **Addison Lee** (www.addisonlee.com), including for fixed-fare airport transfers. Ride service **Uber** also operates all over London, though it has been subject to taxi-driver protests and conflict with the city's transportation regulator. Still, Uber's attractive fares have attracted Londoners en masse. Food delivery service **UberEats** also operates in London.

Fast Facts

APARTMENT RENTALS Alongside the usual global names, **Central London Apartments** (☎ **01524/544-243;** www.central-london-apartments.com) offers serviced apartments in various locations throughout the city. **Home from Home** (☎ **020/7233-8111;** www.homefromhome.co.uk) has a good website that displays all kinds of apartments in numerous London neighborhoods.

ATMS Also known locally as "cashpoints" or "holes in the wall," ATMs are everywhere, and most use global networks such as Cirrus and Plus. Note that you may be charged a fee by your bank for withdrawing pounds from your home currency account.

BABYSITTING Reputable babysitting agencies with vetted employees include **Sitters** (☎ **01202/713-911;** www.sitters.co.uk) and **Universal Aunts** (☎ **020/7738-8937;** www.universalaunts.co.uk). Rates are about £9 per hour during the day and £8 per hour in the evening. Hotel guests must usually pay a booking fee (around £6) and reasonable transportation costs.

BANKING HOURS Most banks are open Monday through Friday from 9am to 5pm; some also have limited Saturday open hours.

BIKE RENTALS Cycling opportunities have increased dramatically since the launch of London's bike-sharing program, now known as **Santander Cycles**—but more popularly known as "the Boris Bikes" after the former mayor, who oversaw the scheme's introduction in 2010. Anyone can hire a bike from one of hundreds of docking stations dotted across town. You can return the bike to any station, making the rental perfect for short trips. Charges are made up of a fixed access fee—£2 per day—and a usage fee—it's free for 30 minutes, and an extra £2 for each 30-minute period thereafter. Buy access with a credit or debit card at the docking station or join online at **https://santandercycles.tfl.gov.uk**. The official app will help you locate the nearest docking stations. At time of writing, newer "dockless" cycle-sharing schemes were also launching, including Singapore's **oBike**, plus **Ofo** and **Mobike** (both Chinese-owned). **London Bicycle Tour Company,** Gabriel's Wharf, South Bank (☎ **020/7928-6838;** www.londonbicycle.com) rents a wide variety of bikes. Rates start at £3.50 per hour and £20 per day (£40 for 3 days).

BUSINESS HOURS Stores generally open at 9am and close around 6pm Monday through Saturday, though they may stay open until 7 or 8pm one night a week (usually Thurs). Sunday opening hours are typically 11am or noon to 5pm, though some places may open longer. Post offices are open 9am to 5:30pm on weekdays.

CLIMATE See "The Weather," earlier in this chapter.

CONSULATES & EMBASSIES **American Embassy,** 24 Grosvenor Sq. (☎ **020/7499-9000;** https://uk.usembassy.gov). **Canadian High Commission,** Canada House, 1 Trafalgar Sq. (☎ **020/7004-6000;** www.canadainternational.gc.ca). **Australian High Commission,** Australia House, Strand (☎ **020/7379-4334;** www.uk.embassy.gov.au). **Irish Embassy,** 17 Grosvenor Place (☎ **020/7235-2171;** www.embassyofireland.co.uk). **New Zealand High Commission,** New Zealand House, 80 Haymarket (☎ **020/7930-8422;** www.mfat.govt.nz).

CUSTOMS Check **www.gov.uk/duty-free-goods** for what foreign visitors may bring into London. For specifics on what you can bring home with you, check with your own country's customs authority.

DENTISTS **Emergency Dentist London:** Branches at 102 Baker St. and three other locations (☎ **020/8748-9365;** www.24hour-emergencydentist.co.uk) offer 24-hour emergency dental service.

DINING Breakfasts range from the traditional "full English" of fried eggs, bacon, sausage, beans, grilled tomato, and toast to a more Continental menu of croissants, baguettes, and coffee. If your hotel doesn't include breakfast in its rates, going to a cafe instead will likely be cheaper. Most cafes are open from 8am to 8pm. Most restaurants open for lunch from noon to 3pm, and for dinner from 6 to 10 or 11pm. Dress codes have become much more relaxed, and except at very expensive restaurants and a few hotel dining rooms, no one will raise an eyebrow at casual clothing. You will encounter general disapproval if you bring small children to the fanciest restaurants, especially at dinnertime.

Many London restaurants take reservations through **www.opentable.co.uk** (or its app). You can also ask your hotel's concierge for help when you arrive, or when you call to reserve a room.

DOCTORS A number of on-call doctor services can treat you and dispense medicine at your lodgings, or you can go to them. **Doctorcall,** 121 Harley St.

(☎ **0844/257-0345;** www.doctorcall.co.uk), makes house calls.

ELECTRICITY Britain uses a 220–240 volt system and alternating current (AC); its electrical plugs have three pins. European appliances will require only a plug adapter, but American 110-volt appliances will need both a transformer and an adapter or they will fry and blow a fuse. Most laptops, phones, and tablets have built-in electrical transformers, but will need an adapter plug.

EMERGENCIES Call ☎ **999** for accidents and dire medical emergencies free of charge from any phone. Hospitals with emergency rooms (known as Accident and Emergency departments, or A&E) in Central London include **University College Hospital,** 235 Euston Rd. (☎ **020/3456-7890**), **Chelsea & Westminster Hospital,** 369 Fulham Rd., Chelsea (☎ **020/3315-8000**), **St. Mary's Hospital,** Praed St., Paddington (☎ **020/3312-6666**), and **St. Thomas's Hospital,** Westminster Bridge Rd., Lambeth (☎ **020/7188-7188**).

FAMILY TRAVEL Look for items tagged with a **kids** icon in this book. Most British hotels accommodate families, and all but the poshest restaurants are usually family-friendly. **Visit London** has a section on its website dedicated to families (www.visitlondon.com/attractions/family) that provides information on family-friendly attractions, events, and restaurants, and offers discounts on various goods and services.

HOLIDAYS Bank holidays, on which some shops, most museums and all banks, public buildings, and services are closed, are as follows: New Year's Day, Good Friday (Fri before Easter), Easter Monday, May Day (first Mon in May), Spring Bank Holiday (last Mon in May), August Bank Holiday (last Mon in Aug), Christmas Day, and Boxing Day (Dec 26). These days, only Christmas Day sees near-total retail shutdown.

INSURANCE Check your existing insurance policies and credit card coverage before buying travel insurance. You may already be covered for lost luggage, canceled tickets, or medical expenses. If you aren't covered, expect to pay 5% to 8% of your trip's cost for insurance.

INTERNET Free Wi-Fi is ever more prevalent, including in most hotels. Cafe chains **Costa Coffee** (www.costa.co.uk), **Pret a Manger** (www.pret.com), and **Starbucks** (www.starbucks.co.uk) offer free Wi-Fi to customers, as do most indie coffee shops. Almost 350 Tube and Overground stations also have Wi-Fi. Though the number of cybercafes has shrunk massively, you'll still find them on many neighborhood high streets. To locate one near you, check out **www.londononline.co.uk/Cybercafes/**.

LGBT TRAVELERS London has one of the most active LGBT scenes in the world. The **Visit London** website (www.visitlondon.com) provides advice on everything from LGBT-friendly lodging to bars and other entertainment.

LOST PROPERTY Be sure to tell all your credit card companies the minute you discover your wallet has been lost or stolen, and file a report at the nearest police station (your insurance company may require a police report before covering any claims). If you've lost all forms of photo ID, call your consulate and airline and explain the situation. It's always best to keep copies of your credit card numbers and passport information in a separate location in case you lose the real items.

Property lost on London public transport (buses, Tube, and taxis) is collected by the **TFL Lost Property Office,** 200 Baker St. (☎ **0343/222-1234**); your first stop should be the enquiry form on their website at **https://tfl.gov.uk/help-and-contact/lost-property**. If you've lost something on an overland train, call the main terminal that serves the train on which you lost your property, or call the above number for help.

LUGGAGE STORAGE If you are staying in an Airbnb or similar, you can store your luggage at a growing number of places across London. Try searching **LuggageHero** (www.luggagehero.com) or **CityStasher** (www.citystasher.com) to find a convenient location. Expect to pay a few pounds per bag, including insurance. Major rail stations usually have a "left luggage" service, too.

MAIL & POSTAGE Stamps for a small letter mailed inside the U.K. cost 65p for first class and 56p for second class. Postage for postcards and letters sent outside the U.K. costs £1.02. You can pay for and print out postage at **www.royalmail.com**. Many newsagents carry stamps, and the city's distinctive red mailboxes are plentiful. The central post office by Trafalgar Square, at 24 William IV St., is open from 8:30am to 6:30pm Monday to Friday, and 9am to 5:30pm Saturday.

MONEY Unlike many of its neighbors, the U.K. maintains its own currency, the pound sterling: £1 consists of 100 pence (pennies). There are 1- and 2-pound coins; silvery 50p, 20p, 10p, and 5p coins; and copper 2p and 1p coins. Banknotes are issued in denominations of £50 (red), £20 (lavender), £10 (orange), and £5 (blue).

Foreign money can be exchanged at most banks and bureaux de change, but you'll be assessed a hefty surcharge or get terrible conversion rates. If you want to arrive with a few pounds in hand, get them from your bank before you leave home. ATMs (known locally as "cashpoints") are located all over the city and offer the best exchange rates; find out your daily withdrawal limit before you leave home. At the time of writing, £1 was worth $1.34. For the most up-to-date currency conversion information, go to **www.xe.com**.

Many stores in London will not take traveler's checks, and those that do often charge stiff fees. It's best to stick to cash and credit cards, though most banks assess a 2% fee above the 1% fee charged by Visa, MasterCard, or American Express for currency conversions. ***Note:*** Be sure to notify your credit card companies before leaving for London, so they don't become suspicious when the card is used overseas and block your account.

PARKING Parking in London is difficult, even for those who have paid for a resident parking permit (yet another reason not to drive here). Metered spaces have time limits of 1 to 4 hours and are hard to find.

Garages (parking lots) are expensive, but plentiful. Look for signs that read **NCP** (for National Car Parks); check **www.ncp.co.uk** for locations and more information.

Always check any warning signs on streets for info on temporary parking suspensions. Parking violations are punished with a hefty fine, tire clamping, or the removal of your car to an impound lot. If your car has been towed, call ☎ **0845/206-8602.**

PASSES The **London Pass** (www.londonpass.com) incorporates free admission to several of London's highest-priced attractions, as well

as an open-top bus tour and other useful discounts. Pass package prices are as follows: 1 day £66 adults, £49 children; 3 days £109 adults, £79 children; 6 days £149 adults, £109 children. You don't need the London Pass for most museums, because they are free. However, you will save quite a lot of money if you cram high-profile, fee-charging attractions into your time here. For example, it's comfortable to see the Tower of London, Westminster Abbey, St. Paul's Cathedral, the Shard, Shakespeare's Globe, and Kensington Palace within 3 days. Entry to just those 6 costs almost £120, versus £109 for those plus much, much more with the London Pass. On the other hand, the total cost of admission to the British Museum, Tate Modern, V&A, Natural History Museum, National Gallery, and Wallace Collection is zero. As a rule of thumb, if you like sights and historic buildings, think seriously about the London Pass. If you prefer art and museums, it's unlikely to represent a good value.
Note, the **London Pass + Oyster** option costs an extra £5 in admin fees over arranging an Oyster yourself (which is easy).

PASSPORTS Citizens of the U.S., Canada, Ireland, Australia, and New Zealand need only a valid passport to enter the U.K.

Always make a copy of your passport's information page and keep it separate from your passport in case of loss or theft. For emergency passport replacement, contact your country's embassy or consulate (see "Consulates & Embassies," on p 168).

PHARMACIES Known here as "chemists," each can fill a valid doctor's prescription. **Zafash Pharmacy,** 233–235 Old Brompton Rd., Earls Court (☎ **020/7373-2798;** www.zafash.co.uk), is open 24 hours. The leading drugstore chain in the U.K., **Boots** (www.boots.com), has branches all over London.

SAFETY London has its share of violent crime, just as any other major city does—its biggest crime-related problems are public intoxication and muggings—but it is usually quite safe for visitors, as long as you take common-sense precautions. Good safety tips include:

- Use your hotel safe.
- Be alert when withdrawing money from ATMs; don't take out more cash than you need, and don't carry around large sums.
- Guard your valuables in public places and keep your wallet in an inner pocket. Pickpockets operate in all the major tourist zones.
- Don't leave pocketbooks dangling from chairs in restaurants or cafes; use a purse that closes securely.
- Avoid conspicuous displays of expensive jewelry.
- Avoid the upper decks of buses late at night. Take a cab if you can afford it.
- Stay alert in high-end shopping areas: Bags from luxury shops are a tip-off to thieves.
- There's safety in numbers—don't wander alone very late at night. And stay out of parks after dark.
- Don't hop in a minicab hailed off the street. Stick to official black cabs (p 167) or licensed services such as Uber.

SENIOR TRAVELERS Discounts (concessions) for seniors over 64 are available (with proof of age) for museums and some entertainment.

SMOKING Smoking is prohibited in shops, all public transportation, and all public buildings. It's also forbidden inside restaurants, pubs, and bars (although these may have dedicated outside smoking areas). Tobacco is expensive in the U.K., so if you smoke, bring your cigarettes from home or buy them in the airport duty-free shop.

SPECTATOR SPORTS London is crazy for football (that's soccer to you Americans) and is home to several professional teams. One of the best places to watch the English lose their decorum (although tickets are hard to come by) is at **Arsenal Football Club,** Emirates Stadium, Drayton Park (☎ **020/7619-5000;** www.arsenal.com). Wear red and you'll fit right in. For a more genteel (albeit confusing) experience, try watching a cricket match at the sport's most hallowed field, **Lords Cricket Club,** St. John's Wood Rd. (☎ **020/7432-81000;** www.lords.org).

The most sacred annual London sporting event is June's **Lawn Tennis Championships at Wimbledon** (☎ **020/8971-2473**; www.wimbledon.com). Check the website for details on how to enter your name for the annual December ticket lottery. Same-day seats to the outside courts are available, but you'll wait in very long lines.

TAXES A 20% value-added tax (VAT) is added on hotel bills and restaurant checks, merchandise, and most services. Non–E.U. visitors are eligible for partial VAT refunds (for details, see p 84). Note that price tags on items in stores already include the VAT (except in some antique shops). Gasoline (petrol) in Britain is further taxed via a Fuel Duty, making it very expensive.

TAXIS See "By Taxi," on p 167.

TELEPHONES London's city code is **020,** but you don't need to dial it within city limits; just dial the eight-digit number. To call London from the rest of the U.K., you must dial the 020 followed by the number. When calling London from abroad, dial the international code (011 from North America, 0011 from Australia, and 00 from New Zealand), followed by 44 (England's country code), followed by 20, and then the eight-digit number.

When calling abroad from London, dial 00, the country code, the area code, and then the number. Directory assistance in London can be reached by calling ☎ **118 180,** but try to dial numbers direct, because connection costs through directory assistance companies are high.

TICKETS See Chapter 8.

TIPPING Tipping is much less common in the U.K. than in many other countries (notably the U.S.). It is not usual to tip chambermaids (though you may certainly do so), bartenders in pubs, or taxi drivers—unless they've helped you with your luggage, in which case a 10% tip should suffice. Hairdressers should be tipped 10%. Hotel porters should get £1 per bag; doormen should get £1 for hailing you a cab. Check restaurant checks for an automatic service charge, which usually runs around 10% to 15%. If service hasn't been included, tip your waiter 10% to 15%, as long as you feel the service merited it. You aren't expected to tip at a pub unless table service is provided.

TOILETS Clean public toilets can be found in most shopping centers and major railway and Tube stations. Some are free, though some charge around 30p for use. Pubs and hotels don't get too fussy if you discreetly nip in to use the loo (especially if you buy a drink first).

Department stores have public restrooms, usually stashed on high floors to discourage traffic. For more information on public restrooms (loos), see p 64.

TOURIST OFFICES Most visitor information resource these days goes into maintaining the excellent **Visit London** website at **www.visitlondon.com**. There is one official walk-in **City Information Centre** just opposite the south side of St. Paul's Cathedral (Tube: St. Paul's). It has information in eight languages, useful leaflets, maps, and an event ticket booking service, as well as free Wi-Fi. It's open Monday to Saturday from 9:30am to 6:30pm, Sunday 10am to 4pm.

TOURIST TRAPS & SCAMS Some of the half-price theatre-ticket shops around Soho are rip-offs (they tag on a heavy commission for poor seats), and most tickets sold on the street are counterfeit; use only the official half-price ticket booth (**tkts,** p 139) at the south end of Leicester Square or official online sellers. Don't buy from street peddlers selling perfume and accessories. See "Safety," above.

TOURS Two similar companies offer good orientation tours of the city from the vantage of a double-decker bus: **London Big Bus** (☎ **020/7808-6753;** www.bigbustours.com) and **Original London Sightseeing Tour** (☎ **020/8877-1722;** www.theoriginaltour.com). Tickets, good for 24 hours, allow visitors to hop on and off buses that stop at most of Central London's major attractions (buses run every 15–30 min.). Both companies' tours cost in the region of £32 and take 2–3 hours; audio commentary is available in a number of languages and there's free Wi-Fi. The ticket also includes a themed walking tour.

Black Taxi Tours of London (☎ **020/7935-9363;** www.blacktaxitours.co.uk) offers personalized 2-hour tours in a genuine black cab for up to five people for £150. The cabs can venture where buses cannot, making it easier to get off the tourist trail.

For walking tours of London geared to particular interests or themes, you can't do better than **London Walks** (☎ **020/7624-3978;** www.walks.com). Expert guides lead visitors on tours ranging from ghost walks to strolls through literary London to historic pub crawls. Walks cost £10 each. **CityGuides** (www.cityoflondonguides.com) offers themed walks of the Square Mile, London's oldest neighborhood, daily at 11am and 2pm. The meeting point is the City Information Centre (no prebooking needed). It costs £7 per person.

If you want to tour London via the Thames, **City Cruises** (☎ **020/7740-0400;** www.citycruises.com) runs sightseeing trips in modern riverboats equipped with audio commentary in eight languages. Tours depart from Westminster, London Eye, Tower, and Greenwich pier and range in duration from 30 minutes to 2½ hours.

Many museums and royal palaces offer daily gallery talks and themed tours inspired by the various objects in their collections. They're often free: Check individual museum websites.

TRAVELERS WITH DISABILITIES Most of London's major museums are fitted with wheelchair ramps, as are almost all buses. Discount (or free) admission ticket for travelers with disabilities are offered by many attractions and theatres. **Tourism for All** (☎ **01539/726-111;** www.tourismforall.org.uk) offers loads of information and advice for travelers with disabilities visiting Britain. Visitors with disabilities planning to travel via public transportation should consult the excellent dedicated section of the **Transport for London** website (http://tfl.gov.uk/transport-accessibility) for downloadable access maps, guides, and other advice.

VAT See "Taxes," above.

A Brief **History**

A.D. 43 Romans invade England and settle Londinium.

61 Queen Boadicea sacks Londinium in a brutal but unsuccessful rebellion against Rome.

200 Romans fortify the city with a wall.

410 Roman troops abandon London as their Empire falls.

600 King Ethelbert builds first St. Paul's Church on ruins of Temple of Diana.

800 Vikings raid Britain.

885 Alfred the Great captures London from the Vikings.

1042 Edward the Confessor is crowned king of England and begins work on Westminster Abbey.

1066 William the Conqueror is crowned king of England in Westminster Abbey after the Battle of Hastings. London becomes seat of political power.

1078 Construction of the Tower of London begins.

1176–1209 London Bridge is built, the first permanent stone crossing linking the two banks of the Thames.

1192 Henry FitzAilwin is elected first lord mayor of London.

1215 Magna Carta is signed by King John.

1240 First Parliament is convened at Westminster.

1348 First outbreak of the Black Death plagues London.

1381 Wat Tyler's Peasant Revolt is mercilessly crushed.

1476 William Caxton, the first English printer, revolutionizes English printing and makes Fleet Street the country's publishing center.

1599 Shakespeare's first play is performed at the Globe Theatre.

1605 The Gunpowder Plot to destroy Parliament is thwarted on November 5.

1642 The Puritan government orders the closure of playhouses such as the Rose and the Globe.

1649 Charles I is beheaded at Whitehall.

1653 Oliver Cromwell is made Lord Protector of the Realm. Puritan rule closes London's theatres, brothels, and gaming halls.

1665 Outbreak of bubonic plague kills 100,000 Londoners.

1666 Great Fire of London sweeps through the city.

1667 Christopher Wren begins work on St. Paul's Cathedral; attempts to redraw London's layout are abandoned.

1675 The Royal Observatory is founded in Greenwich.

1688 James II is banished during the Glorious Revolution; William and Mary move into Kensington Palace.

1694 First Bank of England is established in the City of London.

1735 Dr. Samuel Johnson moves to London and becomes a fixture on the coffeehouse circuit.

1759 The British Museum is opened to the public.

1810 London's first Indian restaurant opens.

1829 Robert Peel sets up Metropolitan Police force, known as "bobbies" in his honor.

1836 Charles Dickens publishes *The Pickwick Papers* and becomes London's favorite novelist.

1837 Eighteen-year-old Queen Victoria ascends the throne and moves into Buckingham Palace.

1851 Great Exhibition takes place in Hyde Park, financing the development of South Kensington.

1854 Cholera epidemic in London results in improved sewage system.

1857 Victoria & Albert (V&A) Museum opens.

1860 London's first public flushing toilet opens.

1863 London opens the world's first Underground Transit System (Tube).

1908 For the first time, London hosts the Olympic games at White City.

1909 American Gordon Selfridge opens London's iconic department store.

1914 World War I starts; zeppelins drop bombs on London.

1939–45 World War II air raids kill thousands in London and destroy much of the city's infrastructure.

1948 London hosts the first postwar Olympic Games.

1951 Festival of Britain held on the South Bank.

1953 Queen Elizabeth II is crowned in Westminster Abbey.

1956 The Routemaster red double-decker bus takes to the streets.

1963 Youth-quake in London: The Beatles and the Rolling Stones rule the day.

1981 Prince Charles marries Lady Diana Spencer in St. Paul's Cathedral.

1986 The M25, London's orbital highway, opens.

1994 London is linked to Paris by rail via the Channel Tunnel.

1997 London mourns the death of Princess Diana.

2000 Traditional pigeon feeding in Trafalgar Square is outlawed.

2002 London celebrates Queen Elizabeth II's Golden Jubilee.

2005 London wins bid for the 2012 Olympics; 55 die in July 7 terrorist attacks on London transport.

2008 "Red" Ken Livingstone is ousted as Mayor of London by Boris Johnson.

2011 Prince William marries Kate Middleton in Westminster Abbey.

2012 London hosts the Olympic Games for the third time (the first time with the Paralympic games).

2016 Londoner Sadiq Khan is the first Muslim elected to be mayor of a European capital city.

2018 London enters its 2nd decade hosting regular season NFL games at Wembley Stadium.

London's Architecture

Norman Period: 1066–1200

The oldest-surviving style of architecture in London dates back to the time of William the Conqueror, when Norman invaders from northern France overran England. Thick walls and masonry were used to support the large interiors needed to accommodate the churchgoing masses. The heavy construction usually gave Norman buildings a dark and foreboding air.

Characteristics of the period include:

- Thick walls with small windows
- Round weight-bearing arches
- Huge piers (square stacks of masonry)
- Chevrons—zigzagging decorations surrounding doorways or wrapped around columns

The Tower of London's **White Tower,** built by William the Conqueror, is a textbook example of a Norman-style castle. **St. John's Chapel** within the White Tower is one of the few remaining Norman-style churches in England.

Gothic: 1200–1550

Also French in origin, the fairytale Gothic style introduced engineering innovations that enabled builders to transfer weight away from a structure's walls so they could be taller and thinner. The style also allowed for the use of larger windows, which allowed more natural light to reach a building's interior.

In addition to the pointed arch, Gothic construction features:

- Vaulted ceilings, using cross vaulting (an "X" design) and fan vaulting (a more conic design)
- Flying buttresses, free-standing exterior pillars that helped support the building's weight
- Carved tracery stonework connecting windows
- Stained-glass windows

You need look no further than **Westminster Abbey,** built in the mid-14th century, for a perfect London example of the Gothic style.

Renaissance: 1550–1650

The Renaissance style, involving proportion and mathematical precision enlivened by decoration, was imported from the Continent by the great Inigo Jones, who was greatly influenced by Italian Palladianism.

Characteristics of Renaissance architecture include:

- A sense of proportion
- A reliance on symmetry
- The use of classical columns—Doric, Ionic, and Corinthian

Top examples of this style include the **Banqueting Hall at Whitehall** and the **arcade** of Covent Garden, both designed by Inigo Jones.

Baroque: 1650–1750

Baroque architects Christopher Wren and Nicholas Hawksmoor had unrivalled opportunities to practice their craft in London when the Great Fire of 1666 provided a clean palette on which to replace medieval wooden structures.

The prime features of the more fanciful baroque style include:

- Classical forms marked by grand curving lines
- Decoration with playful carvings

St. Paul's Cathedral, with its massive dome and complex exterior decor, is Wren's crowning achievement and the finest example of English baroque architecture in London.

Neoclassical & Greek Revival: 1750–1837

Neoclassicism was an 18th-century reaction to the busy nature of baroque architecture. Notable characteristics of neoclassical architecture include:

- Clean, elegant lines, with balance and symmetry
- Use of classical Greek columns
- Crescent layouts (half-circles of identical stone houses with tall windows)

Sir John Soane's Museum and John Nash's curving white stucco **Cumberland Terrace** in Regent's Park are exemplars of these styles.

Gothic Revival: 1820–1900

As industrialization began its inexorable march on London, artists and architects looked back to a supposedly simpler and more romantic, whimsical period for their inspiration.

The features that marked the Gothic Revival style include:

- A confusion of spires, arches, and decorative detail
- Buildings constructed on a grand scale

The **Palace of Westminster,** home to the British Parliament, is the farthest-reaching exponent of this style; the most compact is the **Albert Memorial** in Hyde Park.

20th & Early 21st Century: 1900–Present

The 20th century saw London expanding into its suburbs with uninspired architecture. The Blitz was the period's (far more tragic) version of the Great Fire, and rebuilding took place with postwar austerity. The stark utilitarian style of South Bank's **Royal Festival Hall** is in a style known as **Brutalism. Post-modernism** is a softening of that style, applying the whimsy of the past to the modern, which brought about the inside-out **Lloyd's Building** and the **Gherkin Building.** The best marriage of old and new can be seen in the covered **Great Court** of the British Museum, which managed to put a new hat on an old friend without making it look silly.

Useful London Terms & Phrases

London has one of the world's most famous argots. **Cockney rhyming slang** emerged from the East End during the 19th century and consists of words and phrases constructed using a rhyme—a creative process that makes what you're talking about both less likely to be understood by the uninitiated, and more likely to be humorous. To make the dialect still more obscure, the word that formed the original object of the rhyme is often omitted. For example, "bread" meaning money derives from a rhyme with "bread and honey" and "ruby" meaning curry derives from "Ruby Murray," a 1950s singer. Although some words and phrases have entered common parlance—"barnet," from "Barnet Fair," meaning hair is another—you're unlikely to hear too much pure rhyming slang as you travel the city.

However, London does have a vocabulary of its own—some of it derived from or influenced by Cockney, some disparagingly referred to as "mockney," some related to products, places, and produce that are peculiar to the city, and some just plain slang. You may also notice the liberal use of the F-word on London's streets. Although it certainly isn't considered a polite word, its impact on the local listener is more diluted than in most other English-speaking cities.

Below is a glossary of some London words and phrases you may encounter.

bangers *sausages; usually paired with mashed potato for "bangers and mash"*
banging *good; often applied to music*
barking *crazy or mad; coined from a former asylum in the eastern suburb of Barking*
barney *an argument or disagreement*
bedlam *madness; as in "the roads are bedlam today"; a corruption of "Bethlehem," an asylum formerly at the corner of Moorgate and London Wall, in the City*
black cab *an official London black taxi, as opposed to a private hire "minicab" or an Uber; only black cabs are permitted to tout for fares kerbside*
Boris bikes *rental bicycles that are part of the Santander Cycles bikeshare scheme (see p 167); named after Boris Johnson, London's mayor when the bikes first appeared in 2010*
butcher's *a look (from Cockney "butcher's hook"); as in "can I have a butcher's?"*
BYO *short for "bring your own"; a restaurant that doesn't sell alcoholic drinks but will happily open any you bring along, sometimes for a small corkage fee*
circus *a (usually circular) coming together of streets, as at Piccadilly Circus and Finsbury Circus*
clink *a prison; after the former Clink Prison, on the South Bank*
damage *the cost, check, or bill; as in "what's the damage?"*
dodgy *not to be trusted, suspect; as in "that £20 note looks dodgy"*
dosh *money; also "bread" or "dough"*
gaff *home; "back to my gaff" means "back to my place"*
G 'n' T *gin and tonic; often served with "ice and a slice," i.e. an ice cube and a lemon wedge*
gastrocaff *a fashionable cafe that nevertheless serves traditional English fried breakfasts*
geezer *a man; also "bloke" or "fella"*
greasy spoon *the opposite of "gastrocaff": a basic cafe known for fried food*
gutted *extremely disappointed; as in "I'm gutted Arsenal beat Spurs last night"*
IPA *India Pale Ale; a type of hoppy, light-colored English bitter ale first brewed in the 18th century*
lager *straw-colored, fizzy light beer such as Budweiser and Foster's, served colder than traditional ales (although it's a myth that English beers are served "warm"; they should appear at cool cellar temperature)*
liquor *green parsley sauce served in traditional pie and mash shops*
naff *cheap looking, or unfashionable*
Porter *type of dark, strong ale once popular with London dockers; London brewers including Fuller's and Kernel both brew contemporary versions*
pint *both a measure of beer and a general term for having a drink; as in "do you fancy going for a pint later?"*
quid *one pound; "10 quid" or "a tenner" is £10*
subway *a pedestrian underpass; the underground railway is known as "the Tube"*
wally *a type of pickled gherkin, often paired with fish and chips*

Index

See also Accommodations and Restaurant indexes, below.

X

Y

Accommodations

Restaurants

Photo Credits

p ii top: ©r.nagy; p ii 2nd from top: ©Fedor Selivanov / Shutterstock.com; p ii middle: ©Melissa Baucom; p ii 2nd from bottom: ©T.W. van Urk / Shutterstock.com; p ii bottom: ©Brian Minkoff / Shutterstock.com; p iii top: Courtesy of The Ritz; p iii 2nd from top: Courtesy of THE CONNAUGHT; p iii middle: Courtesy of Royal Albert Hall/ © Paul Sanders; p iii 2nd from bottom: Courtesy of Claridge's; p iii bottom: ©Elizabeth Blanchet; p viii-1: ©Ale Argentieri / Shutterstock.com; p 4: ©fokke baarssen / Shutterstock.com; p 5 top: ©pio3 / Shutterstock.com; p 5 bottom: ©Scott Dexter; p 6 top: ©Richie Chan / Shutterstock.com; p 6 bottom: ©Melissa Baucom; p 7: ©r.nagy; p 10: ©Andres Court; p 11: ©Philip Bird LRPS CPAGB / Shutterstock.com; p 12 top: ©Georgethefourth / Shutterstock.com; p 12 bottom: Courtesy of Visit London / Pawel Libera; p 13: ©Ratikov; p 16: ©Luciano Mortula - LGM; p 17: ©Nataliia Zhekova / Shutterstock.com; p 18: Visitlondonimages / britainonview / Pawel Libera; p 19 top: ©Heather Shimmin / Shutterstock.com; p 19 bottom: ©Gimas / Shutterstock.com; p 21: ©Ivan Mateev / Shutterstock.com; p 22 top: ©Adrian Seal; p 22 bottom: ©PriceM / Shutterstock.com; p 25: ©Fedor Selivanov / Shutterstock.com; p 27: ©Natalya Okorokova / Shutterstock.com; p 29: ©Natalya Okorokova / Shutterstock.com; p 31: ©pio3 / Shutterstock.com; p 32: ©Alex Segre / Shutterstock.com; p 35: ©Luke McKernan; p 37 top: ©Melissa Baucom; p 39: ©Kiev.Victor; p 40: ©Elizabeth Blanchet; p 41: ©Tony Hisgett; p 44: ©Melissa Baucom; p 45: Courtesy of Sea Life London Aquarium / Garry Samuels; p 47: traveljunction; p 49: ©Tracey Hind; p 50: Historic Royal Palaces / Robin Forster; p 51: ©Melissa Baucom; p 54: ©Melissa Baucom; p 55 top: ©Melissa Baucom; p 55 bottom: ©Melissa Baucom; p 56: ©Ron Ellis / Shutterstock; p 57: ©Chrisdorney / Shutterstock; p 59: ©Stephen Finn; p 60 top: ©Bikeworldtravel / Shutterstock.com; p 60 bottom: ©Willy Barton / Shutterstock.com; p 61: ©pio3 / Shutterstock.com; p 63: ©John Blower; p 64: ©Grievous Angel; p 65 top: ©Sean Wallis; p 65 bottom: ©Willy Barton / Shutterstock.com; p 67: ©Elizabeth Blanchet; p 68: ©Dan Breckwoldt / Shutterstock.com; p 72: ©Pcruciatti / Shutterstock; p 73: T©.W. van Urk / Shutterstock.com; p 74: ©Paul Wilkinson; p 78: ©Rain Rabbie; p 79: ©Bex Walton; p 81: ©Dan Breckwoldt / Shutterstock; p 82: ©Elizabeth Blanchet; p 83: ©Lee McCoy; p 85: ©Nito / Shutterstock; p 86: ©Melissa Baucom; p 87: ©Brian Minkoff / Shutterstock.com; p 89: ©Kiev.Victor / Shutterstock; p 90: ©Melissa Baucom; p 93: ©Chrisdorney / Shutterstock; p 94 top: ©R. Fernández; p 94 bottom: ©Kamira / Shutterstock; p 95: Courtesy of The Ritz; p 104: Courtesy of Gordon Ramsay; p 105: ©Karl Florczak; p 107: London on View / Pawel Libera; p 108: ©Niamh Shields; p 109: ©Christian Sosa; p 111 top: ©Ewan Munro; p 111 bottom: ©Elizabeth Blanchet; p 112 top: ©Scott Dexter; p 112 bottom: ©Meghan Lamb; p 113: Courtesy of THE CONNAUGHT; p 121: ©Stephen Kelly; p 122: Courtesy of Bar Kick; p 123: Courtesy of Blue Bar / Jamie McGregor Smith; p 124 top: Courtesy of THE CONNAUGHT; p 124 bottom: Courtesy of The Ned Nickle / Simon Brown; p 126 top: Courtesy of Sky Garden; p 126 bottom: ©Love Art Nouveau; p 127: ©Jim Linwood; p 128: Courtesy of Ronnie Scotts / Ben Amure; p 129: ©Matt Brown; p 131: ©Jon Worth; p 133: Courtesy of Royal Albert Hall / © Paul Sanders; p 138: Courtesy of the O2 Center; p 140: Courtesy of SMITH / Liam Bailey; p 141: Courtesy of Sadlers Wells / Tristram Kenton; p 143: Courtesy of Claridge's; p 152: Courtesy of The Connaught; p 154: Courtesy of Firmdale Hotels; p 155: Courtesy of Dorchester; p 156: Courtesy of The Goring, Belgravia, London; p 157: ©Meghan Lamb; p 158: Courtesy of The Zetter/ Darren Chung; p 159: ©Elizabeth Blanchet.